Stockades in the Wilderness

Stockades in the Wilderness

THE FRONTIER DEFENSES & SETTLEMENTS OF SOUTHWESTERN OHIO, 1788-1795

RICHARD SCAMYHORN

JOHN STEINLE

COMMONWEALTH BOOK COMPANY
St. Martin, Ohio
2015

Copyright © 1986 by Richard Scamyhorn and John Steinle
Copyright © 2015 by Commonwealth Book Company
All rights reserved. Printed in the United States of America

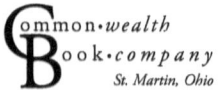
Common·wealth
Book·company
St. Martin, Ohio

Dedicated to Frances Forman, in gratitude from only two of the countless researchers who would have been truly lost without her.

Contents

Foreword • viii

Acknowledgments • ix

Map of the Miami Country • x

List of SW Ohio Stations • xii

Introduction • 1

Beasley's Station • 17

Beedle Station • 21

Bruce's Station • 24

Daraugh's Station • 27

Campbell's Station • 29

Carpenter's Settlement • 30

Columbia & Fort Miami • 33

Covalt Station or Bethany Town • 41

Cunningham's Station • 51

Dunlap's Station or Colerain • 53

Dunn's Station • 63

Freeman's Station • 66

Garrard or Garard Station and Wickerham's and Coleman's Mill Sites • 69

Gregory's Station • 76

Griffin's Station • 78

Hayes' Station • 80

Holes' Station • 85

James Kemper Blockhouse • 89

Ludlow's Station or Mill Creek Village • 93

McFarland Station • 99

McHenry's Blockhouse • 100

Mercer's Station • 101

Morrell's Station • 103

Mounts' Station • 106

Nelson's Station • 107

North Bend (Symmes City) and South Bend • 110

The Paxton Settlement • 122

Pleasant Valley Station • 124

Round Bottom or Clements' Station • 127

Runyon's Station • 129

The Sugar Camp Settlement • 131

Tucker's Station • 134

Turkey Bottom Blockhouse • 136

Voorhees' Station • 137

White's Station • 138

Wood's and Manning's or Miller's Station • 144

Bibliography • 146

Foreword

We began work on this book five years ago. We felt then, and still feel, that the story of the Ohio Valley Frontier during the late 1700s is one of the most fascinating in American history. Many reminders of this time, when the fate of a vast wilderness empire was decided by the clash of arms, remain in our section of Ohio.

Originally, we were fascinated by the correlation between many pioneer settlement sites and the prehistoric villages that antedated them by many centuries. The project grew from that basis to a study of the pioneer struggle for defense against an enemy who seemed to have every advantage. Our text grew much too long for the periodical article we originally intended. As we learned more about the stories of Southwestern Ohio's pioneer families, our desire to rescue from oblivion some basic facts about these people grew stronger. Though many had written about the major military campaigns of Harmar, St. Clair and Wayne, little attention had been paid to the effects of war on the lives of individual settlers.

There seemed to be a need for such a book. Interest in local history was increasing as the Bicentennials of the Northwest Ordinance and of the cities of Marietta and Cincinnati grew near. However, the Bicentennial celebrations appeared to be geared entirely to public relations projects that had little relevance to actual history. The popular outdoor dramas so abundant in Ohio were grossly inaccurate and wildly romanticized. At the other extreme, academic historians were largely uninterested in exploring a time period whose sketchy documentation defied statistical analysis.

That is why we decided—not without frequent doubts about our common sense and sanity—to push ahead with our detective work among the scattered fragments of Southwestern Ohio's early history. In some cases we were able to find only the barest documentation. At other times we found information so detailed that we felt we actually knew the people about whom we were writing. We hope, through this book, to convey that knowledge and perhaps some of our enthusiasm in recreating a pivotal area in the history of our state and our country.

Acknowledgments

Our greatest debt is to the staff of the Cincinnati Historical Society, who always responded with patience and helpfulness to our often unreasonable demands. Laura Chace, Frances Forman, Mary Jane Neely, Mike Isaacs, Anne Shepherd, Barbara Dawson, Beth Gerber and Judy Malone all deserve our gratitude.

Mrs. Ruth Wells of the Colerain Township Historical Society provided invaluable help, including her own transcriptions from the Harmar Papers, in researching the history of Dunlap's Station.

David Simmons of the Ohio Historical Society has given valuable advice and criticism, helping to improve the organization of our book.

We also owe a debt of gratitude to Mike Hagan, Scott Mansfield; David Bosse, Curator of Maps, William L. Clements Library, University of Michigan; Eric Pumroy, head of the Manuscripts Department, Indiana Historical Society; Dale Smalley and the other staff members of the Hamilton County (Ohio) Engineer's Office, Road Records Division; the staff of the Warren County (Ohio) Engineer's and Recorder's Offices; the staffs of the Recorder's and Engineer's Offices, Dearborn County (Indiana); and the employees of the Butler County (Ohio) Recorder's Office.

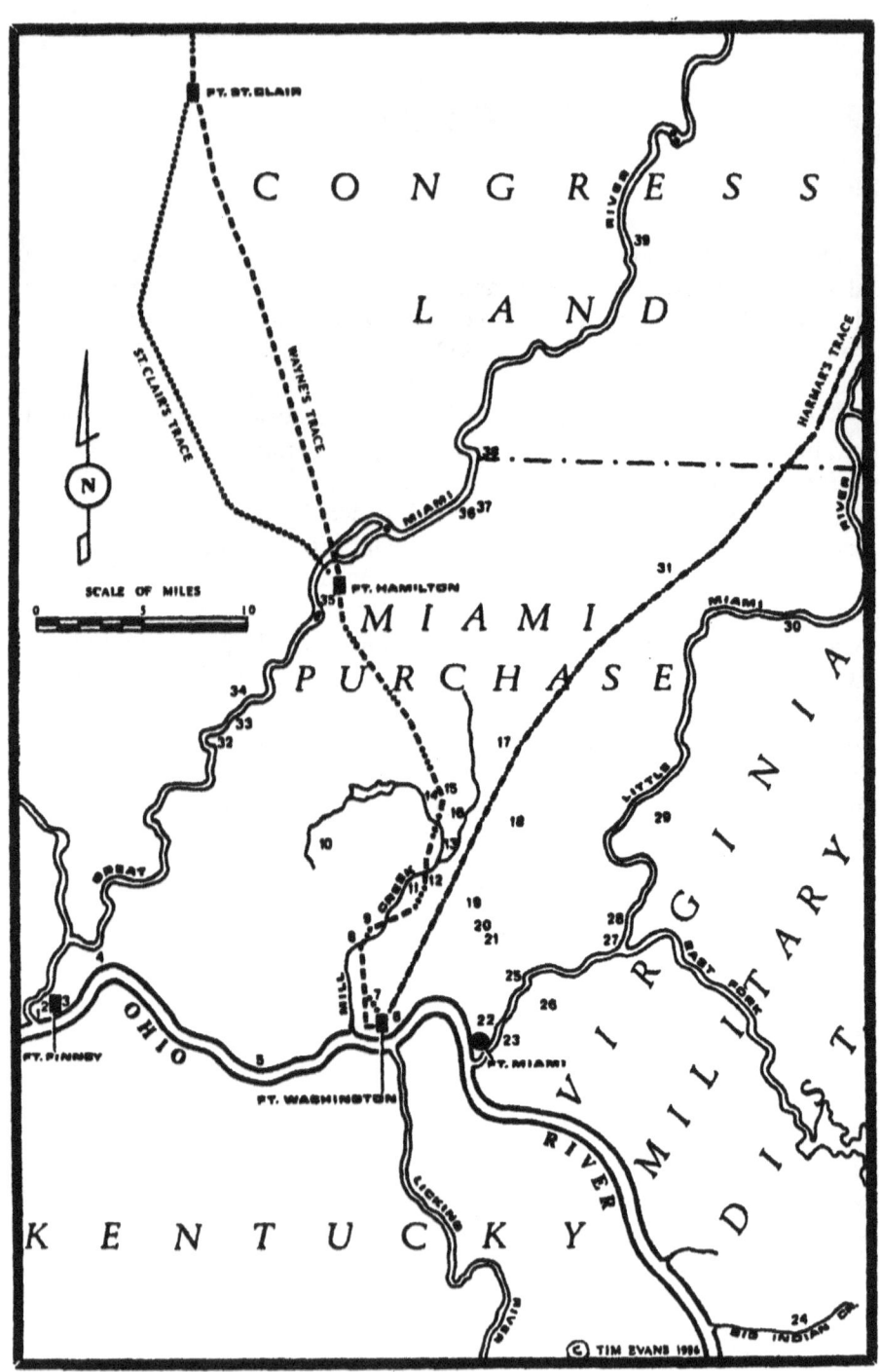

LEGEND

1. HAYES
2. DUNN
3. SUGAR CAMP
4. NORTH BEND
5. SOUTH BEND
6. KEMPER
7. RIDDLE
8. McHENRY
9. LUDLOW
10. KEEN
11. GRIFFEN
12. WHITE
13. VORHEES
14. PLEASANT VALLEY
15. TUCKER
16. CUNNINGHAM
17. RUNYON
18. CARPENTER
19. McFARLAND
20. RED BANK
21. NELSON
22. TURKEY BOTTOM
23. GARRARD
24. WOODS MANNING
25. BEASLEY
26. MERCER'S
27. ROUND BOTTOM
28. COVALT
29. PAXTON
30. MOUNT'S
31. BEEDLE'S
32. DUNLAP
33. CAMPBELL
34. DARAUGH
35. BRUCE
36. GREGORY'S
37. FREEMAN'S
38. MORRELL'S
39. HOLE'S

•••••••• GEN. ARTHUR ST. CLAIR'S TRACE
━ ━ ━ ━ GEN. ANTHONY WAYNE'S TRACE
━•━•━•━ GEN. JOSIAH HARMAR'S TRACE
━•━•━•━ MIAMI PURCHASE BOUNDARY LINE
■ GOVERNMENT FORT SITES
● CIVILIAN FORT SITES

Southwestern Ohio Stations

STATION	FOUNDING DATE	PRESENT LOCATION
Beasley	1792	Plainville
Beedle	1795	Warren County
Bruce	1793	Hamilton, Ohio
Campbell	1793	Opposite Miamitown or Butler County
Carpenter	1793	Blue Ash
Columbia and Fort Miami	1788	Columbia
Covalt	1789	Terrace Park
Cunningham	1793	Evendale
Daraugh	1794 ca.	Ross, Ohio (Butler County)
Dunlap (Colerain)	1790	West of Dunlap
Dunn	1793	Shawnee Lookout
Frazee	1793 ca.	Exact location unknown
Freeman	1792 ca.	LeSourdsville (Butler County)
Garrard	1790	Mt. Washington
Gregory	1791 ca.	LeSourdsville (Butler County)
Griffin	1793	North End of Carthage
Hayes	1791	Shawnee Lookout
Hole	1795	Miamisburg (Montgomery County)
Keen	1795 ca.	North College Hill
Kemper	1793	Walnut Hills
Ludlow	1790	Cumminsville
McFarland	1795	Pleasant Ridge
McHenry	1790	Cumminsville
Mercer	1792	Newtown
Morrell	1795	Excello (Butler County)
Mounts	1795	Warren County
Nelson	1791 ca.	Madisonville
North Bend	1789	North Bend
Paxton	1795	Loveland (Clermont County)
Pleasant Valley	1793	Woodlawn
Red Bank	1791 ca.	Madisonville
Riddle	1792	Brighton
Round Bottom	1789 ca.	Terrace Park
Runyon	1792	North of Sharonville
South Bend	1789	West of Anderson Ferry
Sugar Camp	1789	Shawnee Lookout

Tucker	1792	Woodlawn
Turkey Bottom	1791	Linwood
Voorhees	1794	Reading
White	1790 or 1792	North end of Carthage
Wood's and Manning's	1795	Clermont County

The John Kenton Station near Washington, Kentucky, 1786 was a typical Kentucky station of that period containing cabins with shade type roofs and using the cabin walls as a primary part of the stockade construction. In this case, the roofs sloped out to direct rain away from the compound but this made it easier for attackers to gain the stockade interior. (Plate 65, Lewis Collins, *History of Kentucky*, Covington, Kentucky, 1874, Vol. 2, p. 555.)

Fort Boonesborough as it appeared in 1778, a well-designed stockade with the shade roofs slanting inward for better defense. Ground surrounding the stockade has been cleared to deny cover to attackers. (Drawn by George W. Ranck, in *Filson Club Publication 16*, Louisville, Kentucky, 1901, p. 78.)

Introduction

The ever-present fear of Indian raids meant that defensive fortifications were among the first structures built at the new and vulnerable Southwestern Ohio settlements founded between 1788 and 1795. The story of these defenses is inseparable from that of the people who built them, for settlers spread throughout the area not in the isolated cabins of frontier myth, but in tightly-knit communities often including all the members of an extended family.

These settlements lay in today's Ohio counties of Hamilton, Butler, Warren, Clermont and Montgomery, then part of a larger region known as the Miami Country. That large area embraced the fertile valleys of the Great and Little Miami Rivers, the Mill Creek and the Mad River. Most of the Miami Country was within the original boundaries of Hamilton County as it was first created in January of 1790. To the east lay Washington County and the fledgling Marietta settlement founded in April of 1788.[1]

The flat, fertile bottom lands of the Ohio, the Great and Little Miamis, the Mill Creek and their tributaries not only yielded corn and wheat, but held the promise of water power for grist mills to process the settlers' crops. In locating their settlements, these pioneers often chose the same sites planted by prehistoric farmers a thousand years prior to their arrival. The prehistoric peoples had laboriously carved their furrows in soil deposited in ancient river valleys and built their villages on the broad flat floors of river beds transformed during dramatic glacial epochs.

The Indian trails traversed by the earliest historic adventurers often originated with prehistoric nomadic hunters, who began blazing routes through the area during the last glacial episode. The Miami Country's white pioneers built their settlements on top of and near the villages, burial grounds and ceremonial earthworks of cultures which have become enigmas.[2]

The possibility of making a fortune through the buying and reselling of land impelled many of the Miami Country's early settlers. Lobbying in Congress on behalf of private land companies was promoted by veteran officers of the Revolutionary War army. They felt that the government owed them some consideration in the granting of land since Congress had severely curtailed the benefits it had promised them. Many officers had suffered considerable financial loss in the war and hoped that speculation in Western lands would help them regain some measure of prosperity. Thus, many founders of Miami Country settlements were Revolutionary War veterans of fairly high rank.

Much of the land between the Great and Little Miami Rivers was sold by Congress to the Miami Land Company and was known as the Miami Purchase or Symmes Purchase. Land sales here were administered by Judge John Cleves Symmes of New Jersey, who founded the settlement of North Bend in February of 1789. The availability of land in the Miami Purchase was well publicized in the East by prominent Congressmen such as Jonathan Dayton and Elias Boudinot, who were among the 24 associates governing the land company.

Although Symmes had originally negotiated a purchase of nearly 1,000,000 acres, sloppy surveying and record keeping, his failure to make required payments and frequent changes of land sale conditions by the government drastically reduced the amount of land he had to sell. He eventually lost his large fortune through punitive lawsuits by settlers to whom he had sold land he did not own.

Stretching east from the Little Miami River to the Scioto River was the Virginia Military District. This huge area of more than 4,000,0000 acres was reserved by Congress for grants to Virginia veterans of the Revolutionary War. It was, in a sense, Virginia's last vestige of the enormous tract handed to her under the original colonial charter of 1609. The old English surveying system of "metes and bounds," in which natural landmarks such as rocks, trees and streams were used as boundary markers, later caused much confusion and litigation in the district.

Independent companies conducting land sales in southern Ohio often proved inefficient or even unscrupulous. Congress eventually decided to directly control land sales through government land offices set up at strategic points. The Miami Country lands north and west of the Miami Purchase and the Virginia Military District were sold in this manner as part of the Cincinnati District which reached north to the Greenville Treaty line.

As Southwestern Ohio's first three permanent settlements—Columbia, Losantiville and North Bend—were founded in late 1788 and early 1789, a fragile truce prevailed among the rolling forested hills of the Ohio frontier. The war for American independence had ended only five years earlier, leaving the bitter taste for vengeance among Indian and white in the Ohio Valley. Broken treaties and broken truces, raid and counter-raid, torture, scalping and mutilation were the legacy of the frontier war that had raged into the Indian lands north and west of the Ohio River.[3]

The various treaties negotiated with the Ohio tribes since the end of the Revolutionary War were accepted by some tribes, rejected by others, and opposed by factions within every tribe.[4] Nor were they universally honored by the whites. Most settlers, engulfed by the vast hardwood forest, saw the trees as their greatest enemy to be conquered only by girdling, felling and burning until the land was cleared to plow and plant. The Indian saw the forest as a friend and the white man as a destroyer of all that was sacred.

Despite the tension between white and Indian, initial contacts at the first Southwestern Ohio settlements were cordial. The people of Columbia even gave a Shawnee hunting party a special dinner on Christmas Day of 1788.[5] But the hope for peace soon died. Indian horse-stealing raids into Kentucky provoked retaliatory raids by Kentucky militia who slaughtered hostile and friendly Indian alike.[6]

Settlers at North Bend and Columbia began cheating the Indians of their pelts and selling them bad whiskey.[7] The spread of isolated and vulnerable white settlements up the Great and Little Miami Rivers and the Mill Creek invited attack by Indian warriors opposed to white colonization north of the Ohio River. The first serious attack in the area occurred at North Bend in May of 1789.[8]

The failure of final attempts at negotiation with the hostile tribes led General Arthur St. Clair, Governor of this new Northwest Territory, to declare war in the summer of 1790.[9] The next four years saw incessant Indian raids by war parties ranging in size from two or three men to nearly two hundred warriors. The raids only began to slacken in intensity after the defeat of the united tribes at the Battle of Fallen Timbers on August 20, 1794. Even after this defeat, Indian attacks continued until a final treaty of peace was signed at Greenville on August 3, 1795.[10]

Though many of the first settlers of the Miami Country were troubled by conflicting land claims, poor surveying techniques and the backbreaking labor of clearing away the forest, they also faced the even greater problem of ensuring their own survival against constant hit-and-run attacks by a cunning and resourceful enemy. One solution to the problem lay in the building of sheltering fortifications by the various communities.

Columbia, near the mouth of the Little Miami River, was the first local settlement, founded in November of 1788.[11] Fort Miami, the initial refuge of the Columbia settlers, was a well-planned rectangular fortification with a sturdy blockhouse at each of its four corners. The walls of Fort Miami were actually the outer walls of the log dwellings, which were built end-to-end between the blockhouses to form a protected compound.

The clapboard roofs were of the slanting "shade" fashion, with the clapboards overhanging the outside walls of the houses to prevent the Indians from scaling them.[12] This method of using the walls of the houses to form the defensive walls of a fortification was less expensive and less time-consuming than building picketed stockades. Utilized in Ohio as early as 1778 in the construction of Fort Laurens, the technique was also used in many of the government fortifications built along the Ohio River during and immediately after the Revolutionary War. These included Fort McIntosh in Pennsylvania, Fort Finney (later called Fort Steuben) at Louisville and Fort Washington at Cincinnati.[13]

View of Fort Finney at the Falls of Ohio, from the south east

Fort Miami was also very similar in appearance to at least two of Kentucky's larger civilian forts: Boonesborough and Bryant's Station. At both those settlements the cabin walls formed the outer walls of an enclosed area and the roofs also were built "shade" fashion. In fact, this type of roof gave the defenders of Bryant's Station a distinct advantage during the British and Indian siege of 1782. The high outer roof peak prevented the attackers from picking off the boys who were extinguishing the flaming arrows that had been fired onto the roofs.[14]

Losantiville, the second settlement in the Miami Country, was probably founded in December of 1788 although some evidence suggests January of 1789 as a more likely date.[15] Its name was changed to Cincinnati in January of 1790 by Governor St. Clair.[16] By that time Fort Washington, which General Josiah Harmar called "one of the most solid, substantial wooden fortresses...of any in the Western Territory..." had been built near the town.[17]

Cincinnati, with the nearby protection of Fort Washington and its large garrision of Federal troops, needed no separate fortification of its own. However, Indian raiding parties did sometimes penetrate the Cincinnati environs, and some of the houses in the town were built blockhouse fashion with rifle slits cut in their walls.[18]

North Bend, founded in February of 1789, was the first settlement in the Miami Country to sustain a serious Indian attack. Although few details are recorded concerning the North Bend fortifications, it is clear that the pressing need for defensive works was understood by the community's leader, John Cleves Symmes. At first, North Bend's only fortification was a small blockhouse large enough only to hold the eighteen Federal soldiers assigned to guard the village.[19] However, the local settlers began construction of a stockaded defensive work in June of 1789, after a severe Indian attack the previous month.

Additional defensive structures were built during the next few years and included two of the most unusual fortifications in the Miami Country. A hexagonal blockhouse with an overhanging second story was built sometime before the summer of 1790 on land occupied by Daniel and Eunice Howell. An even more unusual structure was begun on Christmas Day of 1790 at

---

"View of Fort Finney at the Falls of the Ohio, from the South East" by Major Jonathan Heart. Fort Finney (later renamed Fort Steuben) was built near Louisville, Kentucky in 1786. The right side of Major Heart's sketch illustrates how even Federal forts used the walls of crude shade–roofed barracks as part of their curtain walls. Picket-walled forts were few on the Northwest Frontier because of the expense and labor involved in their construction. *(Courtesy of the William Henry Smith Library, Indiana Historical Society, Northwest Territory Collection)*

the instigation of Judge Symmes. This was a sixteen-sided blockhouse, nearly circular in shape to afford the defenders a clear field of fire in every direction.

It was designed by Judge Symmes himself and was something of a nightmare to construct for the eight corner men assigned to notch the logs. One of these men later remarked that he "...thought it was an invention of the old Judge to have something curious and exciting to send back to New Jersey..."[20] By the early 1790s, the increase in population at North Bend, the defensive structures built there and the eighty Federal troops present, apparently brought a fair measure of security to the area.

The smaller settlements which straggled northward up the local rivers and streams were far more vulnerable than Columbia, North Bend or Cincinnati. These tiny communities were founded because of the pressure of the increasing population and the necessity of farming the outlying land to avoid starvation. Judge Jacob Burnet, who arrived in the Miami Country in 1796 as a young lawyer, later recalled the desperate situation of many settlers:

> *A large number of the original adventurers to the Miami Purchase had exhausted their means by paying for their land and removing their families to the country. Others were wholly destitute of property, and came out as volunteers, under the expectation of obtaining, gratuitously, such small tracts of land as might be forfeited by the purchasers...for not making the improvements required... Their situation, therefore, was distressing. To go out into the wilderness to till the soil, appeared to be certain death; to remain in the settlements threatened them with starvation...They depended on game, fish and such products of the earth as could be raised on small patches of ground in the immediate vicinity of the settlements...*
>
> *Having endured these privations as long as they could be borne, the more resolute of them determined to brave the consequences of moving on to their lands. To accomplish the object, with the least exposure, those whose lands were in the same neighborhood, united as one family; and on that principle, a number of associations were formed, amounting to a dozen or more, who went out resolved to maintain their positions.*
>
> *Each party erected a strong blockhouse, near to which their cabins were put up, and the whole was enclosed by strong log pickets. This being done, they commenced clearing their lands, and preparing for planting their*

> *crops. During the day, while they were at work, one person was placed as a sentinel, to warn them of approaching danger. At sunset they retired to the blockhouse and their cabins, taking everything of value within their pickets. In this manner they proceeded from day to day, and week to week, till their improvements were sufficiently extensive to support their families. During this time, they depended for subsistence on wild game, obtained at some hazard, more than on the scanty supplies they were able to procure from the settlements on the river.*[21]

That Burnet did not exaggerate the desperate plight of many settlers is proven by the remarks of Luke Foster, one of Columbia's early pioneers, who recalled in 1819:

> *...being harassed, & pent up by the Indians, that we could take no wild meat, and our corn so frosted, that it would not sprout, neither would a hungry horse eat it...but what was still worse there was not enough of it for every one to have a little there were, perhaps, in Columbia, near 200 persons, of all sex & ages; & I believe not one pound of pork; or any other kind of salted or any other meat; & but little milk, & no flour. In fact, our subsistance, was an insoficiency of such poor corn ground by hand, or boiled whole; & the roots of bargrass, which was found on the rich bottoms, boiled, mashed up, & baked, sometimes with, & sometimes without a mixture of our hand mill meal; but then it was good, I don't know how it would eat now.*[22]

In contemporary usage, the small settlements that Burnet described, crudely fortified and containing about a dozen families each, were called "stations." Such fortified settlements were common on the Pennsylvania, Maryland, Virginia and Kentucky frontiers, where long and bitter experience had taught the area's pioneers to band together for mutual defense.

It is apparent that the fortified settlements of the Miami Country followed in the tradition of similar sites scattered all along the trans-Appalachian frontier and stretching back in time many years before the settlement of Southwestern Ohio had begun. Most of the founders of the Miami Country settlements were Revolutionary War veterans, and many were well acquainted with the civilian fortifications built during that conflict in Western Pennsylvania and Kentucky.

James Elliott, an early visitor to the Miami Country stations, described them in these terms:

> *From the first settlements in America it has been invariable practice on the frontiers for several families to associate together, and build a number of huts generally in the form of a square in order to provide better security against the savages—these settlements on the western waters are called stations and are generally desegnated by the name of the principal proprietor or first projector—some of these stations resemble small garrisons, being inclosed with palisades.*[23]

Joseph Martin, an early settler at Garrard's Station, noted that certain formalities accompanied the organization of a station:

> *The system of starting a station was, by a mutual contract to agree to stand by each other in difficulty—to obey the principal man after whom the station was named—to share equally the dangers of defence—and perform the double duty of soldier and laborer. In addition to these written articles of compact there were inexorable customs prevailing among the stations, which required prompt assistance to be given in case of attack, amounting to a sort of warlike alliance between separate communities. There were also rules relating to capture and recapture of property, as well understood as the system of prize cases of the Admiralty Court.*[24]

The defenses built at these stations in Southwestern Ohio between 1788 and 1795 were strikingly inconsistent in size and quality. At one extreme, Covalt Station near the Little Miami River boasted a stockade fort that rivaled in size Cincinnati's huge Federal installation at Fort Washington. In fact, the Covalt Station was much too large for its tiny garrison to defend and had to be abandoned in time of danger.[25] Other settlements, such as Dunlap's and Mount's Stations, were less effective, smaller-scale versions of Fort Miami at Columbia, using the walls of dwellings to form a protected enclosure.[26]

At least one fortified blockhouse or "station house" was erected at most Southwestern Ohio settlements.[27] In some communities it imitated the Federal military blockhouses of the period, with a second story overhanging the first by several feet so that defenders could fire down through loopholes in the floor at an enemy attempting to enter.[28] At other sites, the blockhouse was simply a strongly-built log house with rifle slits cut in its walls and heavy bulletproof shutters and doors, sometimes with a small stockade to defend its entrance.[29]

At times, sheltering blockhouses were built as vantage points for scouting parties (as at Columbia) or as protection near the fields rather than in the communities themselves. As the Fort Miami stockade became too small to contain all of Columbia's people, many outlying houses were built in blockhouse fashion.[30] Small fortifications were scattered in this way all through the Miami Country, and it is clearly impossible to pinpoint them all.

One of the most puzzling things about the defenses at the local stations was their obvious weakness considering their vulnerable positions. Two of the stations most exposed to danger were Dunlap's and White's, and at both settlements contemporary comments dwelt on the lack of defense preparations. At Dunlap's Station the houses formed a defensive compound but the lower ends of the "shade" fashion roofs extended downward **outside** the fort so that the settlers' dogs could jump atop the roofs to get inside the compound.[31]

The situation was even worse at White's Station, divided by Mill Creek and containing only one fortified cabin, that of proprietor Jacob White.[32] Griffin's Station, near White's settlement and equally vulnerable, was also built in scattered fashion with cabins on both sides of Mill Creek.[33]

The most obvious explanation for the weakness of these defenses was the pressing need of the settlers to construct rudimentary housing while clearing large areas of the virgin forest and to till the resulting fields for sustenance. This daily round of backbreaking labor left little time, energy or ambition to construct more than primitive defensive works. Unfortunately, it also left many settlements painfully vulnerable to Indian attack—so vulnerable that at least four of the Southwestern Ohio communities were hastily abandoned for up to a year during times of threatened Indian aggression.[34]

One factor that contributed to the vulnerability of these settlements was the lack of planning as to their location. Although it has been claimed that surveyor and prominent land speculator Israel Ludlow plotted the positions of the stations to provide a "double ring" of fortifications around Cincinnati, there is no contemporary evidence that any such plan was carried out. The small station settlements, in fact, could be considered an actual liability in terms of local defense since they continually drained able-bodied men from the larger settlements and forced Federal commanders to split their troops into small detachments to guard them.

The stations only began to prove assets in the early 1790s when those communities located near the "Great Road" up the Mill Creek Valley became important staging areas, rest stops and supply depots along the

This sketch of Bryant's Station in Kentucky was drawn in the early 1900s by Miss Jean H. McHenry after an original ground plan of the station by George Rogers Clark. It shows many aspects of traditional station construction, including the use of cabins to form a protected enclosure, slanting shade roofs and projecting blockhouses at the corners to allow a crossfire along the fort walls. *(Courtesy of the Cincinnati Historical Society)*

route northwest to Fort Hamilton for the armies of Arthur St. Clair and Anthony Wayne.[35]

This situation offers a vivid contrast to the reaction at Marietta in January of 1791 after twelve nearby settlers were killed by Indians. The directors of the Ohio Company, who led the Marietta community, ordered the evacuation of all the area's smaller settlements. They concentrated the people into seven large, well-fortified locations grouped close to each other near the mouth of the Muskingum River.[36]

John Cleves Symmes admitted the lack of defense planning in the Miami Country as compared to the Marietta area when he wrote as early as 1789:

> *At the city of Marietta... of course they are much more able to repel an attack, not only from their superior numbers; but from their mode of settlement on the New England plan of connected towns or villages: the settlers with them being restrained by their directors who will not allow them land whereupon to settle at pleasure. The different method adopted for settling Miami, puts it in the power of every purchaser to choose his ground, and convert the same into a station, village or town at pleasure: and nothing controls him but the fear of Indians, therefore whenever ten or twelve men agree to form a station, it is certainly done. This desultory way of settling will soon carry many through the purchase, if the savages do not frustrate them.*[37]

Although a well-organized system of defenses at regular intervals was not built in the Miami Country, the settlers themselves attempted to compensate by organizing to provide advance notice of Indian attack. At least one settlement, Columbia, took the precaution of hiring a group of rangers for the protection of the people working in their fields.[38]

Early in 1790, a local militia force was formally organized by the Federal authorities at Fort Washington. Four companies were established: two at Columbia, commanded by Captains John Stites Gano and James Flinn, one at Cincinnati under Captain Israel Ludlow, and one at North Bend, led by Captain Brice Virgin. The entire force, numbering 410 by May of 1790, was commanded by Lieutenant Colonel Oliver Spencer of Columbia.[39] The men were required to assemble one day each week for two hours of drill and were also required to carry their arms and accouterments to Sunday church in case of surprise Indian attack.[40]

The creation of a militia unit was an improvement in local defense, but the time spent in gathering the troops and traveling to an imperiled community was considerable. The Indian attack on Dunlap's Station began on the morning of January 10, 1791; but it was early afternoon of the 12th before a relief column of Federal troops and militia reached the station.[41] This lag time in communications meant that the shelter of the local forts and blockhouses was still essential to the safety of the area's pioneers.

Even though Southwestern Ohio's frontier settlements were located at irregular intervals, on land chosen rather for its fertility and nearness to water than for any defensive value, most stations were safe against a direct assault. The small size of Indian war parties (most contained less than a dozen men), the shelter of the various forts, and the several hundred militiamen and regular troops available, provided a measure of safety.[42] Even the massive Indian attack against Dunlap's Station was effectively resisted within the fort that General Harmar had described as "shabby" and "in a miserable position for defense."[43]

The man and two children killed during an Indian assault on White's Station in October of 1793 were the only settlers killed during a direct attack on a Miami Country settlement.[44] The many people who were killed or captured by Indian war parties roaming the area were caught while working their fields, making maple sugar, surveying, hunting or traveling between communities.[45] As scattered and isolated as they were, the stations provided a desperately-needed haven until hostilities between white and Indian moved further west toward their final, tragic conclusion.

The Miami Country's settlers were enveloped in forests containing many edible plants, providing them with plentiful raw materials. A long list of available fauna included buffalo, bear, deer, elk and turkey. Considering the abundance all around them the desperate plight of many pioneers is both ironic and tragic. Many had migrated to this wilderness with the bare essentials, some losing possessions along the way. The constant alarms caused by the Indian attacks and the further loss from natural crop disasters left many inhabitants destitute.

As a result, much of the migration from the original settlements was initiated out of sheer desperation to escape starvation. The resulting small settlements scattered throughout the region in turn spawned blockhouses constructed closer to the work areas between and beyond the stockaded stations. Some of these defenses were simply fortified log houses, such as the homes of Oliver M. Spencer, Judge William Goforth and Luke Foster at the Columbia settlement.[46]

There appear to be four distinct phases of early settlement in Southwestern Ohio. The first, beginning in late 1788 and continuing through early 1791, saw the establishment of Columbia, Losantiville and North Bend along the Ohio River. During this time of relative freedom from Indian attack, smaller settlements such as Covalt's, Ludlow's, Garrard's and Dunlap's Stations reached well into the interior along local tributaries of the Ohio.

A second phase began in early 1791 and lasted throughout that year. Serious Indian attacks in the region and the defeat of General St. Clair's army caused panic and uncertainty among the people. Several of the interior settlements were abandoned and few, if any, new ones were begun.

The years 1792 and 1793 comprised a third phase that saw the cautious return to the abandoned settlements. The arrival of General Wayne's army in the spring of 1793 restored confidence and led to the founding of many new communities along the "Great Road" up the Mill Creek Valley toward Fort Hamilton. These settlements proved to be valuable refuges and storehouses for Wayne's army during the following two years of campaigning. Finally, the years 1794 and 1795 saw the establishment of far-flung new stations along army supply routes in today's Butler County and near local rivers or springs in areas of present Warren, Montgomery and Clermont Counties.

The signing of the Treaty of Greenville in 1795 virtually eliminated the need for fortified settlements in Southwestern Ohio. The small stations broke up as their inhabitants moved out onto their individual farms. Thus, there was usually little continuity between the stations and the permanent communities which grew up many years later on the sites they had occupied.

Some of these sites, such as Frazee's Station on the Little Miami River, Keen's Station on St. Clair's Trace five miles above Ludlow's Station, and the blockhouse reportedly built at present-day Brighton in Cincinnati on a site later occupied by the Renner Malt Company, were probably full-fledged communities.[47] However, information on their history is so fragmentary that no clear account can be written.

All these defensive works were destroyed after their usefulness had ended; some through fire, others by settlers themselves who reused the timber in other structures. As important as the frontier defenses of the Miami Country were, some are brought to mind only through folklore while others were forgotten in the infancy of the region's history.

We have included in the following pages all the local settlements for which we could find some evidence of the construction of defensive works. We did not include Cincinnati itself because, as previously noted, the presence of Fort Washington meant that Cincinnati residents had no need to construct fortifications of their own.

We have tried to give some insight into the background and origin of the founders of each settlement, together with an image of how these people coped with the problems of survival in the wilderness.

NOTES

[1] William E. Smith, *History of Southwestern Ohio: The Miami Valleys*, New York, 1964, Vol. 1, p. 7-10; *Early Rosters of Cincinnati and Hamilton County*, Ed. Marjorie Byrnside Burress, Cincinnati, 1984, p. 1- 2; Henry Howe, *Historical Collections of Ohio*, Cincinnati, 1888, Vol. 1, p. 739; Henry A. Ford and Kate B. Ford, *History of Hamilton County, Ohio, With Illustrations and Biographical Sketches*, Cleveland, 1881, p. 67-70.

[2] For the location of settlements near prehistoric earthworks, mounds and burial sites, see the following sections on Beasley's, Dunlap's, Garrard's and Mercer's Stations. Early city maps of Cincinnati show the large complex of earthworks and mounds which once existed on the city's site and which were gradually destroyed by urban encroachment. See especially "A Plan Of Cincinnati Including All the Latest Additions & Subdivisions, Engraved for Drake's Statistical View, 1815," Cincinnati Historical Society Map Collection.

[3] For an excellent account of white-Indian relations during the Revolutionary War, see Randolph C. Downes, *Council Fires on the Upper Ohio: A Narrative of Indian Affairs in the Upper Ohio Valley until 1795*, Pittsburgh, 1968, p. 179-249; also the four volumes of transcriptions from the Draper Manuscripts edited by Reuben Gold Thwaites and Louise Phelps Kellogg entitled *The Revolution on the Upper Ohio, 1775-1777*, Madison, Wisconsin, 1908; *Frontier Advance on the Upper Ohio*, Madison, Wisconsin, 1916; *Frontier Defense on the Upper Ohio*, Madison, Wisconsin, 1912; and *Frontier Retreat on the Upper Ohio*, Madison, Wisconsin, 1917.

[4] Downes, *Council Fires on the Upper Ohio*, p. 184-185.

[5] Letter of I. Dunn to Griffin Yeatman, Dec. 17, 1838, quoted in Daniel Drake, "Memoir of the Miami Country, 1779-1794," Ed. Beverly W. Bond, Jr., *Quarterly Publication of the Historical and Philosophical Society of Ohio*, Vol. 18, (1923), p. 68.

[6] Downes, *Council Fires on the Upper Ohio*, p. 298, 311-312; *The St. Clair Papers*, Ed. William Henry Smith, Cincinnati, 1882, Vol. 2, p. 3-5.

[7] Letter of John Cleves Symmes to Jonathan Dayton, May 18-20, 1789, in "Correspondence of John Cleves Symmes, Original Letters, 1788-1796 Relating to the Miami Purchase and Settlement of Cincinnati," Manuscript Collection, Cincinnati Historical Society, hereafter referred to as "Symmes Correspondence, Cincinnati Historical Society."

[8] Drake, "Memoir of the Miami Country," p. 71-73.

[9] Downes, *Council Fires on the Upper Ohio*, p. 310-315.

[10] Ibid., p. 334-338; Ezra Ferris, *The Early Settlement of the Miami Country*, Indiana Historical Society Publications, Vol. 1, No. 9, Indianapolis, 1897, p. 353; Letter of Judge Francis Dunlavy to Daniel Drake, Dec. 9, 1831, quoted in Drake, "Memoir of the Miami Country," p. 100.

[11] Letter of Luke Foster to Thomas Clark, Esq., May 23, 1819, quoted in Drake, "Memoir of the Miami Country," p. 103; Ferris, *Early Settlement of the Miami Country*, p. 255-256; letter of John Cleves Symmes to Jonathan Dayton, May 18-20, 1789, Symmes Correspondence, Cincinnati Historical Society.

[12] Letter from Ezra Ferris to Griffin Yeatman, Et. Al., Dec. 18, 1838, Lyman Draper Collection, Drake Papers, Microfilm series O, Draper Mss. 1089, Wisconsin Historical Society.

[13] Thomas Smith, *The Mapping of Ohio*, Kent, Ohio, 1977, p. 70-71; Edward G. Williams, *Fort Pitt and the Revolution on the Western Frontier*, Pittsburgh, 1978, p. 123-124; David A. Simmons, *The Forts of Anthony Wayne*, Fort Wayne, Indiana, 1977, p. 5-6; William Guthman, *March to Massacre, a History of the First Seven Years of the United States Army, 1784-1791*, New York, 1970, p. 51.

[14] An excellent artist's impression of Bryant's Station is reproduced in Reuben T. Durrett, *Bryant's Station and the Memorial Proceedings Held on its site...*, Filson Club Publications No. 12, Louisville, 1897, facing page 23. A description of the Bryant's Station fort is included in the same volume, p. 23-25. A plan, illustration and description of Boonesborough are included in George W. Rauck, *Boonesborough: Its Founding, Pioneer Struggles, Indian Experiences, Transylvania Days, and Revolutionary Annals*, Filson Club Publications No. 16, Louisville, 1901, p. 34-37, 52, 78.

15The exact date of Cincinnati's founding was discussed in a court case involving the City of Cincinnati vs. Joel Williams in 1807. Robert Patterson and Israel Ludlow testified that the first settlement took place in January of 1789, while other witnesses (including William McMillan) gave December of 1788 as the correct date. McMillan's estimate of December 28, 1788 has come to be accepted as correct. See Charles Cist, *Sketches and Statistics of Cincinnati in 1859*, Cincinnati, 1859, p. 12-13.
16Drake, "Memoir of the Miami Country," p. 73-74.
17Smith, *The Mapping of Ohio*, p. 81-82.
18Drake, "Memoir of the Miami Country," p. 59, 82-83.
19Letter of John Cleves Symmes to Jonathan Dayton, May 18-20, 1789, Symmes Correspondence, Cincinnati Historical Society.
20Reverend Benjamin W. Chidlaw, "Early Times," 1876, quoted in Marjorie Byrnside Burress, *It Happened 'Round North Bend*, Cincinnati, 1970, Ch. 3, p. 1; Jacob Parkhurst, *Sketches of Jacob Parkhurst 1772- 1863 by Himself*, Knightstown, Indiana, 1976, p. 9.
21Jacob Burnet, *Notes on the Early Settlement of the North-Western Territory*, Cincinnati, 1847, p. 108-110.
22Letter of Luke Foster to Thomas Clark, Esq., May 23, 1819, quoted in Drake, "Memoir of the Miami Country," p. 105-106.
23James Elliott, *Poetical and Miscellaneous Works of James Elliott, A Non-Commissioned Officer in the Legion of the U. S.*, Greenfield, Massachusetts, 1798, p. 136.
24Narrative of Joseph Martin, quoted in article in *The Cincinnati Daily Gazette and Cincinnati Weekly Atlas*, 1844, contained in Charles Whittlesey, "Historical, Topographical and Geological Notices of Hamilton County, Ohio," Manuscript in collection of the Cincinnati Historical Society, hereafter hereafter referred to as Whittlesey, "...Notices of Hamilton County, Ohio."
25Letter of Lieutenant Cornelius Sedam to General Josiah Harmar, Jan. 31, 1791, Vol. 14, Harmar Papers, William Clements Library, University of Michigan.
26Frank A. Bone, *Complete Atlas of Warren County, Ohio*, Lebanon, Ohio, 1891, p. 5; Narrative of William Wiseman, quoted in Cist, *Cincinnati in 1859*, p. 92.
27Charles Greve, *Centennial History of Cincinnati*, Cincinnati, 1904, Vol. 1, p. 281, 290, 292-293; J. G. Olden, *Historical Sketches and Early Reminiscences of Hamilton County, Ohio*, Cincinnati, 1882, p. 59- 60, 73-74, 93, 101, 113-115.
28For an excellent plan of an English military blockhouse of the period see Thomas Anburey, *Travels Through the Interior Parts of America: In a Series of Letter From an Officer*, London, 1789, Vol. 1, p. 137-138. Another English blockhouse plan is illustrated in David A. Armour and Keith R. Widder, *At The Crossroads: Michilimackinac During the American Revolution*, Mackinac Island, Michigan, 1978, p. 128. For descriptions of civilian blockhouses along the Pennsylvania frontier see *Report of the Commission to Locate the Site of the Frontier Forts of Pennsylvania*, Harrisburg, 1896, Vol. 2, p. 389-390, 447. For descriptions of similar blockhouses in the Miami Country see Henry Howe, *Historical Collections of Ohio*, Cincinnati, 1850, p. 236-237; deposition of Thomas Gregory, quoted in Robert Ralston Jones, *Fort Washington at Cincinnati, Ohio*, Cincinnati, 1902, p. 77-78; Narrative of Isaac Dunn, John S. Gano Papers, Vol. 3, p. 164-165, Cincinnati Historical Society; Reverend Benjamin W. Chidlaw, "Early Times," 1876, quoted in Burress, *It Happened 'Round North Bend*, Ch. 3, p. 1; Ford, *History of Hamilton County, Ohio*, p. 364.
29Oliver M. Spencer, *Indian Captivity of O. M. Spencer*, New York, 1834, p. 14; Ferris, *Early Settlement of the Miami Country*, p. 267, 312-314; Drake, "Memoir of the Miami Country," p. 59, 63.
30Ferris, *Early Settlement of the Miami Country*, p. 267, 281, 291.
31Narrative of William Wiseman, quoted in Cist, *Cincinnati in 1859*, p. 92.
32Ibid., p. 84; *The Centinel of the North-Western Territory*, Nov. 9, 1793.
33J. G. Olden, *Historical Sketches*, p. 111-112.
34The four abandoned settlements were Dunlap's, Covalt's, Ludlow's and Tucker's Stations; see narrative of Mary Covalt Jones, "Reminiscences of Early Days," manuscript in collection of Cin-

cinnati Historical Society, p. 6, 8; letter of "Inhabitants of the Settlement Called Dunlap's Station," to General Josiah Harmar, Jan. 16, 1791; and letter of Lieutenant Jacob Kingsbury to General Josiah Harmar, Jan. 17, 1791; Vol. 14, Harmar Papers, William Clements Library, University of Michigan; narrative of William Wiseman, quoted in Cist, *Cincinnati in 1859*, p. 101-102; J. G. Olden, *Historical Sketches*, p. 113-114.

[35]Arthur G. King, "Origins of Some Cincinnati Streets—A Street in Clifton," *Bulletin of the Historical and Philosophical Society of Ohio*, Vol. 10, (1952), p. 146-147.

[36]Rufus Putnam, *The Memoirs of Rufus Putnam*, Ed. Rowena Buell, Boston and New York, 1903, p. 113-115; Smith, *The Mapping of Ohio*, p. 78-79.

[37]Letter of John Cleves Symmes to Jonathan Dayton, May 18-20, 1789, Symmes Correspondence, Cincinnati Historical Society.

[38]Drake, "Memoir of the Miami Country," p. 111.

[39]Letter of John Reily to Daniel Drake, Dec. 21, 1831, quoted in Drake, "Memoir of the Miami Country," p. 110; letter of Dr. William Goforth, Sept. 3, 1791, quoted in Charles Cist, *The Cincinnati Miscellany*, Cincinnati, 1845, Vol. 1, p. 200.

[40]Drake, "Memoir of the Miami Country," p. 107, 111, 116; Winthrop Sargent, "Order to the Militia of Hamilton County," Dec. 21, 1791, quoted in *Quarterly Publication of the Historical and Philosophical Society of Ohio*, Vol. 13, (1918), p. 117.

[41]Narrative of William Wiseman, quoted in Cist, *Cincinnati in 1859*, p. 97-98; letter of Dr. William Goforth to General Josiah Harmar, Jan. 13, 1791, Vol. 14, Harmar Papers, William Clements Library, University of Michigan.

[42]For the size of Indian war parties see Drake, "Memoir of the Miami Country," p. 64-65, 69, 104, 110; Cist, *Cincinnati in 1859*, p. 107; for numbers of militia see Drake, "Memoir of the Miami Country," p. 80; letter of Dr. Goforth, Sept. 3, 1791, quoted in Charles Cist, *The Cincinnati Miscellany*, Cincinnati, 1845, Vol. 1, p. 200.

[43]Letter of General Josiah Harmar to General Henry Knox, Jan. 25, 1791, Folio Letter Book A, Letter X, Harmar Papers, William Clements Library, University of Michigan.

[44]*The Centinel of the North-Western Territory*, Nov. 9, 1793.

[45]Letter of Judge Francis Dunlavy to Dr. Daniel Drake, Dec. 9, 1831, quoted in Drake, "Memoir of the Miami Country," p. 100-101; letter of Luke Foster to Thomas Clark, Esq., May 23, 1819, quoted in Ibid., p. 105-106; letter of Oliver M. Spencer to Dr. Daniel Drake, Dec. 23, 1831, quoted in Ibid., p. 108-110; narratives of Joseph Martin and Enoch Buckingham, quoted in articles in *The Cincinnati Daily Gazette and Cincinnati Weekly Atlas*, 1844, contained in Whittlesey, "...Notices of Hamilton County, Ohio,"; Ferris, *Early Settlement of the Miami Country*, p. 312-314, 318-321, 343-345.

[46]Letter of Luke Foster to Thomas Clark, Esq., May 23, 1819, quoted in Drake, "Memoirs of the Miami Country," p. 105; Ferris, *Early Settlement of the Miami Country*, p. 267.

[47]*The Centinel of the North-Western Territory*, Jan. 9, 1796; Max Mosler, Jacob Hoffman and James D. Smith, *Historic Brighton*, Cincinnati, 1902, p. 11.

Beasley's Station
1792

Captain John Beasley, a Revolutionary War veteran like so many other early settlers in the Miami Purchase, was among a group which emigrated in the late fall of 1779 from Spotsylvania County, Virginia to Bryant's Station near Lexington, Kentucky. He later served several tours of duty with Captain William Hagan's company of Bryant's Station militia in 1780 and 1782.[1]

Captain Beasley and his large family, including his second wife and children from both marriages, later moved to the Miami Country and made up the inhabitants of Beasley's Station. In 1792, he erected a large blockhouse on the north bank of the Little Miami River near its confluence with Walton Creek. The blockhouse was located south of present Wooster Pike and east of Walton Creek Road, in Section 3, Township 4, Fractional Range 1, Columbia Township.[2]

Captain Beasley related to Dr. Ezra Ferris the details of one hostile incident which occurred at the station. The attack originated between the river and the blockhouse during the construction of Beasley's grist mill in 1793. The number of Indians involved in the attack is unknown, but Beasley reportedly was wounded during the running skirmish. Although Joseph Martin of Garrard's Station stated that Beasley was not wounded by the Indian gunfire, Dr. Ferris received his information in person and saw the ball still embedded in Captain Beasley's hand.[3]

Beasley's first mill was completed and operating in 1793. There was an island opposite the mill and a dam was built to connect them.[4] The Beasley family was an enterprising one and they continued to improve and expand their business interests.

John Beasley held certificates of purchase for his original 119 acres, one rod and five square perches of land, valued at 100 dollars. He received his deed from John Cleves Symmes on May 20, 1796.[5] He purchased an additional 49 acres from William Goforth on November 3, 1797 for a price of 124 dollars and 50 cents.[6]

An advertisement in a Cincinnati newspaper illustrates the improvements made at Beasley's Station by 1801:

> *for Sale: a plantation lying on the bank of the Little Miami about 5 mile from Columbia with a orchard of*

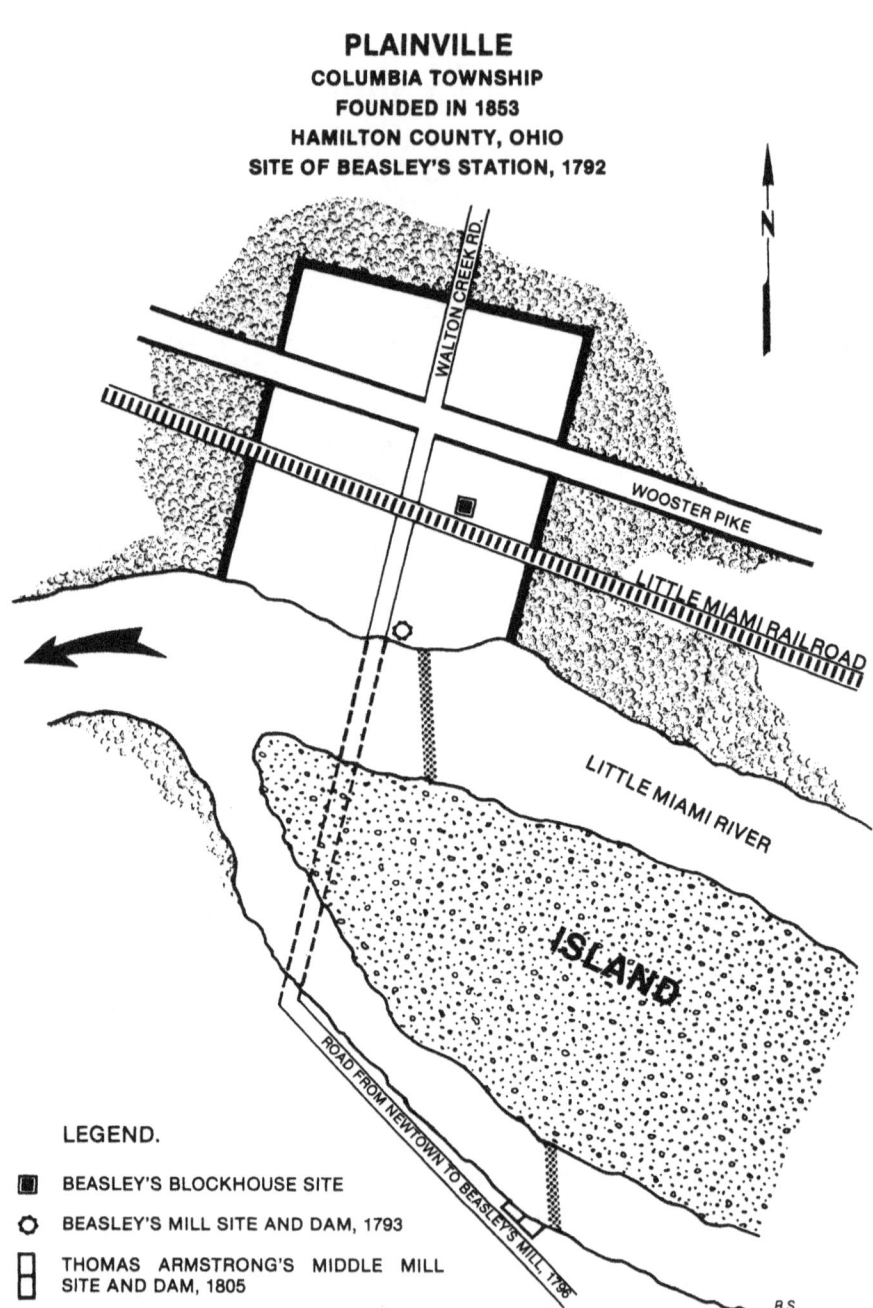

John Beasley's blockhouse and mill are shown on this composite plan of Plainville, as they relate to two present roads and the Little Miami Railroad. (Illustration by Richard Scamyhorn)

200 apple trees and 200 peach trees, uncompleted new house, saw mill, grist mill, 2 pair of stones - Boats can go most of the year from Ohio to the tailrace of the mill.
Aug. 12, John Beezley[7]

The station farm was sold to the Armstrong family and became their lower mill site.[8] In 1857 Henry Debolt surveyed his subdivision within the village of Plainville, encompassing the site of Beasley's Station. This survey helps to pinpoint the location of Beasley's Station.[9] The settlement was surrounded by prehistoric and historic Indian trails, habitation sites and ceremonial earthworks.[10]

During the years that the Beasley family occupied their station their neighbors were residing at Round Bottom and Covalt's Stations to the northeast, and Mercer's Station (Newtown) to which a connecting road was surveyed and established in 1796.[11]

Notes
[1] Bettye Lee Mastin, *Lexington, 1779: Pioneer Kentucky as Described by Early Settlers*, Cincinnati, 1979, p. 103; *George Rogers Clark And His Men: Military Records, 1778-1784*, Comp. Margery Heberling Harding, Frankfort, Kentucky, 1981, p. 50, 76.
[2] Lula Anna Strome, "The Story of the Pioneer Settlement of Plainville, Ohio, in 1794, and the Founding of Plainville Presbyterian Church, in 1880," manuscript in collection of Cincinnati Historical Society; Ferris, *Early Settlement of the Miami Country*, pp. 330-331; *Plat Book 1*, p. 311, Hamilton County Recorder's Office; *Road Record Book, Vol. 1-1B, 1793-1850*, p. 134, Hamilton County Engineer's Office, Road Records Division.
[3] Ferris, *Early Settlement of the Miami Country*, p. 330-332; narrative of Joseph Martin, quoted in Whittlesey, "...Notices of Hamilton County, Ohio."
[4] Narrative of Joseph Martin, quoted in Whittlesey, "...Notices of Hamilton County, Ohio"; *Plat Book 1*, p. 311, Hamilton County Recorder's Office.
[5] *Deed Book A*, p. 558; Hamilton County Recorder's Office.
[6] *Deed Book E-2*, p. 12, Hamilton County Recorder's Office.
[7] *Western Spy and Hamilton Gazette*, Aug, 12, 1801.
[8] Ferris, *Early Settlement of the Miami Country*, p. 330.
[9] "Plat of Plainville, Ohio, Henry Debolt surveyor," Oct. 15, 1857, *Plat Book 1*, p. 239-312, Hamilton County Recorder's Office.
[10] S. F. Starr, "The Archaeology of Hamilton County," *The Journal of the Cincinnati Museum of Natural History*, Vol. 23 (1960) p. 18-20, 27- 36, 43, 47, 75-80; William C. Mills, *Archaeological Atlas of Ohio*, Columbus, Ohio, 1914, p. 31.
[11] *Road Record Book, Vol. 1-1B, 1793-1850*, p. 134, Hamilton County Engineer's Office, Road Records Division.

Site of Beedle Station in Warren County as it appears in 1986. (See map) Beedle Station, Turtlecreek Township, Warren County. (Map by Richard Scamyhorn)

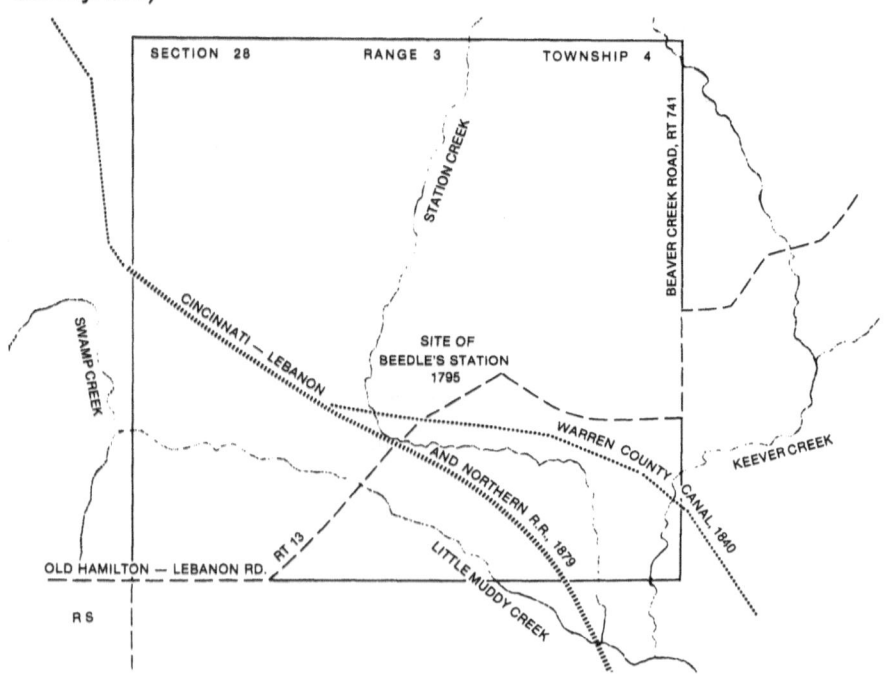

Beedle Station
1795

In the latter part of 1795 William Beedle founded a station which may have been the first settlement within the limits of present Warren County, Ohio. Beedle was a native of the Passaic Valley in New Jersey and sold his land there to his brother-in-law, Nathaniel Littell, in 1792.[1]

William Beedle may have arrived in the Miami Purchase as early as 1789, considering that he is listed as one of the original lot owners in Losantiville in 1789 and 1790.[2]

In October of 1791, Beedle applied as a volunteer settler for 106 acres of land forfeited by Hugh Gaston in the northeast corner of Section 10, Township 2, Range 4. The records show that he received a Gaston forfeiture of 106 acres in Section 33, Township 3, Range 1.[3]

On November 13, 1795, William Beedle purchased from Jonathan Dayton the entire Section 28 in Township 4, Range 3 in what is now Turtle Creek Township, Warren County. It was here, approximately five miles southwest of present Lebanon, that Beedle established his station.[4]

Prior to establishing his settlement, Beedle was a surveyor with two surveying parties sent from Cincinnati up the Mill Creek to do field work in the Mad River region. Daniel C. Cooper (who later laid out the city of Dayton) was in charge of one group and John Dunlap the other.

Beedle was in the Dunlap party and while encamped at Voorhees' Station on Mill Creek the surveying team decided to follow General Josiah Harmar's Trace. At some unknown point on Harmar's Trace Beedle, with his brother Francis, left the survey party and continued eastward, probably to locate a suitable site for his settlement.[5]

The first settlers at this station included William Beedle and his wife Esther, their son James, four daughters and sons-in-law and their children. There are several spelling variations of the family surname in publications and records, with Bedle the most commonly used. However, the surname Beedle is used by William on his deed from Jonathan Dayton, dated November 13, 1795, and in his Last Will and Testament, dated March 9, 1812.[6]

The families at Beedle's Station were mostly of the Presbyterian faith. Isaac Miller and Francis Beedle are among those persons credited with establishing the first church at or near the station about 1797. This Presbyterian assembly was known as the Turtle Creek congregation.[7]

The first building erected at the station site undoubtedly was the blockhouse, which is said to have been built in the style of many other defensive structures in the Miami Purchase. The upper part of the building extended over the lower part.

The residents of Beedle Station, like the inhabitants of most other contemporaneous settlements in the Northwest Territory, lived in primitive conditions. Primary clothing material used at the station in the beginning was dressed deerskin. Most of the children's clothing, including that of the young women, was fashioned from buckskin.[9]

The station soon became well known as other settlements were established and more roads were surveyed to and within present Warren County. Sections of the original roads or traces from Hamilton, Cincinnati and elsewhere were either altered or abandoned by 1800. At a later date many improved township, county, state and federal highways were laid along the general course of the original traces.[10]

A section of an old Cincinnati-Lebanon road which passed by the station was, as late as 1831, commonly called the Beedle Station Road. This road presently is Warren County Road 13 to its junction with Warren County Road 21. From that point, the old road to Cincinnati took a southwesterly course and crossed the Butler County line above the Tylersville Road. William Beedle and other settlers were petitioning for alterations of the roads passing through his settlement as early as 1806.[11]

The Beedle blockhouse stood west of today's State Route 741, north of the Hamilton Road (County Road 13), east of Station Creek and about one and three-quarter miles south of State Route 63.[12] Reverend James Kemper may have traveled over the old Cincinnati-Lebanon Road when he left his home in Cincinnati to pastor the Turtle Creek congregation at Beedle Station in 1799, an office which he held until 1801.[13]

James Kemper's successor, Richard McNemar, had a dramatic impact on the Beedle settlement and the Calvinists at Turtle Creek. McNemar was converted to the Shaker faith in 1805 by three Shaker missionaries from New York, the first people of that religion to visit the area. McNemar's double cabin was used by the Shakers for their religious services; the open space between the cabins sheltered the typical Shaker dance services which had given their nickname.

McNemar, after his own conversion to Shakerism, converted some of William Beedle's children and grandchildren as well as the Turtle Creek congregation. This split the family and William Beedle's resentment is manifest in his Last Will and Testament. Those family members who had converted to Shakerism were left very small legacies, while the others received generous bequests.[14]

Notes

[1] *A Genealogical Index of Pioneers in the Miami Valley, Ohio: Miami Co., Montgomery Co., Preble Co., and Warren Co., Ohio*, Ed. Lindsay M. Brien, Dayton, Ohio, 1970, p. 19.
[2] *Early Rosters of Cincinnati and Hamilton County*, p. 9.
[3] *Symmes Purchase Records*, Ed. Chris McHenry, Lawrenceburg, Indiana, 1979, p. 54, 74.
[4] *Transcribed Records Vol. F*, p. 369-370, Warren County Recorder's Office.
[5] "Extracts of B. Van Cleve's Memoranda," *The American Pioneer*, Ed. John S. Williams, Cincinnati, 1843-1844, Vol. 2, p. 294.
[6] *Miami Valley Will Abstracts: Miami, Montgomery, Warren and Preble Co. 1803-1850*, Ed. Lindsay M. Brien, Dayton, Ohio, 1940, Will Book 1, March 1812, p. 58, 120; *Transcribed Records Vol. F*, p. 369-370, Warren County Recorder's Office; *Will Records Book 1*, p. 57-60, Warren County Courthouse, Will Books and Administration Division.
[7] Reverend William M. Johnson, *175 Years at the Lebanon Presbyterian Church 1806-1981*, Centerville, Ohio, 1981, p. 3.
[8] *The History of Warren County, Ohio*, Chicago, 1882, p. 240.
[9] Henry Howe, *Historical Collections of Ohio*, Columbus, 1891, Vol. 2, p. 431.
[10] *Road Record Book Vol. 1, 1793-1850*, p. 194, Hamilton County Engineer's Office, Road Records Division; *Road Record Book 1*, p. 155-158, 186-187, 201, 258-259, *Road Record Book 1-2*, p. 27, 31, 35, 53, 86, Warren County Engineer's Office; *Will Record Book 1*, p. 57- 60, Warren County Courthouse, Will Books and Administrations Division; *Deed Book 5*, p. 30C, 57, 71-72, *Deed Book 6*, p. 125, 229, *Deed Book 9*, p. 263-264, *Deed Book E*, p. 30, Warren County Recorder's Office; *Plats, Descriptions and Valuations of Lands and Real Property in Turtle Creek Township, 1910*, p. 20, *Survey Book 4*, p. 86-87, Warren County Auditor's Office; U. S. Geological Survey 1898, revised 1906, Mason, Ohio Quad., 7.5' series; P. O. Beirne, C. E., "Map of Warren County, Ohio," Philadelphia, 1856, Warren County Engineer's Office; L. H. Everts, *Combination Atlas Map of Warren County, Ohio*, Philadelphia, 1875, p. 51, 64-65; Frank A. Bone, *Complete Atlas of Warren County, Ohio*, Lebanon, Ohio, 1891, p. 15, 22-23; Warren County Commissioner's Journals, Volumes for 1804-1822; *Index for Vol. 1*, p. 252-253, *Vol. 1*, p. 11, 34, 53, 110-111, 150-151; *Vol. 8*, p. 342, 346-348; *Vol. 13*, p. 320-321, 365, 368, 370.
[11] Ibid.
[12] Ibid.; Warren County Engineer's Official Highway Map, 1983.
[13] Hazel Spencer Phillips, *Richard The Shaker*, Oxford, Ohio, 1972, p. 20, 35.
[14] Ibid., p. 47-50; *Will Record Book 1*, p. 57-60, Warren County Courthouse, Wills and Administrations Division.

Bruce's Station
1793

On the 4th of March, 1791, Arthur St. Clair was appointed Major General in the United States Army. He relieved General Josiah Harmar as supreme commander of troops then guarding the Northwest Territory.[1]

Gen. St. Clair immediately began planning an assault on the primary Indian towns to the north of his headquarters in Cincinnati. In August he had gathered an army of regulars and militia at Fort Washington.[2] By September the troops were encamped at the present site of Hamilton in Butler County, where they constructed Fort Hamilton.[3] This military installation was intended to protect the supply route on the Great Miami River, act as a provision depot and maintain a communications link between the forward army posts and Fort Washington.[4]

The civilian population between 1791 and 1795 in what is now Butler County consisted mainly of transients such as surveyors, scouts, militia and employees of the army supply contractors. Some of the actual settlers then present were probably squatting on their original settlement sites.[5]

One early settler near Fort Hamilton was Charles Bruce. He was listed in the 1790-91 Census of Hamilton County, Ohio and was a private in a company of volunteer militia under the command of Captain Brice Virgin. Bruce's name appears on the muster roll call held by Colonel Charles Mentges, Inspector of the Army, at Fort Hamilton on January 27, 1792.[6]

Charles Bruce may have resided at one of the settlements along the Little Miami River before starting his own station. In April 1791, Bruce, along with several other men from Little Miami River stations, openly defied a ban on indiscriminate target practice even when challenged by militia Lieutenant Luke Foster. He was hauled before Judge William Goforth and fined two dollars for his misconduct. Unable to pay even this small fine, Bruce had to ask the court for twenty days leeway in coming up with the cash.[7]

According to reports, Bruce in 1793[8] built a station one and one-half miles below Fort Hamilton on the east side of the Great Miami River at the outlet of a large pond adjacent to a 300-acre prairie.[9] This pond was mistaken for the river by surveyor John Dunlap in 1789, while running the meridian line between the first and second townships in the second range for John Cleves Symmes. The pond is plotted on an official road protraction plan of 1808.[10]

Charles Bruce purchased the north part of Fractional Section 6 in Township 1, Range 2, in present Fairfield Township. The deed for the 200 acres he bought from Symmes was signed on April 1, 1795.[11] Bruce's Station stood on what is now part of the Hamilton campus of Miami University.[12]

The station was used by the cattle drovers supplying General Anthony Wayne's troops during the Indian campaigns of 1793-94. Benjamin Van Cleve delivered a herd of cattle to Fort Greenville on July 31, 1794 and began his return to Cincinnati on August 2. He and his five men passed Fort St. Clair on August 3 and stayed over at Bruce's.[13] The army may have detached a few soldiers from the complement at nearby Fort Hamilton to act as a guard for Bruce's Station.

Whether the army also detached troops to protect William Daraugh's Station on the Great Miami River near Fort Hamilton is not known. However, on Thursday, September 25, 1794, seven horses were stolen by Indians from Daraugh's Station.[14] Daraugh was listed as a resident of Ross Township, Butler County, in the county census of 1807.

During the year of 1795 more pioneers were venturing out from the older settlements, prompting an increase in advertisements for property. On February 7, 1795 one such advertisement appeared in *The Centinel of the North-Western Territory* which read:

> *Sale: Section of land in the Miami Purchase near Fort Hamilton on Pleasant Run Bottom about one mile from Bruce's Station. Wm. Muir.*[15]

In May 1796 Charles Bruce petitioned for a road 66 feet wide from his station to the "Great Road" leading from Fort Washington to Fort Hamilton. The road was initially established ten feet wide. The survey reports were reviewed by the Court of Sessions March 1797 and May 1798 and the road was widened.[16]

Bruce continued to improve his original settlement and acquired additions to his property. He purchased 160 acres of mortgaged land adjoining his property from George Adams, who had been an army bugler during the Revolutionary War. The deed was signed January 8, 1807, the same year that Bruce was listed in the Butler County census.[17]

Following his death, Charles Bruce's property was sold. The sale notice appeared in the *Western Spy and Hamilton Gazette* March 28, 1817 and read:

> *For Sale; that very valuable Farm belonging to the estate of Charles Bruce, late of Butler County, deceased, situate on the east bank of the Great Miami River, between*

one and two miles below Hamilton, containing three hundred acres. Cont. Excellent apple orchard, about 120 acres cleared and fenced. Hamilton; Feb. 10, 1817.
       Joseph Hough
       John Reilly executors"[18]

Notes
[1]*A History and Biographical Cyclopaedia of Butler County, Ohio*, Cincinnati, 1882, p. 4.
[2]Ibid.
[3]Ibid., p. 4-5.
[4]Ibid., p. 4.
[5]*Deed Book A*, p. 4, Butler County Recorder's Office; *Deed Book A*, p. 534-535, Hamilton County Recorder's Office.
[6]*Early Rosters of Cincinnati and Hamilton County*, p. 11,; "Selections From the Torrence Papers, VIII," *Quarterly Publication of The Historical and Philosophical Society of Ohio*, Vol. 13 (1918), p. 97-98.
[7]*Judge William Goforth's* Notebook of Court Cases, entries for April 6 and 7, 1791, John Armstrong Collection, Box 19, Indiana Historical Society.
[8]*Centennial History of Butler County, Ohio*, Ed. Bert S. Bartlow, W. H. Todhunter, Stephen D. Cone, Joseph I. Pater, Frederick Schneider, Etc., Cincinnati, 1905, p. 229; *History and Biographical Cyclopaedia of Butler County, Ohio*, p. 284-285.
[9]James McBride, *Notes on Hamilton, From An Original Manuscript Written in 1831*, reprinted by Republican Publishers, Hamilton, Ohio, 1898, p. 4; *History and Biographical Cyclopaedia of Butler County, Ohio*, p. 25.
[10]*Road Record Book, Vol. 1, 1793-1850*, p. 14-15, Hamilton County Engineer's Office, Road Records Division; James McBride, *Pioneer Biography: Sketches of the Lives of Some of the Early Settlers in Butler County, Ohio*, Cincinnati, 1869, Vol. 1., p. 4.
[11]*Deed Book A*, p. 4, Butler County Recorder's Office.
[12]Butler County Road Maps; U. S. Geological Survey, Hamilton, Ohio Quad., 7.5' series; L. H. Everts, *Combination Atlas Map of Butler County, Ohio*, Philadelphia, 1875, p. 30-31; *Road Record Book Vol. 1, 1793-1850*, p. 130, Hamilton County Engineer's Office, Road Records Division.
[13]"Memoirs of Benjamin Van Cleve," *Quarterly Publication of The Historical and Philosophical Society of Ohio*, Vol. 17 (1922), p. 51.
[14]*Copy of Diary of Major Winthrop Sargent, Number 2*, commencing at New York Oct. 1, 1793 and ending in Philadelphia Jan. 1, 1796, entry of Sat., Sept. 27, 1794, Manuscript in Collection of Cincinnati Historical Society; Alta Harvey Heiser, *West to Ohio*, Yellow Springs, Ohio, 1954, Ch. 1, p. 12; *Census of 1807 Butler County, Ohio*, Ed. Willard Heiss and R. Thomas Mayhill, Knightstown, Indiana, 1986, p. 7.
[15]*Centinel of the North-Western Territory*, Feb. 7, 1795.
[16]*Road Record Book Vol. 1, 1793-1850*, p. 130, 135, Hamilton County Engineer's Office, Road Records Division.
[17]McBride, *Pioneer Biography*, Vol. 1, p. 173; *Deed Book A*, p. 355, Butler County Recorder's Office; *Census of 1807 Butler County, Ohio*, p. 6.
[18]*The Western Spy and Hamilton Gazette*, March 28, 1817.

Daraugh's Station
1792

John Daraugh (the name is also spelled Darraugh, Dorrough, Deurow, Dorough, and Derrah in old records) was among the first property owners in Losantiville in the years 1789-1790. He and William Daraugh were active in forming the first Presbyterian church in Cincinnati from 1792 to 1794. On January 20, 1790, Israel Ludlow applied for a forfeiture of land owned by William Burnet on behalf of John Daraugh. He received 106 acres in the northeast corner of Section 7, Township 2, Second Entire Range, in present-day Crosby Township, Hamilton County.[1]

However, a memoir by James Felton indicates that the station was not at the site of John Daraugh's actual land holdings but was a "squatter" settlement located on the west bank of the Great Miami River near the mouth of Indian Creek and the old Colerain Road. This location would be in Section 34, Ross Township, Butler County, near today's Ross, Ohio.[2]

James Felton's parents William and Margaret, natives of Germany and Ireland respectively, were among the founders of Daraugh's Station, with their young children Kate, John, and Robert. Other members of the Daraugh's Station community mentioned by James Felton include Charles Mansfield, Margaret Felton's brother; Robert McLeland; William Crumm; Henry Whitaker; John Larison; Nancy Swimm, and Rebecca Goble.[3]

Many of these people are also mentioned in accounts of Dunlap's Station or Colerain, so it may be that they resided there before feeling safe enough to venture north to their own settlement. However, it is unlikely that Daraugh's Station was founded before the spring of 1792, since Dunlap's Station itself was abandoned in January of 1791 after a savage Indian attack and not repopulated until January of 1792.[4]

Felton's memoir indicates that the danger of Indian attack was keenly felt by the Daraugh's Station inhabitants. They built a strong blockhouse near their cabins and fled to it in times of danger. Church services were held in the blockhouse, to which the men carried their firearms, stacking them in the corner in case of an attack.[5]

Several people narrowly escaped death or capture by Indians near Daraugh's Station. A young boy named John Crumm was captured while picking wild grapes near the station. After spending several years with the Indians and being adopted by an Indian couple, Crumm was ransomed and returned to his original family, not without much hesitation and reluctance to abandon his adopted Indian parents.[6]

Whether the army may have detached some troops from nearby Fort Hamilton to protect Daraugh's Station is not known. However, on Thursday, September 25, 1794, seven horses were stolen by Indians from the station.[7]

It is also uncertain whether the Daraughs ever finalized their land titles to the area around the station. An early Butler County Census does reveal that William Daraugh was still living in Ross Township, Butler County, as late as 1807.[8]

Notes
[1] *Early Rosters of Cincinnati and Hamilton County*, p. 9, 11, 20, 164; *Symmes Purchase Records*, p. 21.
[2] "A Sketch of the Life of Jacob Felton," courtesy of Mr. Scott Mansfield, San Gabriel, California, p. 1.
[3] Ibid. p. 1-3.
[4] James McBride, *Pioneer Biography*, Vol. 1, p. 86.
[5] "Sketch of the Life of Jacob Felton," p. 2
[6] Ibid. p. 2-3.
[7] *Copy of Diary of Major Winthrop Sargent, Number 2*, Entry of Saturday, Sept. 27, 1794, Cincinnati Historical Society; Alta Harvey Heiser, *West to Ohio*, Yellow Springs, Ohio, 1945, Ch. 1, p. 12.
[8] *Census of 1807, Butler County, Ohio*, Ed. Willard Heiss and R. Thomas Mayhill, Knightstown, Indiana, 1968, p. 7.

Campbell's Station
1793

On November 16, 1792 John Campbell, a resident of Columbia, applied for 106 acres of Adam Lee's land, by forfeit, in the northeast corner of Section 20, Range 1, Township 4, present Sycamore Township.[1]

The terms of the Miami Land Company stipulated that any section of land contracted for in the Miami Purchase must be improved within two years after the date of purchase or be subject to forfeiture. If a purchaser applied under this rule as John Campbell did, his initial acquisition automatically came from the northeast corner of the section unless the entire section was acquired.[2]

After acquiring the 106 Sycamore Township acres he had applied for, Campbell is supposed to have built his blockhouse in Colerain Township, on the east side of the Great Miami River opposite present-day Miamitown.[3] A Revolutionary War veteran, he had served at least three tours of duty with different companies of Kentucky militia from 1779 to 1783, eventually earning the rank of sergeant.[4]

Campbell reportedly built his blockhouse opposite Captain James Henry's cabin, one mile north of a spring and salt lick located near the residence of Jerimiah Chandler.[5] The information source for this account could not be ascertained, but by using an old plat of Miamitown and calculating the described distances, the blockhouse would have stood in Fractional Section 1, Range 1 East, Township 1 North, in present Colerain Township.[6]

However, if John Campbell was adjacent to Capt. Henry, then it is feasible that he built in Fractional Section 20, Range 2, Township 1, in present Fairfield Township, Butler County. His station site may have been established in an advertisement by John Dunlap in *The Centinel of the North-Western Territory* in December of 1793:

> *for settlers at the new station on the Great Miami 3 miles above Colerain on the property of Capt. James Henry...John Dunlap. N. B. A plan of the above will be shown to anyone who wishes to become settlers, by applying J. D.*[7]

Notes
[1] *Symmes Purchase Records*, p. 59-60.
[2] Ibid., p. 9.
[3] Greve, *Centennial History of Cincinnati*, Vol. 1, p. 292.
[4] *George Rogers Clark and His Men*, p. 20, 115, 120.
[5] Henry Hale, "Suburbs of Cincinnati," *The Cincinnati Enquirer*, Feb. 12, 1961.
[6] J. G. Olden, *Historical Sketches*, p. 41, 118; maps of Hamilton County, Ohio, by S. Morrison and J. Williams, 1835; William D. Emerson, 1847; A. W. Gilbert, 1848; *Titus' Atlas of Hamilton County, Ohio*, Philadelphia, 1869, p. 17; U. S. Geological Surveys, Addyston, Ohio, Shandon, Ohio, Greenhills, Ohio Quadrangles, 7.5' series.
[7] *Centinel of the North-Western Territory*, Dec. 14, 1793.

Carpenter's Settlement circa 1793

James Carpenter, an early settler at Columbia, applied for warrant number 250 in the Miami Purchase on November 28, 1789. This warrant was located in Township 4, Range 1, in present Sycamore Township and consisted of the entire 640 acres in Section 15.[1]

It is not clear at what date Carpenter began his improvements; however, he may have left Columbia in the spring of 1793 along with Abner Denman, Brice Thompson, Richard Ayers and others to establish a settlement.[2]

Brice Thompson was a veteran of the Revolution who migrated from Essex County, New Jersey to Mason County, Kentucky in 1790. On November 26, 1792 he applied for 106 acres in Section 21, Township 4, Range 1 (warrant number 103) adjoining Carpenter's land.[3]

Richard Ayers obtained Section 22 in 1972 and Abner Denman purchased land in 1793. All of the inhabitants of the settlement built their ordinary log cabins very close to each other.[4]

The only reference to a defensive stockade at this settlement is from a history of Blue Ash written in 1968 by Pliny A. Johnston, superintendent of the Hamilton County School District. In his description of the defensive arrangement, Johnston related that in addition to positioning the cabins to form a small square, a palisade with two gates was built around the four dwellings.[6]

Johnston also intimated that the first Baptist church built at this settlement, Carpenter's Run Church, was constructed blockhouse fashion even though it was completed in 1798, three years after the signing of the Greenville Treaty. There are no records of Indian hostilities at this settlement.

The site remained agricultural for many years and was known at one time as Plainfield. The first cabins here stood at the intersection of today's Cooper and Plainfield Roads.[8]

Notes
[1] *Symmes Purchase Records*, p. 19.
[2] Marion S. Kjellenberg, *Blue Ash, 1968 History and Directory, 1793-1968. The Fastest Growing City in Southwestern Ohio*, Montgomery, Ohio, 1968, p. 6.
[3] Ibid., p. 6; *Symmes Purchase Records*, p. 60; J. G. Olden, *Historical Sketches*, Cincinnati, 1880, p. 117-118.
[4] *Blue Ash, 1968 History and Directory*, p. 6.
[5] Ibid.
[6] Ibid.
[7] Ibid.
[8] Maps of Hamilton County, Ohio, S. Morrison and J. Williams, 1835; William D. Emerson, 1847; A. W. Gilbert, 1848; R. C. Phillips, 1865; C. S. Mendenhall, ca. 1877; City of Cincinnati and Hamilton County Metropolitan Topographic survey maps, Hamilton County Engineer's Office, Roads Records Division; U. S. Geological Survey, Madeira, Ohio Quad. 7.5' series.

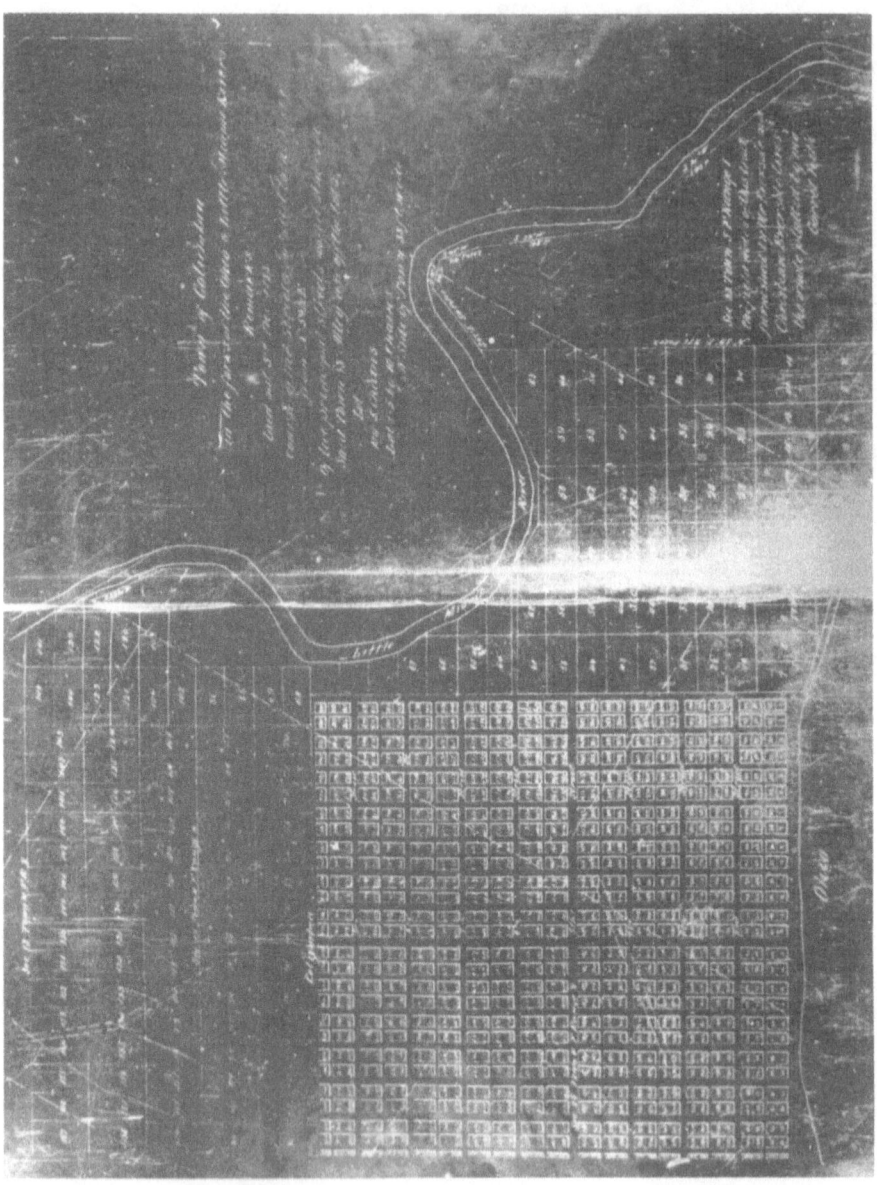
Copy of the original plan of the town of Columbia at the confluence of the Ohio and Little Miami Rivers as originally laid out Dec. 3, 1788.

Columbia and Fort Miami 1788

Columbia was the first of three settlements begun along the Ohio River in the Miami Purchase during 1788 and 1789. Columbia's founder was Benjamin Stites, born at Scotch Plains, Essex County, New Jersey in 1734.[1]

During Benjamin's youth the Stites family migrated to Ten Mile Creek, in western Pennsylvania, and settled at Red Stone Fort (Brownsville). During the Revolutionary War, Benjamin served with the Pennsylvania militia under the command of General James Irvine, earning the rank of captain.[2] Listed as Captain in the Washington County, Pennsylvania Militia Roster of 1782-85, he later attained the rank of major.[3]

Benjamin Stites apparently was the first "booster" of organized settlements in the Miami Purchase. Having seen that countryside in 1786, Stites returned to his native New Jersey and interested John Cleves Symmes, one of the state's Congressmen, in purchasing and developing large tracts of this western land. While Symmes was still negotiating the purchase with the U. S. Treasury, Stites bought 20,000 acres from him, located on the west bank of the Little Miami River from its mouth some distance upstream, and west along the Ohio River. The deal led to later embarrassment when Symmes was unable to secure title to the land. After much negotiation and political maneuvering, Symmes finally legalized his holdings in 1794.[4]

The first settlement, Columbia, was begun on November 18, 1788 but provisions for its defense had been planned beforehand.[5] While enroute to the site near the mouth of the Little Miami, Stites and his party stopped at Limestone, Kentucky (now Maysville) and cut a large quantity of oak clapboards to be used as roofing for a fort. The heartwood of the trees was prepared for use as chinking the open spaces in the walls of the blockhouses they planned to erect; the doors were to be of double boat planks.[6]

While the party was gathering the necessary materials at Limestone, an Indian attack killed two of them. One was Nehemiah Stites, a nephew of the leader.[7] But the settlers did not allow this tragedy to deter them and one of them later recalled:

> *We remained their in order to get some clabboards to cover the blockhouses that was contemplated for our safety, the trees then standing in the forest, however the*

This crude sketch of the first blockhouse at Columbia, although done in the late 1800s, may be based on eyewitness descriptions. One of the Columbia blockhouses survived until 1838, when it toppled into the Ohio River by bank erosion. Illustration from A. E. Jones, *Extracts From the History of Cincinnati*, Cincinnati, 1888. *(Courtesy of the Cincinnati Historical Society)*

> *men with their usual energy and industry persevered and cut down the timber of sturdy oaks and rived out a large quantity of clabboards and made a raft and secured them and then we embarked again.*[8]

Hezekiah Stites, Benjamin's brother, confirmed that the Columbia settlers "brought down clapboards and doors for 4 houses."[9]

The erection of the blockhouses and stockade at Columbia was described much later by Ezra Ferris, one of the area's early settlers:

> *They commenced building a blockhouse on the bank of the river and before night, had the body of it raised and the door (previously prepared) hung... the first blockhouse being finished they erected 3 others at proper distances, and in proper form for a fort; filling the intermediate spaces with cabins about 14 or possibly 16 feet square: with the roofs pitching inward and projecting over the outside wall so that it could not be passed over without great difficulty, leaving spaces for 3 gates, one next to*

The house in which Benjamin Stites, founder of Columbia, died in 1804. Built in 1800 for his daughter, Mrs. Anna Carter, the house was torn down in April, 1915. It stood at 4136 Davis Lane (Airport Road) about one and one half miles northwest of where Stites originally landed. *(Photo courtesy Greene County District Library, Xenia)*

> *the river and one at each end, the cabins probably might number thirty or more.*[10]

In other notes, Ferris described the fort upon his arrival in December of 1789:

> *An apartment in the fort (of about 16 feet square) was assigned each family, in which for the time, they resided. Fort Miami consisted of four long buildings, for they were all connected together, but divided into different apartments, with a blockhouse at each corner, projecting a few feet beyond the range of other buildings, so that no Indian could approach any part in the ring without exposing himself to the fire of the white people from the blockhouse.*[11]

One of the blockhouses at Columbia survived until 1838 and was described by Thomas Gregory of Cincinnati, who had lived in the house for several years:

> *The blockhouse was about eighteen feet wide and twenty four feet long with the gable end towards the Ohio River and very close to the edge of the bank.*
>
> *The building was constructed of round logs about the size of a man's body, unhewed, but notched together at the corners. It contained two rooms divided by a rough partition of split logs, afterwards changed to a board partition, and above the first story was a high garret or attic. The roof was covered with split logs secured by wooden pins, afterwards replaced by clapboards. There was a puncheon floor, later removed for a more modern substitute. The attic projected over the lower story and was provided with port or loop holes for rifles. A large stone chimney stood in the middle of the gable end furthest from the river. This chimney was built outside of the logwork, but the fireplace opened into the lower room. This fireplace was large enough to take in logs about four feet in length and at night it furnished our light, for lamps of any kind were very scarce. The front of the house, facing the Ohio River, had a window and door in the lower story and a small window in the attic.*
>
> *There was a window opening on each side of the house in the back room and another small window in the attic facing away from the river. The door was a heavy one secured by a bar, and the windows were protected by heavy plank shutters.*[12]

The blockhouse was occupied by the Hart family in 1832, Hart's oldest daughter having married Athan Stites, then owner of the land and the blockhouse. Athan was the son of Hezekiah and nephew of Benjamin Stites.

The site lies in Section 29, Township 5, Fractional Range 1, Spencer Township. High water and bank erosion toppled the blockhouse into the river. The area today would be adjacent to Tucker Marine Company, 4603 Kellogg Avenue. Athan's brick house was one hundred feet behind the blockhouse, with the west half of the house at the center line of the blockhouse.[13]

The entire oblong structure of Fort Miami was completed about one month after the landing. It stood about three quarters of a mile below the mouth of the Little Miami River. A letter dated September 30, 1791 states that "Just below the mouth of the Little Miami River is a garrison called Fort Miami. At a small distance below the garrison is the town of Columbia."[14]

The completed Fort Miami bore a striking resemblance to the Kentucky station forts. Like them, it boasted of a walled compound created by building crude shade-roofed cabins end-to-end, with projecting blockhouses at the corners to provide a clear crossfire along the walls. A further refinement was the extending of the clapboard roofs beyond the edges of the cabins to prevent Indians from scaling them.

References to heavy bulletproof wooden doors and shutters at Columbia are numerous. Oliver M. Spencer noted concerning his father's cabin that:

> *Its narrow doors of thick oak plank, turning on stout wooden hinges, and secured with strong bars braced with timber from the floor, formed a safe barrier to the entrance below; while above, on every side, were port holes, or small embrasures, from which we might see, and fire upon the enemy. Of windows we had but two, containing only four panes of glass each, in openings so small, that any attempt to enter them by force must have proved fatal to an assailant.*[15]

Even the horses at Columbia were protected from possible Indian attack, as Hezekiah Stites recalled:

> *Several blockhouses and cabins were built and stockades erected adjoining to them for the protection of their horses from the Indians. The wooden hinges of the massive doors or gates of these enclosures were so made that they could not be opened without a grating that would awaken the inmates of the cabin. Care was taken to cut down the trees to a considerable distance around them that the Indians should, in making an approach, be at once without the means of concealment and protection.*[16]

The fortifications erected by the settlers at Columbia seem to have been superior in workmanship to many of the other stations in the Miami Valley. The government troops sent to the settlement did not fare so well, as Ezra Ferris recalled:

> *...A few days after Major Stites' party made their landing*

> *Lieutenant (since General) Kingsbury with a... company of soldiers landed about a mile below the fort and built a blockhouse on a low bank near the river which they surrounded in part with pickets, but being unfortunate in his location the water having raised over his works he reimbarked his men either Christmas or New Year's Day and floated down below the mouth of Deer Creek and on the next day, commenced building a picket fort on the bank of the Ohio River near the spot... where the steam mill was afterward erected which was then said to be the first settlement made at Cincinnati (now so called).*[17]

John Cleves Symmes corroborated this occurrence in a letter to Jonathan Dayton. Describing his arrival at Columbia, he wrote that:

> *The soldiers had been drove from the ground floor of their blockhouse into the loft, and from the loft into a boat which they had wisely preserved from the destruction of the previous ice, and the then raging torrent of the Ohio.*[18]

The location of Kingsbury's blockhouse was west of the intersection of present Kellogg Avenue and Wilmer Street (Turkey Bottom Road). This site has always been recorded as a low swampy area on the topographical maps and was near the Kellogg Avenue toll gate.[19]

Despite the precautions taken to build adequate defenses at Columbia, including the hiring of "spies" or rangers to scout for Indian war parties, John Reily recalled that "it was almost impossible to keep any horse-creatures at Columbia." News items in *The Centinel of the North-Western Territory* indicate that the Indians were stealing horses from Columbia as late as May of 1794.[20]

By 1789 the influx of settlers filled the fort and many of the apartments were shared by two or three families. Several cabins were built outside the fort as a result. These cabins, such as the one built by Major Goforth, were as well prepared for defense as the blockhouses. During the following year many families ventured down to the inlots of Columbia, about one mile below the fort.[21]

In 1790, a road was petitioned "three poles wide from Fort Miami to Captain Mercer's lots, along the line of the other five acre lots to the Little Miami, then along several courses of the river to William Flinn's house and from there along Turkey Bottom to the most convenient ford to Wickerham's

Mill."[22] This was the beginning of the extensive road system which eventually connected many of the southwestern Ohio station communities.

After General St. Clair's defeat by the Indians in 1791, the settlers erected blockhouses on the hills beyond the outlots of Columbia. These were manned by the local militia as lookout and signal stations.[23]

The layout of the town of Columbia was planned as carefully as the fortifications, as Ezra Ferris noted:

> *Major Stites has nearly all the bottom lands at Columbia laid off in five acre lots from Miami Fort down to the plat of that part he laid off in half acres for the town, and from the river back to Turkey Bottom.*[24]

A microfilm copy of the original plan of Columbia and a map of the Miami Purchase circa 1790, show the in-lots and the out-lots there plotted in segments of entire and fractional sections of old Columbia Township.[25]

The exact date of the demise of Fort Miami as a defensive stockade is not known. However, its importance in the development of Southwestern Ohio is quite apparent. During 1792, it was reported by one visitor at Columbia that the settlement contained 1,100 residents with many well-built houses, a boatyard on the Little Miami, and two military posts which had been erected several miles behind the town.[26]

Although today most attention is focused on Cincinnati proper as the progenitor and protector of all the early Hamilton County villages, in actuality Columbia was the seedbed that spawned a profusion of satellite stations, some of which became permanent communities. Many of the proprietors of these new stations formed their plans at, and drew their tenants from, the Columbia settlement.

Columbia provided the primary protection between the Miamis prior to Fort Washington, supplemented for short periods by a few government troops. There was a flourishing community here when Cincinnati was a struggling hamlet. The unfortunate frequent flooding and Indian harassment that the settlement endured hastened the migration to safer and drier environs.

Notes
[1]R. Pierce Beaver, "The Miami Purchase of John Cleves Symmes," *Ohio Archaeological and Historical Society Quarterly*, Vol. 40 (1931), p. 284-288; "Family Papers of Major Benjamin Stites," quoted in Esther Benzing, *Fairfield, Ohio*, Mt. Healthy, Ohio, 1978, p. 33, 36.
[2]Ibid., p. 34, 36; *Official Roster of Soldiers of the American Revolution Buried in the State of Ohio*, Ed. Frank D. Henderson, John D. Rea, Jane Dowd Dailey, Columbus, Ohio, 1929, Vol. 1, p. 353; *Pennsylvania Archives*, Ed. Wm. H. Engle, M. D. and John B. Linn, Harrisburg, 1898, series 2, Vol. 14, p. 765.
[3]*Pennsylvania Archives*, series 2, Vol. 14, p. 765; Benzing, *Fairfield, Ohio*, p. 34.

[4] Beaver, "Miami Purchase," p. 248-288.
[5] Ferris, *Early Settlement of the Miami Country*, p. 255-256; Letter of John Cleves Symmes to Jonathan Dayton, May 18-20, 1789, Symmes Correspondence, Cincinnati Historical Society; *Fairfield, Ohio*, p. 34.
[6] Letter from an unidentified person to Daniel and John Gano, undated, Lyman Draper Collection, Drake Papers, Microfilm series O, Draper Mss. 1088, Wisconsin Historical Society, p. 2; *Fairfield, Ohio*, p. 34.
[7] Ibid.
[8] Letter from an unidentified person to Daniel and John Gano, undated, Lyman Draper Collection, Drake Papers, Microfilm series O, Draper Mss. 1088, Wisconsin Historical Society.
[9] Narrative of Hezekiah Stites, Lyman Draper Collection, Drake Papers, Microfilm series O, Draper Mss. 1021-1027, Wisconsin Historical Society.
[10] Letter from Ezra Ferris to Griffin Yeatman, et. al., Dec. 18, 1838, Lyman Draper Collection, Drake Papers, Microfilm series O, Draper Mss. 1089, Wisconsin Historical Society.
[11] Ferris, *Early Settlement*, p. 250.
[12] Deposition of Thomas Gregory, quoted in Jones, *Fort Washington at Cincinnati, Ohio*, p. 76-78.
[13] Ibid.; *Road Record Book, Vol. 1-1B 1790-1850*, p. 92; *Road Record Book, Vol. 2*, p. 78; *Road Records 1855-1871*, p. 543, Hamilton County Engineer's Office, Road Records Division; Map of Hamilton County by Wm. Emerson, 1847; *Titus' Atlas of Hamilton County, Ohio*, p. 39, 47; George Moessinger and Fred Bertsch, *Map of Hamilton County, Ohio*, New York, 1884 (Atlas), hereafter known as Atlas of Hamilton County, Ohio, 1884, p. 2.
[14] Ferris, *Early Settlement*, p. 250, 257; Letter printed in *Philadelphia Daily General Advertiser*, Oct. 18, 1791, included in Robert Clarke Papers, Box 1, Folder 3, No. 448, Cincinnati Historical Society.
[15] Oliver M. Spencer, *Indian Captivity of O. M. Spencer*, New York, 1834, p. 14.
[16] Drake, "Memoir of the Miami Country," p. 63.
[17] Letter of Ezra Ferris to Griffin Yeatman, et. al., Dec. 18, 1838.
[18] Letter of John Cleves Symmes to Jonathan Dayton, May 18-20, 1789.
[19] A. E. Jones, *Extracts from the History of Cincinnati*, Cincinnati, 1888, p. 54.
[20] Drake, "Memoir of the Miami Country," p. 111; *Centinel of the North-Western Territory*, May 24, 1794.
[21] Ferris, *Early Settlement*, p. 267, 281.
[22] *Road Record Book, Vol. 1-1B 1790-1850*, p. 92, Hamilton County Engineer's Office, Road Records Division.
[23] Ferris, *Early Settlement*, p. 291.
[24] Ibid., p. 266.
[25] Manuscript map of the Miami Purchase, ca. 1790, Cincinnati Historical Society; Microfilm copy of original plat of Columbia, Hamilton County Recorder's Office.
[26] John Heckewelder, *A Narrative of the Mission of the United Brethren among the Delaware and Mohegan Indians*, Ed. William Elsey Connelly, Cleveland, 1907, p. 68.

Covalt Station or Bethany Town 1789

Abraham Covalt was born in 1743 at Egg Harbor, New Jersey, where he spent his youth. After his marriage, Covalt and his wife moved to Bedford County, Pennsylvania.[1]

During the Revolutionary War, Covalt served in the Bedford County Militia, and in 1777 held the rank of Captain in the Sixth Company, Second Battalion, under the command of Colonel George Ashman.[2] Captain Covalt's son Bethuel held the rank of Ensign in the same company, and later served under Captain Henry Rush, as did another son, Timothy.[3]

Abraham Covalt apparently entered into a land transaction with John Cleves Symmes prior to 1789 and persuaded seven families to leave Pennsylvania and settle with him in the Miami Purchase.[4]

Of the 45 persons in his party, twelve were members of his family, including seven sons and three daughters.[5]

Covalt, like other early pioneers with a background of military discipline, prepared well for his trip. The party traveled in two flat boats, one being 55 feet in length and the other 40 feet. One boat held the farm implements and twenty head of livestock including cattle, swine, sheep and seven horses. Also aboard one of the boats were mill stones for the grist mill which Covalt obviously had included in his plans before leaving Pennsylvania.[6]

The party landed at the mouth of the Little Miami River in January of 1789 and a temporary camp was established there while cabins were being constructed at their permanent settlement. The seventeen dwellings erected at the settlement were soon enclosed in a large stockade including four blockhouses. It was not only one of the largest fortifications at any of the frontier settlements in Hamilton County but possibly the first one in the interior of the Miami Purchase. The site was known as Covalt Station or Bethany Town.[7]

A secondary source dating from 1844 places the station approximately 240 feet below where the Little Miami Railroad bridge crossed Covalt's Mill Run. This source also states the station's cemetery was about sixty feet below the fort.

The traditional setting for Covalt Station is on the property of St. Thomas Episcopal Church at Terrace Place and Miami Avenue, Terrace Park.[8]

Captain Covalt proceeded to have his millwright, Joseph Hinkle, construct a grist mill on Covalt's Run (Red Bird Creek) between the fort and the Little Miami River, making it the only standing mill at that time servicing the settlements in the Miami Purchase. The Covalt mill was probably constructed of round logs and equipped with a tub wheel or a small overshot wheel. Early mills of this type were commonly called corncrackers, and were capable of grinding two or three bushels of meal a day.[10] The mill reportedly stood about 60 feet from the old Covalt cemetery.[10] Its hopper was filled every morning and the millstone left to turn non-stop 24 hours a day.[11]

The inhabitants apparently hung tobacco to dry in this structure. On one occasion the Indians occupied the mill overnight waiting to seize the miller, who at that time was Mr. S. Gerston. During their vigil, the Indians emptied grain sacks and stripped and crushed the drying tobacco leaves.[12] Whether the inhabitants of the station built an additional blockhouse to protect the mill is not known.

Although the Indian attacks were increasing, Captain Covalt continued to encourage new settlers to invest in his land holdings and offered them a tract of half a section each at his cost. He had purchased four tracts from John Cleves Symmes on the west side of the Little Miami River, including Fractional Sections 22, 23, 28 and the entire Section 30, all located in Township 5, Fractional Range 2, Columbia Township.[13]

Captain Covalt entered into a partnership with Levi Buckingham at the Station, with both sharing the costs for property line surveys. Their receipt for the surveying fees is dated May 24, 1790.[14]

Small bands of Indians were active around the Columbia Township settlements throughout 1789 and 1790 stealing livestock and killing or capturing settlers, usually by ambush. This was especially true of the stations at Columbia, Round Bottom and Covalt's. At the time of the attack on Dunlap's Station in January, 1791, General Harmar sent Captain Cornelius Ryker Sedam with twelve soldiers from Fort Washington to the Covalt settlement as a guard.[15] Sedam reported to Harmar:

> *Sir. Yours of the twenty second came to hand where in you informed me you wold wish to have the strength of this plase thare is 17 fighting men beside the troopes and one half of them is a hunting Every Day so you may judg my situation at this plase the Fort is as larg as Fort Washington and in very bad repare it is not in my power to put it in a plase of defense with out more men in I in*

close you a plan of it the hunters Daly in forms me of Sines as thay Call it that thay Si when thay are out the 25 in the morning the sentinel Saw one nere the Fort but if thay com I hope I will be abel to in form you how the affare went.[16]

The plan enclosed by Sedam shows a large rectangular stockade with a blockhouse at each corner. Attached to each of the two shorter ends of the stockade is a triangular extension marked "Place for Cattle." He also drew lines of fire from each loop hole in the stockade and blockhouses to show that every portion of the fort was covered by a crossfire. Sedam's statement that this fort and Fort Washington were comparative in size implied that the stockaded area of Covalt's fort encompassed 40,000 square feet.[17]

Abraham Covalt Jr. and his close friend Abel Cook were appointed as hunters for the settlement and early in 1791 they left Covalt Station with three other hunters, tracking game along the Little Miami River. There are conflicting reports as to the direction they took. A contemporary narrative by William Fitzwater states they chose an area north of the station near today's Miamiville.[18]

During the hunt the party separated and the younger Covalt was killed and scalped opposite the site of the grist mill later constructed by Enoch Buckingham. This mill was on the Little Miami River south of Miamiville in Fractional Section 20, Symmes Township.[19]

While three members of the hunting party fled in a direct route to Covalt Station, Levi Buckingham escaped up a steep ravine and finally reached the Little Miami River again at a site later known as Quail's railroad crossing. This location was east of the site where the party had been ambushed by the Indians.[20]

Various dates, with a wide range, have been published concerning this incident and the murder of Abel Cook. Despite the inconsistencies, most accounts agree that Abel Cook was killed one month after his friend and that they were both buried at Covalt Station.[20]

The indefensible size of the fort and the killing of Abel Cook by a small band of Indians on February 27, 1791 led the inhabitants to petition General Harmar for further aid. They wrote:

We the inhabitance of Bethany Town and Else where do once more Etempt to Solicite The Most honourable General Harmer Commander in Chief in the Western territory to whome we your humble petetionars are in Duty Bound Shall Ever Pray That your Excellancy Would

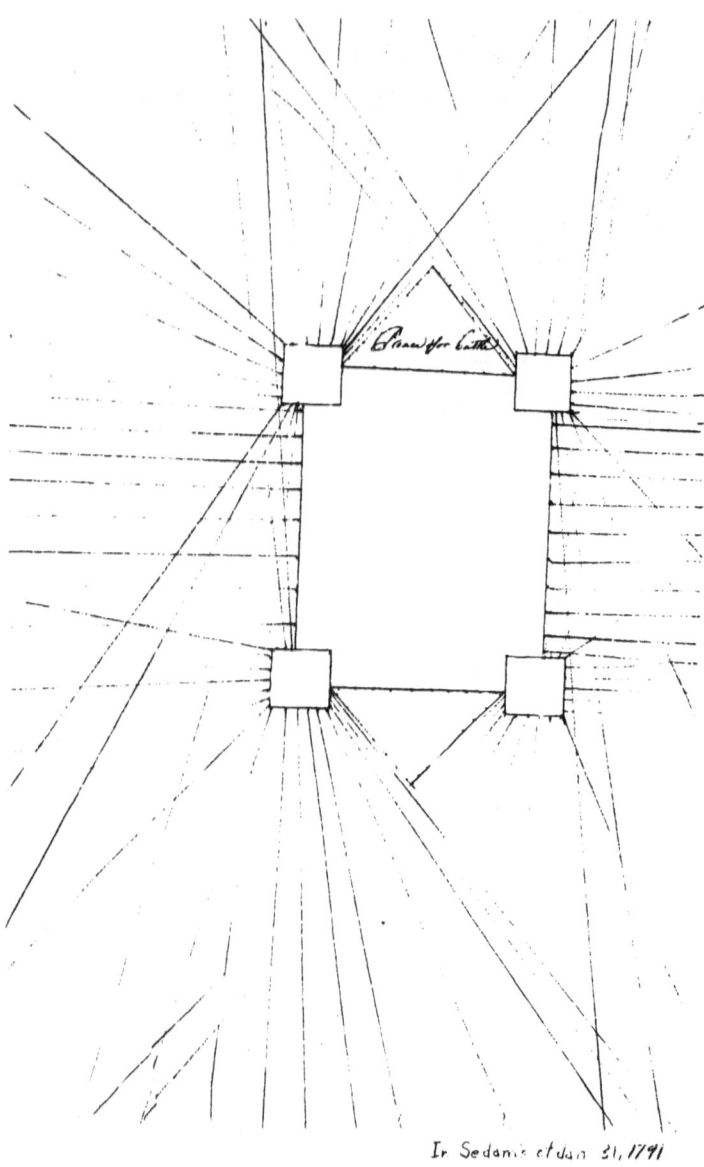

Plan of Covalt's Station, included in a letter from Lieutenant Cornelius Sedam to General Josiah Harmar, January 31, 1791. Perhaps the most interesting aspect of the plan is the indication of lines of fire from the Fort's loopholes to show how the entire area could be swept by crossfire. The triangular extensions at both ends of the Fort are marked "Place for Cattle." *(Courtesy of the William L. Clements Library, University of Michigan, Josiah Harmar Papers)*

> *take our Situation into your most Serious Consideration and Send us som few Troopes and Suffer us not to Brak up for we dont do our Selves a kindness by keeping our garesn but the Collumbia people and your Town also by our mill in Supplying them in bread and if we move from hear our mill is usless Either to our Selves or to the Enterer Part of the inhabitene further we humble Petetionars Do younaneusly agre to build a blockhous outside of the gareson near the mill if your honour think it best If your Excelancy doth not Simpethise with us then we must make the best Shift we can &c but if your honour ples to aprebate our Request on our part we do all in our power to Defend This Settlement in hopes of address we your humble Petetionars as in Duty Bound Shall Every Pray. February the 28th day 1791.*
>
> *N B yesterday the Indians have killed Abel Cook in the Narrows betwixt Collumbia and the big botom gareson yesterday.*[22]

The soldiers garrisoned at Covalt's Station were supposedly ordered to protect the inhabitants of the fort and the mill and not to allow themselves to be drawn away from the stockade in pursuit of marauding Indians; however, they were lured away on more than one occasion by ruse. Mary Covalt related one such incident and described how she closed the fort gate although the Indians were firing at the stockade at the time:[23]

> *The soldiers, being always in readiness at the report of guns, started in the direction of the sound in pursuit of the Indians. The savages saw them coming. They ran around the hill and attacked the fort, knowing that the soldiers would have to return to the fort to protect it. They shot several bullets in the gate of the fort. I was the one that shut the gate, the men all being absent.*

Despite the problems with the Indians, Captain Covalt decided to build a house for his family outside the fort and this decision proved fatal. Enoch Buckingham related years later the circumstances surrounding Captain Covalt's death in 1791:

> *Covalt and another man went up the hill fronting the Station, and along the base of which the railroad and*

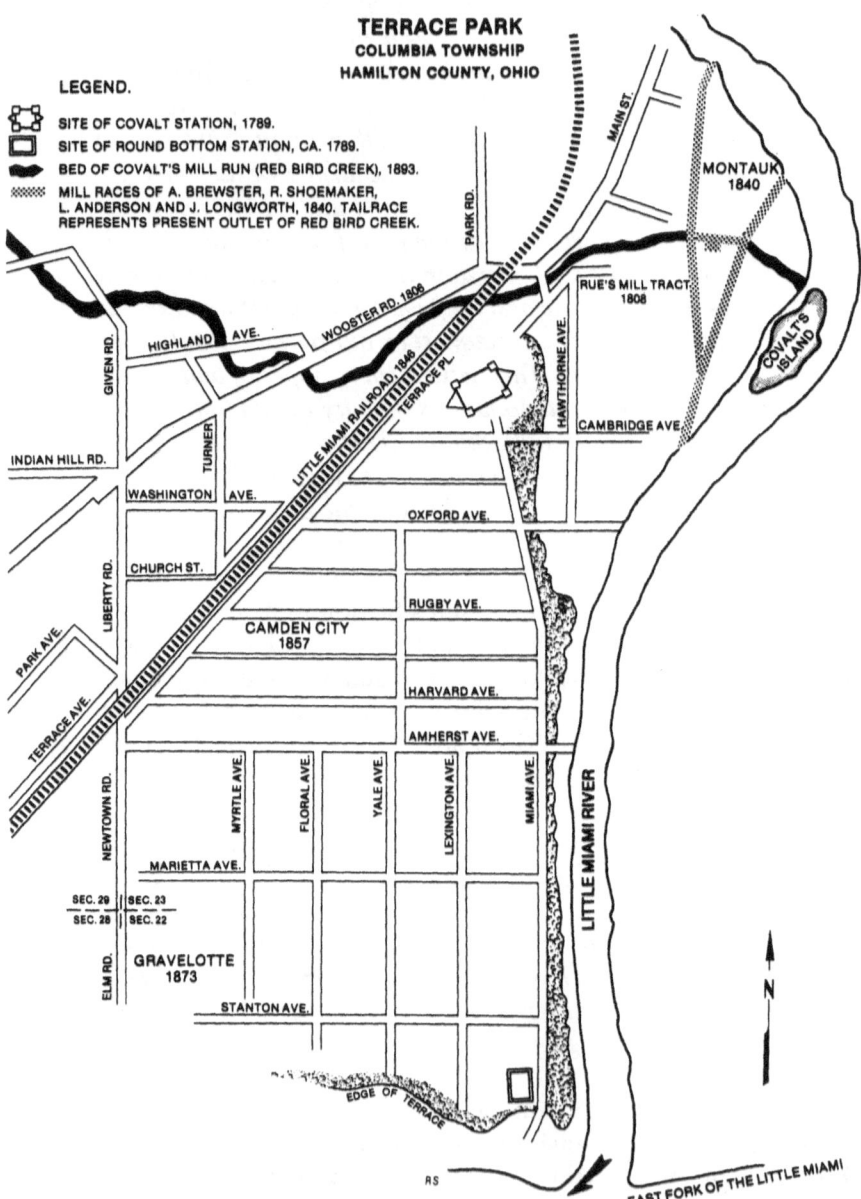

Composite plat of Terrace Park, Columbia Township, showing sites of Covalt and Round Bottom stations and several millraces. (Illustration by Richard Scamyhorn)

turnpike (Wooster Pike) are now established, to split shingles or to get timber. Covalt was shot in the back, but not killed, and as he ran he made a brave resistance, but was soon dispatched. Hinkle was killed and scalped.[24]

There are several versions of this episode and probably the most reliable one states that along with Covalt and the millwright Joseph Hinkle were two of Covalt's sons, who escaped to the fort. Hinkle reportedly was not shot but nearly beheaded with a tomahawk. Although Joseph Martin in one of his narratives states that Covalt was not scalped, one would tend to favor Mary Covalt's description of the event which states that Covalt's scalp was taken. It is hard to believe that the Indians would have taken Hinkle's scalp and left one like Covalt's, with auburn hair. Luke Foster was a resident of Columbia at the time of Captain Covalt's death. In a letter to Thomas Clark dated May 23, 1819 Foster recalled that he had attended the funeral of Covalt and Hinkle, with fifty of his fellow militiamen from Columbia.[25]

Based on the postscript of the letter of petition to General Harmar from the inhabitants of Covalt's Station or Bethany Town dated February 28, 1791, stating that Abel Cook was killed the previous day, and the narratives fixing the time span between his death and that of Abraham Covalt, Jr., the proper chronological order of their demise should read:[26]

Abraham Covalt, Jr, latter part of January, 1791.
Abel Cook, February 27, 1791.
Abraham Covalt, Sr., March, 1791.

Following Captain Covalt's death the inhabitants of the Station became very restless. In the fall of 1791 the federal troops and the militia were being withdrawn to join General St. Clair's hapless expedition against the Indians and the settlers began to move out of the stockade. It was abandoned until the spring of 1792 at which time they returned to their settlement, still apprehensive about their future there.[27]

The bulk of these pioneers had gathered at Garrard Station, east of Fort Miami. This was a wise move as the manpower at Garrard Station was probably also depleted and the influx from Covalt Station increased the number of inhabitants capable of making an effective mutual defense.[29]

According to Mary Covalt, the militia left Covalt Station under the command of Lieutenant Spears to join St. Clair. Only one returned from the battlefield of St. Clair's defeat, her brother Cheniah (or Chenaniah).[29] Cheniah served under Captain Brice Virgin in a company of volunteer militia and was number 44 on the muster list at Fort Hamilton on January 7, 1792. Cheniah Covalt must have been considered a skilled scout and Indian fighter, since he was chosen to be one of Captain Ephraim Kibbey's Company of

Guides and Spies, the vanguard of General Anthony Wayne's army during the triumphant campaign of summer, 1794.[30]

In 1794 a road was petitioned from Covalt's Station to White's Station on Mill Creek, but neither field notes nor a protraction of this road have been located. However, the petition may have been dismissed by the Court of Sessions.[31]

Like many of the other fortifications in Hamilton County, the stockade was abandoned following General Wayne's victory and the signing of the Greenville Treaty in 1795. The fort reportedly burned to the ground about 1810 after the property had changed owners.[32]

Prior to the demise of the fort, the property on which it stood passed from the Covalt family to Samuel Heighway. On January 29, 1796 Cheneniah Covalt gave his brother Bethuel power of attorney over the tract, and on that same day Bethuel sold the parcel to Heighway for $200. (Both transfers were recorded July 16, 1799.)[33] A description of the property sold reads:

> *One tract or parcel of land lying in the county of Hamilton and known as Covalt's Station including an Island being part of the 23rd. Fraction situated on the north east corner & bounded by the Little Miami until it crosses the run known by the name of Covalt's Mill run & up said run by fence to a stake at corner of the station and westward ____ Poles—to corner of fence on the improved land across the said run from thence North ____ Poles—from thence East until it strikes the Little Miami containing together fifty acres with a small cabin on the adjoining premises with fence round the improved land.*[34]

Samuel Heighway was a well educated and prosperous emigrant from England. He and two partners (John Smith & Evan Banes) purchased from John Cleves Symmes approximately 40,000 acres of land in present Warren County on February 3, 1796. Heighway laid out the town of Waynesville in one of his tracts, and with fourteen settlers (the majority English emigrants) established that Quaker settlement in the spring of 1797. It may have been on impulse that he purchased the Covalt Station tract while negotiating with Symmes for the Warren County land.[35] Heighway certainly could not have devoted much time to the Covalt property between the date of purchase and 1801 because during that period his energies were focused on the improvements at Waynesville and designing, with his partner John Poole, a steam engine intended for navigational purposes. Samuel Heighway sold the 50 acre-Covalt Station tract to Christian Rue and other Rue family members on July 24, 1806 for $959.[36]

Notes

[1] Narrative of Mary Covalt Jones, "Reminiscences of Early Days," Manuscript in collection of Cincinnati Historical Society, p. 7, 8.
[2] *Official Roster of Soldiers of the American Revolution Buried in the State of Ohio*, p. 89; "Muster Rolls and Papers Relating to the Associators & Militia of the County of Bedford," quoted in the *Pennsylvania Archives*, Series 5, Vol. 5, p. 68, 70, 106.
[3] *Pennsylvania Archives*, Series 5, Vol. 5, p. 70, 106, 117-118.
[4] Narrative of Mary Covalt Jones, p. 1-2, 7-8.
[5] Ibid.
[6] Ibid., p. 1-2.
[7] Ibid., p. 1-3; J. G. Olden, *Historical Sketches*, p. 74-75; Drake, "Memoir of the Miami Country," p. 64, 76, 110-111; Letter of Cornelius Ryker Sedam to General Josiah Harmar, Jan. 31, 1791; Petition of the inhabitants of Covalt Station to General Harmar, Feb. 28, 1791, Vol. 14, Harmar Papers, Clements Library, University of Michigan; Benjamin Drake, *Tales and Sketches of the Queen City*, Cincinnati, 1838, p. 157.
[8] Whittlesey, "Notices of Hamilton County, Ohio," p. 14-19; *Road Record Book 1-1B, 1793-1863*, p. 110, and *Restored Records, Decrees and Plats Affecting Real Estate, Vol. 1, 1798-1863*, p. 56, both Hamilton County Engineer's Office, Road Records Division; *Plat Book 12*, p. 44, Hamilton County Recorder's Office.
[9] Narrative of Mary Covalt Jones, p. 2; *Deed Book C*, p. 136-139, Hamilton County Recorder's Office; Petition of the inhabitants of Covalt Station to General Harmar; Dwight Wesley Garber, *Waterwheels and Millstones; A History of Ohio Grist Mills and Milling*, Historic Ohio Buildings, Series 2, Columbus, 1970, p. 132.
[10] Narrative of Mary Covalt Jones, p. 1-2; Whittlesey, "Notices of Hamilton County, Ohio," p. 14-19.
[11] Ibid.; *Cist's Weekly Advertiser*, Cincinnati, Dec. 14, 1847, p. 155.
[12] Narrative of Mary Covalt Jones, p. 12.
[13] *Hamilton County, Ohio Court and Other Records*, compiled by Virginia Cummins, Cincinnati, 1967, Vol. 2, p. 159-160; Letter of Luke Foster to Thomas Clark, May 23, 1819, quoted in Drake, Memoir of Miami Country," p. 65, 104; *Deed Book C*, Hamilton County Recorder's Office; *Columbia Township Record Book, Ministerial Funds, Township 5, 1809-1923*, Manuscript in collection of Cincinnati Historical Society.
[14] Stites Receipt Book, Manuscript in collection of Cincinnati Historical Society.
[15] Letter of General Josiah Harmar to General Henry Knox, Jan. 25, 1791, Vol. 14, Harmar Papers, William Clements Library, University of Michigan; Letter of Ezra Ferris to Griffin Yeatman, et al., Dec. 18, 1838, Lyman Draper Collection, Drake Papers, Microfilm series O, Draper Mss. 1089, Wisconsin Historical Society.
[16] Letter of Cornelius Sedam to General Harmar, Jan. 31, 1791.
[17] "Plan of Covalt's Station," by Sedam, included in letter to General Harmar, Jan. 31, 1791.
[18] Narrative of Mary Covalt Jones, p. 5; William Fitzwater, quoted in J. L. Rockey and R. J. Bancroft, *History of Clermont County, Ohio*, Philadelphia, 1880, p. 462, 470.
[19] Ibid.; maps of Hamilton County, Ohio by William D. Emerson, 1847; R. C. Phillips, 1865; C. S. Mendenhall, ca. 1877.
[20] Ibid.
[21] Narrative of Mary Covalt Jones, p. 5-6; Narrative of Enoch Buckingham, quoted in Whittlesey, "Notices of Hamilton County, Ohio," p. 19; A. E. Jones, *Extracts from the History of Cincinnati*, p. 59; Excerpts from the diary of Dr. William Goforth, quoted in Charles Cist, *The Cincinnati Miscellany*, Vol. 1, Cincinnati, 1845, p. 172.
[22] Petition of the inhabitants of Covalt Station to General Harmar, Feb. 28, 1791.
[23] Narrative of Mary Covalt Jones, p. 11-12.
[24] Narrative of Enoch Buckingham, quoted in Whittlesey, "Notices of Hamilton County, Ohio," p. 19.
[25] Narrative of Mary Covalt Jones, p. 6-8; narratives of Enoch Buckingham and Joseph Martin, quoted in Whittlesey, "Notices of Hamilton County, Ohio," p. 19.

[26] Petition of the inhabitants of Covalt Station to General Harmar, Feb. 28, 1791.
[27] Narrative of Mary Covalt Jones, p. 10.
[28] Ibid.
[29] Ibid., p. 10, 13.
[30] Ibid., p. 13; "Selections from the Torrence Papers, VIII," *Quarterly Publication of the Historical and Philosophical Society of Ohio*, Vol. 13 (1918) p. 97-98; Muster roll of Captain Ephriam Kibbey's Company of Guides and Spies, Manuscript, Cincinnati Historical Society.
[31] *Road Record Book 1, 1793-1850*, p. 110, Hamilton County Engineer's Office, Road Records Division.
[32] Narrative of Mary Covalt Jones, p.17; *Deed Book C*, p. 136-139, Hamilton County Recorder's Office.
[33] Ibid.
[34] Ibid.
[35] Francis Baily, *Journal of a Tour in the Unsettled Parts of North America in 1796 and 1797*, London, 1856, p. 195-196, 211, 215; Elizabeth Faries, "The Miami Country, 1750-1815, as described in Journals and Letters," *Ohio Archaeological and Historical Society Quarterly*, Vol. 57 (1948) p. 58; Rverend James Smith, "Tours into Kentucky and the Northwest Territory, Ohio," *Ohio Archaeological and Historical Publications*, Vol. 16 (1907) p. 395; *History of Warren County, Ohio*, p. 555-557.
[36] Letter of John Cleves Symmes to Thomas Jefferson, March 4, 1801, quoted from copy in Manuscript Collection of Cincinnati Historical Society; original in Huntington Library, San Marina, California; *Deed Book G*, p. 155-156, Hamilton County Recorder's Office.

Cunningham's Station
1790

James Cunningham migrated from Scotland to Lancaster County, Pennsylvania with his brothers John and Robert. During the Revolutionary War James joined the 3rd Battalion of Lancaster County Militia and earned the rank of Lieutenant Colonel. He served as Colonel of a regiment of Pennsylvania Militia under the command of Brigadier General High Mercer during the Jersey Campaign of 1776, and was listed as a Colonel at Fort Constitution. Following his military service, James Cunningham was appointed on October 21, 1777 as a commissioner of Lancaster County, Pennsylvania. His duty was to seize the personal effects of all traitors.[1]

Cunningham moved to Jefferson County, Kentucky in 1785 and later to Cincinnati. On May 26, 1789. he entered warrant number 382 for 640 acres in Section 28, Township 4, Range 1, in present Sycamore Township. Together with his brothers-in-law he made improvements at his station site in the west half of Section 28, which today would be located along the west side of Reading Road, on the west side of the east fork of Mill Creek, between Cooper and Glendale-Milford Roads. Cunningham reportedly moved his family to the station site where they remained through the winter of 1789-90. At some interval in 1790 he purchased lots 181 and 182 between present Vine and Walnut Street, north of Second Street in Cincinnati and moved his family there.[2]

Cunningham may not have returned to his station site until 1792. However, by that year he petitioned for a road from Cincinnati, up Mill Creek, by Ludlow's Station, past White's Station at the third crossing of Mill Creek, on to Cunningham's and then to Runyan's improvements.[3] The Cunningham family built a grist mill on Mill Creek prior to 1825 and it appears on an official plat in the Hamilton County survey records.[4]

The Cunningham Station was on an important road leading past Runyan's Station to the Mad River (Dayton and Springfield) area and beyond. Like other stations in the Mill Creek Valley, Cunningham's may have been used as a storage depot or bivouac area by the military troops during the Indian campaigns of 1793-94. Benjamin Van Cleve, who had been an employee of a company supplying the army during those campaigns, was well acquainted with Cunningham's settlement. Enroute to Cincinnati, following a survey assignment on the Mad River, Van Cleve's party stopped at Cunningham's

Station on October 5, 1795 where they were fed a hearty meal of milk and mush at John Clawson's house.[5]

James Cunningham died in 1812 and on April 17, 1813 a notice was placed in a Cincinnati newspaper which read:

> *to be sold at action May 2, 1813, 64 acres and .17 in sec. 28 T4, R1 on Mill Creek - Also 16 acres .13 in same sect. being the property of James Cunningham dec. these tracts lying on the state road Cincinnati to Dayton. April 17, 1813*
>
>   **Janet Cunningham exec.**[6]

Notes

[1] *Official Roster of Soldiers of the American Revolution Buried in the State of Ohio*, Vol. 1, p. 98; J. G. Olden, *Historical Sketches*, p. 95; Eric Manders, "Notes on Troop Units in the Army at New York City, 1776," *Military Collector and Historian*, Vol. 26, No. 2 (1974), p. 91; *Official Roster of Soldiers of the American Revolution Buried in the State of Ohio*, p. 98; *Pennsylvania Archives*, series 2, Vol. 2, Ed. John B. Linn and Wm. H. Engle, M. D., Harrisburg, 1895, p. 777-778; *The St. Clair Papers*, Vol. 2, p. 156; *Pennsylvania Archives*, series 2, Vol. 3, p. 704.

[2] *Symmes Purchase Records*, p. 17; J. G. Olden, *Historical Sketches*, p. 95; Ibid., p. 41, 59, 95-97, 99; A. E. Jones, *Extracts from the History of Cincinnati*, p. 47-49; *Road Record Book, Vol. 1-1B, 1793-1850*, p. 45, 51, 54, 58; *Road Record Book, 1853-1871*, p. 535; *Hamilton County Survey Book No. 16*, p. 75-76, Hamilton County Engineer's Office, Road Records Division; U. S. Geological Survey, Cincinnati East Quad, 7.5' series; maps of Hamilton County, Ohio by S. Morrison & J. Williams, Cincinnati, 1835; Wm. D. Emerson, Cincinnati, 1847; A. W. Gilbert, Cincinnati, 1848; Atlas of Hamilton County, Ohio, 1884, p. 5; A. E. Jones, *Extracts from the History of Cincinnati*, p. 49.

[3] *Road Record Book Vol. 1 1793-1850*, p. 94-95, Hamilton County Engineer's Office, Road Records Division.

[4] *Hamilton County, Ohio Survey Book, 1825-1830*, p. 223, Hamilton County Engineer's Office, Road Records Division.

[5] "Memoirs of Bemjamin Van Cleve," quoted in *Quarterly Publication of the Historical and Philosophical Society of Ohio, Vol. 17* (1922) p. 58.

[6] *Western Spy and Hamilton Gazette*, April 17, 1813; *Revolutionary War Soldiers in Hamilton County, Ohio*, Ed. Robert D. Craig, Salt Lake City, 1965, p. 8.

Dunlap's Station or Colerain 1790

John Dunlap, a surveyor in the employ of John Cleves Symmes, was appointed a deputy registrar in Symmes' Miami Land Office on May 2, 1789 and left that office on November 28, 1789 to form a settlement in present Colerain Township.[1]

In the spring of 1790 Dunlap laid out a town along the bank of the Great Miami where the river formed an enormous horseshoe bend. The settlement sat on a gravelly terrace deposited by the Wisconsin glacier. From the station approximately 200 paces north in this same great bend sat a prehistoric earthwork enclosing 95 acres. The walls of the ancient enclosure still measured nine feet in height in 1838 and were recorded on maps as late as 1848.[2]

Dunlap persuaded eleven families totaling about thirty people to join him in founding a town named Colerain after his birthplace in County Londonderry, northern Ireland.[3] The village was located, according to General Josiah Harmar, "...five and forty miles up the Great Miami, and 17 miles from this post (Fort Washington)..."[4] The present location is near East Miami River Road, Colerain Township, Section 30, Township 2, Range 1.[5]

General Harmar described the fortification at Colerain as "...11 families and as many houses thrown together in a miserable position for defense, having 3 ill constructed block houses for their protection."[6] William Wiseman, one of the Federal soldiers detached to guard the station, recalled many years later that General Harmar's low opinion of the fortification was correct:

> *The fort, or station, consisted of a few cabins lying in a square of perhaps an acre or more. These had been built for convenience sake, facing each other, and with the roofs, of course, sloping outward; the very reverse of what they should have been for efficient defence. The outer edges of these were so low, that it was not uncommon for the dogs, which had been shut out, to spring from adjacent stumps on to the roof, and thence, side-*

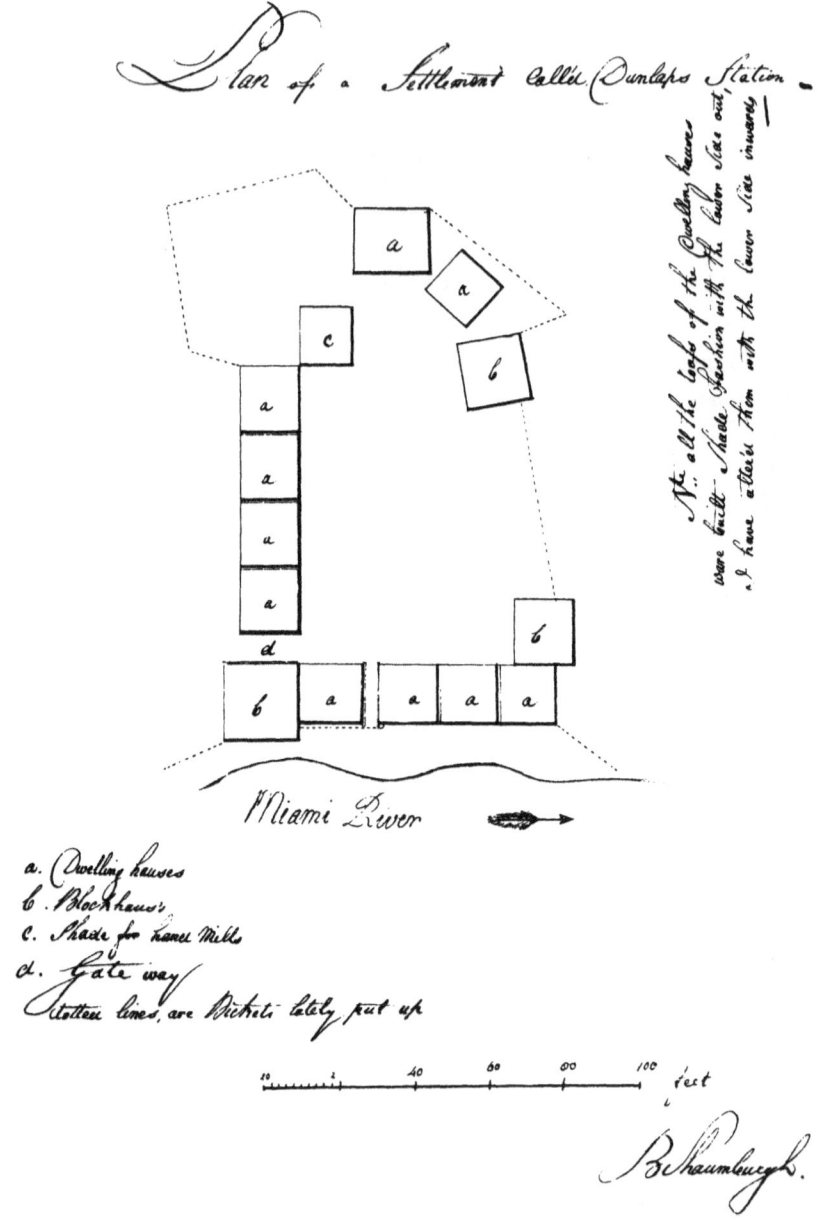

"Plan of a Settlement Call'd Dunlaps Station" by Lieutenant Bartholomew Shaumburgh, 1791. This plan shows how the houses at Dunlap's Station (or Colerain) were arranged to form a defensive compound and connected by a picket wall for added protection. *(Courtesy of the William L. Clements Library, University of Michigan, Josiah Harmar Papers)*

> *ways, into the inclosure. At the corners of the square, blockhouses had been constructed, and pickets, very weak and insufficient for defence against a resolute and active enemy, filled up the intervening spaces inclosing the whole.*[7]

Michael Hahn, whose family had lived in Colerain, remembered that "...The families built their cabins together, and facing each other with the lower ends to the outside. These were connected together with pickets eight feet high, composed of small timber, split in half, sharpened at the ends, and set a sufficient depth into the ground."[8]

An early settler at Columbia stated the cabins at Colerain were "...what they call half faced cabbins the lowest part of the roof outside, very injudiciously done the intention was to throw the water off the garrison but giving the Indians great advantage..."[9]

A plan of the station drawn by Lt. Bartholomew Shaumburg in 1791 shows the dwelling houses and one shelter for a hand mill, arranged in an "L"-shaped enclosure and protected by three slightly larger blockhouses and a bastion-shaped line of pickets "lately put up."

Shaumburg noted on the plan that "all the roofs of the dwelling houses were built shade fashion with the lower side out, I have alter'd them with the lower Side inwards."[10]

The obvious weakness of the fort at Colerain is surprising considering the exposed situation of the settlement. At the time it was built it was the northernmost station in the area and farthest from any assistance by militia or federal troops. The station eventually endured the most severe attack by Indians in the Hamilton County area.

On December 6, 1790, an Indian party was seen scouting in the vicinity of Colerain. A force of 58 federal troops was sent to protect the settlement, but the Indians appeared to have fled the area. Lieutenant Jacob Kingsbury and a dozen soldiers were left at the station as a guard, with orders to "repair and somewhat amend" the fortification.[11] The troops set to work in clearing the trees immediately adjacent to the fort so that they would not afford cover to the Indians. This work was not completed before the fort was surrounded and attacked.

On January 8th a surveying party which included Abner Hunt, John Wallace, and two men named Sloan and Cunningham was ambushed by Indians. Cunningham was killed, Hunt was thrown from his horse and captured, and Sloan, though wounded, managed to mount his horse and escape to Dunlap's Station. He was given Lieutenant Kingsbury's quarters, and the next day several soldiers were sent out to bury Cunningham.[12]

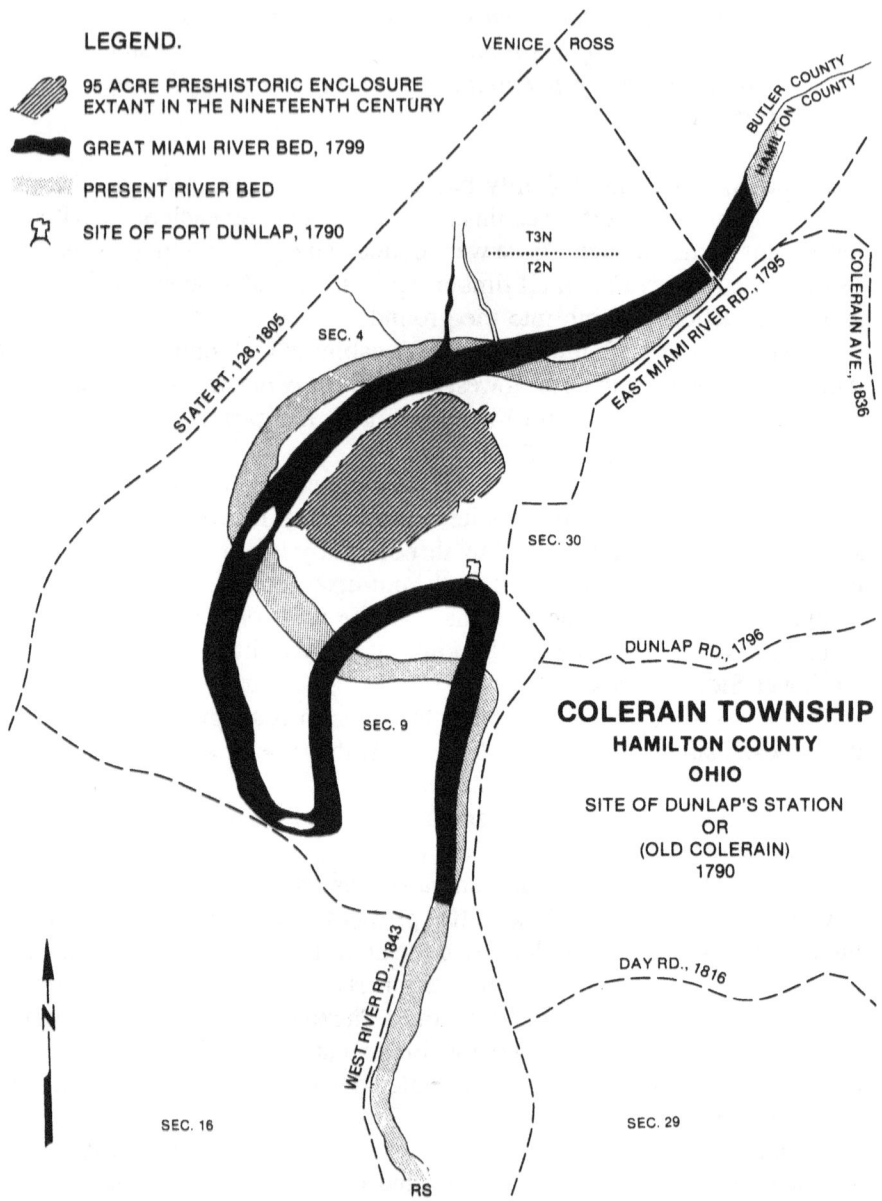

Composite map of Colerain Township, site of Dunlap's Station or Old Colerain, including a 95-acre prehistoric enclosure. (Illustration by Richard Scamyhorn)

On the following morning—Monday, January 10th—a large Indian war party surrounded and attacked Dunlap's Station. The attack has been so magnified and embroidered by folklore that Lieutenant Kingsbury's own terse report to General Harmar, written just after the attack, remains the best source:

> *Dunlaps Station 12th January, 1791*
> *Dear General,*
> *Monday morning (about Sunrise) at half past Seven The Indians Surrounded this Garrison the Indians consisting of nearly Two Hundred after they had compleatly surrounded us Mr. Hunt a prisoner (taken last Saturday within one Mile of this place) demanded this Garrison by order of the Indians I informed them that we were happy to see them that we had plenty of Men Arms Ammunition and provisions and had been waiting impatiently for them for several days they then began a very heavy fire but have wounded but one man which is McVicar of Capt. Truemans Compy shot through the arm they demanded the Garrison several times but to no purpose we have killed and wounded not less than Twelve or fifteen the savages have kill'd most part of the Cattle belonging to the Station and burnt all the buildings the outside of the Garrison and have destroyed most part of the Corn belonging to the inhabitants the Indians appeared to come prepared for a Siege as they had a number of pack Horses with heavy Loads on them and were Loaded themselves with Large packs on their backs The Savages raised their Siege yesterday Morning about Eight oClock after keeping up a very heavy fire for nearly twenty five hours They threatened to starve us out or storm our works and to set fire to our Garrison they attempted to set fire to our garrison with arrows but could not bring any of their plans to bear they informed me that Girty was there and called me by name and told me they would wish to see me outside of the Garrison Hunt the prisoner they Murdered within Two hundred yards of the Garrison I have the pleasure of sending you Two scalps hope before long to send you several more but have them to take first. The Inhabitants will some of them leave this place others will remain here. I had of my men and the inhabitants*

> in the Garrison in the Attack thirty five men old and young sick and well I shall now be a little weakened by the loss of some of the Inhabitants who are about to leave this place - Captain Sloan the bearer Recd a wound in his Side but was of very great Service to me in the attack - I yesterday morning sent off an Express to you but they met the Militia and returned -
> I am dear general,
> With ther utmost Respect -
> Your most obdt, Humbl Servt-
> Jacob Kingsbury Lieut.
> Comdg Dunlaps Station -
> NB Capt. Sloan killed the Indian with the large Scalp and will be glad to keep it after you have seen it[13]

William Wiseman later recalled that during the night of the attack, the Indians tied Abner Hunt between the fort and the prehistoric earthwork nearby, and tortured him to death:

> Here they stripped him naked, pinioning his outstretch hands and feet to the earth, kindling a fire on his naked abdomen, and thus, in lingering tortures they allowed him to die. His screams of agony were ringing in our ears during the remainder of the night, becoming gradually weaker and weaker till towards daylight, when they ceased.[14]

After the attack, General Harmar resolved to improve the Colerain fortifications and wrote to Lieutenant Kingsbury:

> I now order Mr. Shaumburg to join you as an Engineer for the space of one week, he will show a plan of a stockade wall, which if you can get the inhabitants to execute will be a solid protection for them. If not Mr. Shamburgh will consult with you and put the present old miserable Stockage in the best defensible order possible...Mr. Foster with the Columbia militia now sent on for fatigue in order to render the Post more secure.[15]

However, the settlers at Colerain decided to abandon the station and move to the comparative safety of North Bend, They signed a petition which read:

> *We the Inhabitants at the Settlement Called Dunlaps Station, have duly Considered under what great Disadvantages we are to labor for the great part of this year, after the reduction of our Live Stock, graine and all other necessarys for live, by an attack lately made upon us by a party of Savages - and therefore have concluded to lieve this place as soon as we can possibly built craft to remove ourself down the Miami River - Jan 16th 1791*[16]

The reluctance of the settlers to remain at the station is understandable, considering the ordeal they had been through and the fact that they had lost 75 head of cattle and 1,500 bushels of corn as a result of the attack.[17] Lieutenant Kingsbury, unsure whether he should remain at Dunlap's Station and continue to improve the fortifications, wrote to General Harmar:

> *The inhabitants of this Station are determined to move down to Judge Sims's, with their effects as soon as they can make Rafts, and Canoes, to carry them down the Miami River, as they have nothing to subsist on, but a little corn... there is not one will remain here. I thought it my Duty to inform you of the movement of the Inhabitants, and would wish to know by the bearer whether I am to remain here after their Departure or not,... Agreeably to your Orders I have Commenced repairing the Old Stockade, this Morning, but I cannot expect any help from the Inhabitants as they are preparing to move...*[18]

Apparently the militia sent to work on the defenses were also of little help, as General Harmar notified General Henry Knox,

> *I sent an officer, with some of the militia of Cincinnati and Columbia to put the works of Colerain in a better posture of defence. This he has but partially effected, as the Militia were, as usual impatient to be done.*[19]

Ironically, there was no one to defend, since the station had been abandoned.

John Dunlap, however, did not give up the idea of fostering a settlement at Colerain. In January 1792 he reestablished the station even during a period of great apprehension following General St. Clair's defeat by the combined tribes the previous November.

Aerial view of the Dunlap's Station site in 1986.

John Cleves Symmes wrote to his friend Jonathan Dayton on January 17, 1792 that

> ...on my arrival in the purchase about the 20th of November I found the settlers in the greatest consternation on account of the late defeat. Several had fled into Kentucky and many others were preparing to follow them—and it was with the greatest difficulty that I prevailed with people to stand their ground. The timely arrival of Mr. Dunlap greatly contributed to this sucess, as he had the good fortune to prevail with his settlers, who had abandoned Colerain, to return again with him and re-establish their station. Colerain has ever been considered as the best barrier to all the settlements—& when that place became re-peopled the inhabitants of the other Stations became more reconciled to stay.[20]

Dunlap thus combined a military victory over Indian attack with a moral victory in encouraging many settlers to remain in the area.

Although no further attacks were made by the Indians, Dunlap did have one more fight to wage: a legal battle with those settlers who refused to fulfill their obligations to him. An advertisement in *The Centinel of the North-Western Territory* in January 1794 states:

> The Subscriber finding it highly necessary to inform all those holding donation lots of whatever kind in the town of Colerain, that they must comply with the terms of settling said place by the first day of May next ensuing this date or look upon their lots as forefeited. And all those holding donation lots by virtue of the first terms of settling at Colerain and has been of no service in protecting said place since the last settlement which was in January 1792, must look upon their lots as forefeited at this present time. John Dunlap Colerain, January 9, 1794.[21]

There were several early roads petitioned and surveyed to Dunlap's Station. In 1792, a road was petitioned from "Cincinnati to Dunlap's Station beginning at the nine-mile run on General St. Clair's Trace toward Fort Hamilton and extending the nearest and best way to Dunlop's Station." In 1795, a survey was made to establish the road from Fairfield (present-day Hamilton) to Colerain, four poles wide.[22]

The fort was abandoned at the end of the Indian hostilities in 1795 and by the summer of 1801 no remains of it could be seen among the cornfields.[23]

Notes

[1] *Symmes Purchase Records*, p. 14; Drake, "Memoir of the Miami Country," p. 81; Cist, *Cincinnati in 1859*, p. 92, 104.
[2] E. G. Squier and E. H. Davis, *Prehistoric Antiquities of the Mississippi Valley*, reproduction by AMS Press, New York, 1973, Vol. 2, Plate 3, No. 2, 35-36; *Soil Survey of Hamilton County, O. 1975-1979*, Cincinnati, 1979; maps of Hamilton county by S. Morrison and J. Williams, 1835; Wm. Emerson, 1847; A. W. Gilbert, 1848; *Survey Book 5*, p. 42-45; "Survey of the Meanders of The Great Miami River," Hamilton County Enginer's Office, Road Records Division.
[3] Letter of General Josiah Harmar to General Henry Knox, Jan. 25, 1791, Letter Book A, Harmar Papers, William Clements Library, University of Michigan; Cist, *Cincinnati in 1859*, p. 92, 104.
[4] Ibid.
[5] United States Geological Survey, Shandon, Ohio Quad, 7.5' series.
[6] Letter of General Harmar to General Knox, Jan. 25, 1791, Harmar Papers, University of Michigan.
[7] Cist, *Cincinnati in 1859*, p. 92.
[8] Ibid., p. 104.
[9] Letter of M. Gano to A. Gano, Dec. 18, 1838, Lyman Draper Collection, Drake Papers, Microfilm Series O, Draper Mss 1086, Wisconsin Historical Society.
[10] "Plan of a Settlement Called Dunlap's Station" by Lieutenant Bartholomew Shaumburgh, Harmar Papers, University of Michigan.
[11] Letter of General Harmar to General Knox, Jan. 25, 1791, Harmar Papers, University of Michigan.
[12] Cist, *Cincinnati in 1859*, p. 92-93, 105.
[13] Letter of Lieutenant Jacob Kingsbury to General Josiah Harmar, Jan. 12, 1791, Vol. 14, Harmar Papers, University of Michigan.
[14] Cist, *Cincinnati in 1859*, p. 95.
[15] Letter of General Harmar to Lieutenant Kingsbury, Jan. 15, 1791, Vol. 14, Harmar Papers, University of Michigan.
[16] Letter of "Inhabitants of the Settlement Called Dunlap's Station" to General Josiah Harmar, Jan. 16, 1791, Vol. 14, Harmar Papers, University of Michigan.
[17] Letter of General Harmar to General Knox, Jan. 25, 1791, Letter Book A, Harmar Papers, University of Michigan.
[18] Letter of Lieutenant Kingsbury to General Harmar, Jan. 17, 1791, Vol. 14, Harmar Papers, University of Michigan.
[19] Letter of General Harmar to General Knox, Jan. 25, 1791, Letter Book A, Harmar Papers, University of Michigan.
[20] Symmes Correspondence, Cincinnati Historical Society.
[21] *Centinel of the North-Western Territory*, Jan. 18, 1794.
[22] *Road Record Book, Vol. 1-1B, 1790-1850*, p. 95, 123, 133, Hamilton County Engineer's Office, Road Records Division.
[23] Cist, *Cincinnati in 1859*, p. 103.

Dunn's Station 1793

Captain Hugh Dunn served in the 13th Regiment of the Continental Line during the Revolutionary War and like many other veterans of that war was left destitute when paid for his services in depreciated Continental currency.[1]

Dunn left Newark, New Jersey in 1788 with his family—wife, four sons and one daughter—and eventually proceeded down the Ohio River toward the new Miami settlement of Columbia. Once during the trip they were attacked by Indians; later their boat was nearly destroyed in a storm.[2]

The party arrived at Columbia on December 15, 1788 and they resided there until the spring of 1793,[3] when a disastrous flood of the Ohio River inundated most of the town. In March, during the peak of the flood, Dunn was forced to evacuate his family and their belongings through the roof of their cabin. They managed to save themselves and all the household goods aboard two canoes which they lashed together. As they drifted downstream in the swift current, they watched the flood waters sweep away their cabin, smokehouse and henhouse.[4]

The Dunn family moved from Columbia to the mouth of the Great Miami River, taking with them to a new settlement families from Columbia, Cincinnati and North Bend. Those who left Columbia with Dunn included Benjamin Randolph, Isaac Mills, Joseph Kitchel, Benjamin Cox and Thomas Walters. The latter two were among the last persons reported killed by Indians in the Miami Purchase in a February 2, 1795 incident.[5]

The Dunn party arrived at the mouth of the Great Miami and found the bottoms inundated. They also found a small settlement, established by Captain Joseph Hayes, where they took refuge until that fall.[6] During the summer, the Dunn party built a blockhouse about one-quarter mile north of the Hayes settlement.

The blockhouse was a two story log structure, the upper story projecting over the lower by about four feet. Port holes were cut in the loft projection and the first floor walls which permitted the settlers to direct variable angles of gunfire. The overhang also made it difficult for any attacker to reach the roof of the blockhouse.[7]

After the fall harvest, the Dunn party moved to their own station. This was located at the base of Fort Hill (Miami Fort or Shawnee Lookout), near the northwest end of that prehistoric enclosure and habitation site, and southwest of the Goose Pond. Both of these landmarks were well known to the early settlers and surveyors.[8] The blockhouse probably stood in the southwest quarter of Fractional Section 6, Fractional Range 1 East, Township 1, in Miami Township, near present Brower Road.[9]

During the summer of 1794 Benjamin Randal, Garrett Vanness, William and Samuel Harper and Frederick Nutts joined Dunn's Station and cabins were soon strung out from the Goose Pond to the First Principal Meridian.[10]

Earlier, during the previous winter and early spring, a military stockade and storage facility had been erected on the west bank of the Great Miami River in Section 11, Township 5 North, Range 1 West, in present Lawrenceburg Township, Dearborn County, Indiana. General Anthony Wayne had ordered the defenses built and manned by regular army personnel under the command of a Major Byrd.[11]

The garrison was to act as a communication link between the Miami settlements and Fort Greenville, and would also deter Indians from attacking keel boats carrying military supplies to Fort Hamilton.[12] The troops stationed at the stockade may not have been the most disciplined of soldiers. The settlers referred to the garrison as the "Rowdy Camp" and the "Rowdy Regiment."[13] The installation stood approximately one and one-half miles southwest of Dunn's Station.

Although the presence of the soldiers and a stockaded defense may have offered some measure of protection to the inhabitants of Hayes' and Dunn's Stations from 1794 to 1795, it did not eliminate sporadic Indian attacks on the settlers. Dunn's Station received some determined forays from the Indians.[14] In narratives by Isaac Dunn, son of the founder, and Abram Brower it was related that they were greatly exposed to attack from small bands of Indians who stole what they could and killed at least one of the settlers.[15]

Captain Dunn owned a pack of dogs that he had trained to attack on command. The pack leader was an enormous black dog of unknown pedigree. In order to prevent theft of his horses, Captain Dunn tethered them outside the blockhouse on chain halters leading inside through the port holes cut in the log walls.[16] Anyone attempting to free the horses would alert the residents by the rattling of the chains inside the cabin. Captain Dunn's strategy was to get a shot at the thieves through a port hole. If this failed, he would set his attack dogs on the would-be thieves.[17]

On one occasion the Indians tried in vain to destroy the station just to steal the horses. Isaac Mills was one of the defenders that day and the dogs were exceptionally effective. The huge black leader of the pack returned to the blockhouse with clothing he had ripped from one of the attackers.[18] After the Greenville Treaty was signed, Shawnee Chief Captain Blackfish offered

Hugh Dunn a horse valued at one hundred dollars in exchange for Dunn's large black dog. Captain Blackfish admitted he had been the unwilling donor of clothing to the dog during the attack on the station.[19]

Dunn's settlement might have been called a temporary one since several years later the family moved to a tract the Captain had purchased earlier in Section 30, Range 2, Township 4. Near present Elizabethtown in Whitewater Township, Dunn had bought the land on June 15, 1791.[20]

The landform has changed dramatically through the past two centuries; the Great Miami River has changed course many times, one of the most dramatic changes occurring on November 23, 1847 during a severe flood. The village of Hardinsburg (or Hardentown), Dearborn County, Indiana, an import-export landing for steamboats, was left high and dry as a new channel was cut in the Great Miami near Dunn's Station. Captain Dunn would be hard pressed to identify his station site today.[21]

Notes
[1]John H. Gwathmey, *Historical Register of Virginians in the Revolution, 1775-1783*, Richmond, 1938, p. 241; Charles W. Fletcher, *History of Dearborn and Ohio Counties, Indiana*, Chicago, 1885, p. 598.
[2]Ibid., p. 697.
[3]Ibid.; Ferris, *Early Settlement of the Miami Country*, p. 261.
[4]Narrative of Isaac Dunn, in the John S. Gano Papers, Vol. 3, p. 164-165, Cincinnati Historical Society; Fletcher, *Dearborn and Ohio Countues*, p. 697-698.
[5]Ibid., p. 698; Ferris, *Early Settlement*, p. 261; *The Centinel of the North-Western Territory*, Feb. 7, 1795.
[6]Ferris, *Early Settlement*, p. 343-345, 359; Fletcher, *Dearborn and Ohio Counties*, p. 697-898; Narrative of Ezra Hayes, in the William Henry Harrison Papers, Albert J. Green Manuscript Collection, Cincinnati Historical Society.
[7]Narrative of Isaac Dunn, in the John S. Gano Papers, Vol. 3, p. 164-165, Cincinnati Historical Society.
[8]William Henry Harrison, *A Discourse on the Aborigines of the Valley of the Ohio*, Cincinnati, 1838; maps of Hamilton County, Ohio by S. Morrison and J. Williams, 1835; C. S. Mendenhall, ca. 1848; Wm. D. Emerson, 1847; A. W. Gilbert, 1848; R. C. Phillips, 1869; C. S. Mendenhall, ca. 1877; *Hamilton County, Ohio Survey Book 9*, p. 68; *Hamilton County, Ohio Survey Book 3*, p. 221-236, Hamilton County Engineer's Office, Road Records Division; Archibald Shaw, *History of Dearborn County, Indiana*, Indianapolis, 1915, p. 226; *The Restored Records, Decrees & Plats Affecting Real Estate, 1798-1863*, Vol. 1, p. 27; Vol. 47, p. 1-6, Hamilton County Engineer's Office, Road Records Division.
[9]Ibid., Hamilton County maps, Footnote 8; City of Cincinnati and Hamilton County Metropolitan Topographical Survey Maps, Miami Township, Hamilton County Engineer's Office, Road Records Division; *Titus' Atlas of Hamilton County, Ohio*, p. 9; copy of field notes of Benjamin Chambers and William Ludlow, survey of the Great Miami, Township 5, Range 1 west, 1838, Engineer's Office, Dearborn County, Indiana; U. S. Geological Survey Maps, 1914-1970, Hooven and Lawrenceburg, Ohio, Kentucky, Indiana Quad. 7.5' series; R. R. Jones, "The Ohio River, 1700-1914," Manuscript in collection of the Cincinnati Historical Society, p. 130; Ferris, *Early Settlement*, p. 261, 330, 343-345, 358-360; Fletcher, *Dearborn and Ohio Counties*, p. 698; Narrative of Isaac Dunn, Gano Papers, Vol. 3, p. 164-165, Cincinnati Historical Society.
[10]Ibid.; Field Notes of Israel Ludlow, "Survey of the proposed state line between Indiana and Ohio, Oct. 11, 1798," Cincinnati Historical Society.

[11]Fletcher, *Dearborn and Ohio Counties*, p. 96.
[12]Ibid.
[13]Ibid.
[14]*The Hayes Family, Origin, History and Genealogy*, comp. Royal S. Hayes, Cincinnati, 1927, p. 299; Narrative of Isaac Dunn, *The Lawrenceburg Press*, July 21, 1870; Jones, "The Ohio River," p. 130-131; Narrative of Isaac Dunn, in Gano Papers, Vol. 3, p. 164-165, Cincinnati Historical Society.
[15]*The Hayes Family*, p. 299; Narratives of Isaac Dunn, *The Lawrenceburg Press*, July 21, 1870 and Gano Papers, Vol. 3, p. 164-165, Cincinnati Historical Society; Jones, "The Ohio River," p. 130-131.
[16]Ibid.
[17]Narrative of Isaac Dunn, Gano Papers, Vol. 3, p. 164-165, Cincinnati Historical Society.
[18]Ibid.
[19]Ibid.
[20]*Symmes Purchase Records*, p. 102-103.
[21]*The Hayes Family*, p. 98-99; "Archaeological Survey Report at the Miami Fort Power Plant, Hamilton County, Ohio, July 11, 1977," unpublished manuscript prepared by Timothy S. Dalbey, Consulting Archaeologist; Maps of Hamilton County, Ohio by C. S. Mendenhall, ca. 1835; Wm. D. Emerson, 1847; A. W. Gilbert, 1848; Narrative of Ezra Hayes, in the William Henry Harrison Papers, Albert J. Green Collection, Cincinnati Historical Society.

Freeman's Station circa 1792

Abraham Freeman was born on October 10, 1743 in Woodridge, New Jersey. Abraham and his seven brothers reportedly served in the Continental Army during the Revolutionary War.[1] Following the war, Captain Freeman migrated first to Lancaster County, Pennsylvania and then to the Miami Purchase. His family eventually included six sons and six daughters.[2]

Captain Freeman probably purchased his first section from the Miami Land Company sight unseen in 1788. He contracted for this land in the Symmes Purchase from Jonathan Dayton, as did many other Pennsylvania and New Jersey residents.[3] At least three of Freeman's sons were of age to negotiate for their own land by 1790.[4] Freeman's 1788 land transaction included tracts which presently encompass Cincinnati Union Terminal, Mill Creek and segments of lower Price Hill.[5]

The Freeman family arrived in the Miami Purchase prior to January 7, 1789. Abraham's son Isaac was the recipient of two of the first 30 donation in-lots and out-lots offered in present day Cincinnati while another son, Samuel, purchased three lots near his brother's.[6] Another son, Dr. Clarkson Freeman, was not a part of the family's early land deals in the Symmes Purchase as he was incarcerated in 1791 for counterfeiting.[7]

Although the Freeman family initially settled in the Mill Creek Valley, their land holdings soon included property in today's Butler and Warren Counties.[8] Abraham senior soon moved to his property in present Lemon Township, Butler County and is recorded as probably the first resident in that part of the county.[9] It is only conjecture that he was the first settler there; however, prior to 1800 he did build a house north of Coldwater Creek, about one mile north of Gregory's Station and one half mile north of the present village of Lesourdsville. It stood near the road originally opened between Fort Hamilton and Morrell's Station in 1796 (old Hamilton-Middletown Road).[10]

Freeman's station, which consisted of five families, was definitely established by 1793 and was included in an official census of persons residing north of the Ohio River in that year.[11] Freeman may have established his settlement during a lull in the hostile Indian activities in the Miami Purchase and prior to the death of his son, Isaac, who with other members of a truce party dispatched by the commandant of Fort Washington, was killed by Indians in 1792.[12]

Although Freeman's activities have been traced, the actual location of his station remains debatable. In May 1796 Samuel Freeman and Joel Williams petitioned that a street be opened from the Ohio River, between the homes of John Stewart and John Hamilton in Cincinnati, to the Public Ground, intersecting the Great Road to Freeman's Station.[13]

Freeman owned large tracts of widely separated land in the Miami Purchase but his activities are centered primarily in Sections 35 and 36, Township 3, Range 3 and Section 26, Township 2, Range 4, Lemon Township, Butler County.[14] His station possibly stood in Section 35 near Gregory or Coldwater Creek, east of David Gregory's settlement. It was at this location that Captain Freeman later sold land to Benjamin Lesourd, who founded LeSourdsville.[15]

On November 12, 1799 Abraham Freeman ran an ad in *The Western Spy* at Cincinnati announcing the opening of his inn and general store at Freemansburg. The ad located Freemansburg on the Great Road to the Mad River, twenty three miles from Cincinnati and three miles below the Great Prairie. This description indicates that his inn may have become the Red Buck Tavern, later operated by his son John, and that Freemansburg stood on the later site of LeSourdsville, three miles below the prairie at today's Middletown.[16]

By 1800 Captain Freeman, through the petition of eighty residents of present Butler County, purchased one half of reserved Section 26 on Dick's Creek near today's Amanda and east of Dr. Calvin Morrell's Station. Freeman built and operated a mill there which was later deeded to his son Clarkson. The Captain moved to Sangamon County, Illinois in 1836 where he spent the remainder of his life near his son Abraham, junior.[17]

Notes

[1]Joseph Wallace, *Past and Present of the City of Springfield and Sangamon County, Illinois*, Chicago, 1904, Vol. 1, p. 153-155, quoted in Freeman Family Records, Manuscript Collection, Cincinnati Historical Society.
[2]Alta Harvey Heiser, *Hamilton in the Making*, Oxford, Ohio, 1941, p. 94; *History and Biographical Cyclopaedia of Bulter County, Ohio*, p. 643; Freeman Family Records, Cincinnati Historical Society; *Deed Book A*, p. 218, Hamilton County Recorder's Office.
[3]*Symmes Purchase Records*, p. 70.
[4]Ibid., p. 44, 78, 87, 99, 102-105; *Deed Book A*, p. 218, *Deed Book BI*, p. 55, Hamilton County Recorder's Office.
[5]*Symmes Purchase Records*, p. 70; U. S. Geological Survey Map, Covington, Kentucky Quad. 7.5' series.
[6]A. E. Jones, *Extracts from the History of Cincinnati*, p. 43, 50; John S. Gano Papers, Vol. 3, p. 103, Cincinnati Historical Society.
[7]Freeman Family Records, Cincinnati Historical Society; *Territorial Papers of the United States: The Territory Northwest of the Ohio River, 1787-1803*, Ed. Clarence Edwin Carter, Washington, D. C., 1934, Vol. 2, p. 478-479.
[8]Ibid., Vol. 2, p. 470 and Vol. 3, p. 72-74; *Deed Book C-1*, p. 66, Butler County Recorder's Office; *History and Biographical Cyclopaedia of Butler County*, p. 643; Copy of Israel Ludlow's Survey Between the Miami Rivers, Manuscript Collection, Cincinnati Historical Society; Copy Symmes Purchase Map, Cincinnati Historical Society (Original in National Archives Records, Group 49, Ohio #2); *Symmes Purchase Records*, p. 105.
[9]*History and Biographical Cyclopaedia of Bulter County, Ohio*, p. 643; Freeman Family Records, Cincinnati Historical Society.
[10]Ibid., see chapters on Bruce's, Gregory's and Morrell's Stations.
[11]*Territorial Papers of the United States*, Vol. 2, p. 740.
[12]Ibid., Vol. 2, p. 478-479.
[13]*Road Record Book Vol. 1, 1793-1850*, p. 130, Hamilton County Engineer's Office, Road Records Division.
[14]Freeman Family Records, Cincinnati Historical Society; *Territorial Papers of the United States*, Vol. 3, p. 72-74; Copy of Israel Ludlow Survey Between the Miami Rivers, Cincinnati Historical Society; *History and Biographical Cyclopaedia of Butler County, Ohio*, p. 643; *Deed Book B*, p. 66, Butler County Recorder's Office; *The Western Spy and Hamilton Gazette*, Nov. 12, 1799.
[15]*History and Biographical Cyclopaedia of Butler County, Ohio*, p. 643; Freeman Family Records, Cincinnati Historical Society.
[16]*The Western Spy and Hamilton Gazette*, Nov. 12, 1799; U. S. Geological Survey Maps, Hamilton and Mason, Ohio Quad., 7.5' series.
[17]*Territorial Papers of the United States*, Vol. 3, p. 72-74; Freeman Family Records, Cincinnati Historical Society; Map of Butler County, Ohio, 1836, by James McBride.

Garrard or Garard Station Wickerham's and Coleman's Mill Sites 1790-1791

Anderson Township of Hamilton County was originally part of the Virginia Military District. This was an area between the Scioto and Little Miami Rivers set aside by Virginia for allotment to her citizens who had served with the Continental Army during the Revolutionary War. It was actually a holding area to be used if the lands south of the Ohio River reserved for that purpose proved insufficient.

The land was the remnant left after Virginia ceded her land claims in the west to the Federal Government, part of the arrangement which ultimately led to the adoption of the U. S. Constitution. The original lands had been granted under the King James Charter of 1609 creating the Virginia Colony.[1]

In the spring and summer of 1788, Major John O'Bannon surveyed two tracts of land now located in Anderson Township. He assigned the surveys to Lieutenant John Steel under Military Land Warrant Number 602 for 666⅔ acres. The survey numbers were 536 and 1723 and the surveys were completed on August 22 and 29 of 1788, almost two years before Congress authorized surveying and settlement in this area of the Virginia Military District.[2]

The illegally-surveyed Steel tract was also illegally settled by a group of pioneers led by Jonathan Garrard. While a soldier in Braddock's army during the French and Indian War, Jonathan Garrard had been badly disfigured by a wound to the chin. There are several versions of how and when the Garrards arrived at survey number 536. Stephen Gerrard, a great-grandson of Jonathan, said that:

> *About 1792 some of the family emigrated to the territory of Ohio. Landing at the mouth of the Miami River, and ascending about two miles, Jonathan Garrard, son of*

Reverend John Garrard, built a fort or Block House, which afterwards was known as Garrard's Station.[3]

His account further says that the Garrard family, originally from Pennsylvania, settled at Gerrardstown in Berkely County, Virginia in 1754 and traveled from there to Ohio.[4]

A more reliable version states that in the spring of 1790 the Garrard family emigrated from Fort Garrard, Green County, Green Township, in the Monongahela Valley of Pennsylvania. Fort Garrard was a well known frontier Pennsylvania settlement where an especially gruesome Indian attack in 1782 claimed the lives of most of the Corbly family.[5]

Garrard's Ohio settlement consisted of possibly fifteen families illegally squatting on John Steel's tract. Prior to their arrival, John Bridges and Samuel Welch had built a cabin about 220 yards south of the site where Garrard would build his fort. Later, in the spring of 1792, the Reynolds, Raridon and Smith families and Thomas Smalley built cabins about one half mile below the fort.[6]

The settlement lay on the east side of the Little Miami River at the base of a hill overlooking a horseshoe bend and a well known river ford named after James Flinn, a captain of the Columbia militia. The crossing of the Little Miami connected Garrard's and Mercer's Stations with Columbia and Fort Washington.[7]

The site of Garrard's Station was purchased on October 23, 1806 from John Steel by General James Taylor of Newport, Kentucky and by 1814, when a road was built from Garrard's Station to the Clermont County line, the site was being called Allen's Fording and Robert's Ferry.[8] The course of the Little Miami River and Clough Creek have been radically altered and the horseshoe bend and the ford now lie under the jet runway at Lunken Airport.[9]

Garrard's settlement was close to no less than six prehistoric habitation sites and during the survey of two of them during the latter part of the nineteenth century the location of the fort was recorded in relation to them. The fort site today is located on the property of Henry Moeller, 2049 Elstun Road.[10]

Joseph Martin, one of the pioneers in Garrard's party, later reported:

> *John Garard and myself built the Station immediately after we arrived, and we had brought down the planks for roofs in our boats. We met Harmar's men going up the Ohio in boats. We used to pronounce the name Jarrard and it was originally Jarrat, a French name.*[11]

Mary Covalt, daughter of Abraham Covalt of Covalt's Station, used the name Gerret Station in describing the settlement.[12] An 1820 Census of Anderson Township listed the names as Jonathan and John Jarret.[13]

Garrard's Station was apparently considered a safe refuge. Many of the people from Covalt's and possibly the Round Bottom fort temporarily joined the settlement for mutual protection after the death of Captain Covalt and the defeat of General St. Clair's army in the fall of 1791.[14]

Ezra Ferris related an Indian encounter below the fort in 1792. A man named Welch (probably the Samuel Welch who had settled nearby with John Bridges) was making sugar at his cabin on January 7, 1792. He went up a hill near his residence to check the taps on the maple trees, was captured by several Indians and taken to an encampment of twenty five or thirty warriors. His life was spared by the intervention of an Indian elder. The entire war party had intended attacking the families living below Garrard's fort and stealing their horses. The Indians aborted their plan, fearing that the settlers might have been alerted by the activities of three of their scouts.

This proved a wise decision since a hunting party from Garrard's Station, led by Captain Hall, a scout from Covalt's Station, discovered the Indians. Hall tried to lure the warriors into an ambush after dark by hobbling a white horse among several fallen trees. A bell was attached to the horse while the settlers remained hidden. One Indian was wounded in the atttempt to steal the bait.[15] Welch was taken north by his captors but managed to escape months later with the help of a Canadian fur trader. He returned home in the late fall of 1792.[16]

In 1792 General James Taylor of Newport crossed the Ohio River with two bags of corn to be ground at one of the mills on the Little Miami.[17] He described in a later narrative Garrard's Station and the two mills he found nearby. Taylor identified Garrard as a Virginian and related how he had established his station and fort:

> *The river forms a bend in the form of a horseshoe embracing near 200 acres of rich bottom land with spare growth of Buckeye, box elder, sugar trees and c. of great fertility and easy to clear. Without knowing or caring to whom the land belonged he established his station and this rich bottom was mostly cleared and put in corm and was cultivated as I passed near it on my way to Wickham's Mill.*[18]

Jacob Wickham or Wickerham or Wickersham, listed as a resident of Columbia in the spring of 1790, had previously served in William Harrod's and Squire Boone's companies of Kentucky militia during the Revolutionary

Copy of a road survey from a north-south meridian line near the mouth of the Little Miami River past Flinn's Ford, terminating at Garrard's Station in 1826. Lewis Broadwell was the surveyor. *(Hamilton County Engineer's Office, Road Records Division)*

War.[19] Wickerham may have had a fortified settlement of his own near the Little Miami River, since in 1792 a petition was submitted to the Court of Sessions for a road from Wickerham's Station to Mercersburg (now Newtown).[20] The mill and possible station site was sold on December 14, 1796 to Jacob Frazee. This 200 acre tract lay just north of Garrard's Station and the property lines adjoined.[21]

Wickerham's mill was in operation as early as 1790 and a road was petitioned from it to Fort Miami (Columbia) in that year. The residents of Columbia were so anxious for a road to the mill that they asked that the road be opened within a month following approval of the petition.[22]

The first mill at Wickerham's was a floating affair constructed on two flat-boats, or Kentucky boats, moored in the Little Miami. However, the boats had sunk prior to General Taylor's inspection of the site in 1792 and a crude standing mill had been erected on the river bank. General Taylor described the mill in these terms:

> *The first fall of the Little Miami is about three miles from the mouth and immediately behind Columbia. We proceded to the mill we found no Kentucky boats, it had been so erected the two boats had been moved close up to the ripple of about five feet fall which was increased by some bush and rock to raise a head in the river, had sunk the boats as the cables did not permit them to rise with the tide. Jacob Wickam was the proprietor. He had raised a cob of small logs at the shore on the east side had filled it with rocks sufficient to make it stable, had fixed a huge block in the stream just wide enough for a full wheel to ply on a wide apron, had broke up his boats and made a half fence Shelby in which his mill stones of 18 inches by two feet diameter were running, he subsequently put up more valuable work, but nothing more than country work, he some four or five years later sold out. Some ten or twelve after the seat got into the hands of two Yankees by name of Samuel and Josiah Holly, who built a good merchant mill on the site. They broke and it got into the hands of Phillip Turpin.*[23]

Ezra Ferris described Wickerham's mill as a tub mill, meaning that the mill wheel was a small horizontal one, similar to later water turbines in some respects. He located it not on the Little Miami itself, but east of the river on Clough Creek near its mouth.[24] Oliver Spencer, a youthful resident of Columbia, stated in a narrative published in 1835:

> *Wickerham's Mill near Turpin's Mill site had a flat boat tied to the bank and a piroque anchored in the stream, the shaft rested on the piroque and flatboat. Hand mills were used mostly during low water.*[25]

A second mill of the same type was built by Neniad Coleman in 1791 while he resided at Columbia. Coleman was born in Loudon County, Virginia in 1746. He was attached to the Third Virginia Regiment commanded by Colonel Heath during the Revolutionary War and disabled in 1779. General Taylor's account describes this mill:

> *There was in 1791 a temporary grist mill but at a small ripple about two miles from the mouth opposite a place called Garrard's Station. Opposite the back part of Columbia, but the high water of that winter carried it off and it was not rebuilt.*[26]

J. G. Olden and Ezra Ferris, early historians of the Miami country, agree that Coleman built this floating mill but disagree on the method of construction. Ferris remembered the mill as being contained in one flat-bottomed boat while Olden described it as using one boat for the grain and meal and another for the machinery, with the water wheel in between.[27] Floating mills of this type were usually operated by an undershot water wheel with about thirty per cent efficiency.

Notes
[1]C. E. Sherman, *Original Ohio Land Subdivisions, Vol. III of the Final Report*, Columbus, 1925, p. 16, 19-20.
[2]Nelson W. Evans, "Colonel John O'Bannon," *Ohio Archaeological and Historical Society Publications*, Vol. 14 (1905) p. 321-326; Copy of original 1788 survey by John O'Bannon, *Hamilton County, Ohio Survey Book No. II*, p. 235-236, Hamilton County Engineer's Office, Road Records Division.
[3]Anna Russell Des Cognets, *Governor Garrard of Kentucky, His Descendants and Relatives*, Lexington, Kentucky, 1898, p. 131.
[4]Ibid.; Narrative of Stephen Dye, quoted in the Simon Kenton Papers, Series 4BB, p. 36-38, Lyman Draper Collection, Wisconsin Historical Society.
[5]W. F. Horn, "Early Western Movement on the Monongahela and Upper Ohio 1765-1795," quoted in *The Horn Papers*, Vol. 1, Scottsdale, Pennsylvania, 1945, p. 347-348; Narrative of Joseph Martin, quoted in Whittlesey, "Notices of Hamilton County, Ohio;" Narrative of General James Taylor, Manuscript in Collection of Cincinnati Historical Society, p. 45; *Report of the Commission to Locate the Site of the Frontier Forts of Pennsylvania*, Vol. 2, p. 439-441.
[6]Narrative of Joseph Martin, quoted in Whittlesey, "Notices of Hamilton County, Ohio;" Ferris, *Early Settlement of the Miami Country*, p. 281, 319.
[7]Ibid., p. 340; Narrative of General Taylor, p. 45; Berry Day, "Records of a Past Generation," copies from *The Miamisburg Bulletin*, July 13, 1883, p. 2-3, Manuscript in Collection of Cincinnati Historical

Society; *Road Record Book I, 1793-1850*, p. 6, 94, 112-113, 120, Hamilton County Engineer's Office, Road Records Division.
[8]Property Deed with description, *Deed Book G*, p. 165-166, Hamilton County Recorder's Office; *Hamilton County, Ohio Survey Book 22*, p. 2, 12, Case No. 93287, Common Pleas Court and *Road Record Book 1811-1816*, p. 237-244, Hamilton County Engineer's Office, Road Records Division; Columbia Township Records, Manuscript in Collection Cincinnati Historical Society; Lewis S. Collins, *Historical Sketches of Kentucky*, revised by Richard H. Collins, Covington, Kentucky, 1874, Vol. 1, p. 355-357.
[9]*Road Record Book 1-1B, 1790-1850*, p. 67, 92, 112-114, 138; *Road Record Book 1850-1871*, p. 543; *Hamilton County Survey Book, 1825-1830*, p. 109-115, Hamilton County Engineer's Office, Road Records Division; Maps of Hamilton County by S. Morrison and J. Williams, 1835, and Wm D. Emerson, 1847; *Titus' Atlas of Hamilton County, Ohio*, p. 43.
[10]Ibid., Maps of Hamilton County, Ohio as in Footnote 9; Mills, *Archaeological Atlas of Ohio*, p. 31; Starr, "Archaeology of Hamilton County, Ohio," p. 44-47, 60-70, 75-79; Cincinnati Art Museum Library Files, Record Group 3, Series 5, Folder 2, 1889.
[11]Narrative of Joseph Martin, quoted in Whittlesey, "Notices of Hamilton County, Ohio."
[12]Narrative of Mary Covalt Jones, p. 6, Cincinnati Historical Society.
[13]U. S. Census Office, *4th Census, 1820*, Population Schedules, Ohio, Washington, 1820, Vol. 2, Anderson Township, Hamilton County, Ohio.
[14]Narrative of Mary Covalt Jones, p. 6, Cincinnati Historical Society.
[15]Narrative of Joseph Martin, quoted in Whittlesey, "Notices;" Ferris, *Early Settlement*, p. 281, 318-319, 321; Cist, *The Cincinnati Miscellany*, Vol. 1, p. 174.
[16]Ferris, *Early Settlement*, p. 320-321.
[17]A. E. Jones, *Reminiscences of the Early Days of the Little Miami Valley*, Cincinnati, 1878, p. 19; A. E. Jones, "Semi-Centennial Anniversary of the Birth of Cincinnati," Dec. 26, 1838, Manuscript in Collection of Cincinnati Historical Society.
[18]Narrative of General Taylor, p. 45.
[19]Collins, *Historical Sketches of Kentucky*, p. 12-13; Jones, *Extracts from the History of Cincinnati*, p. 18; Letter of John Reily to Daniel Drake, quoted in *The Bulletin of the Historical and Philosophical Society of Ohio*, Vol. 16-18 (1921-1923) p. 15.
[20]*Road Record Book 1, 1793-1850*, p. 6, 94, 112-113, 120, Hamilton County Engineer's Office, Road Records Division.
[21]*Hamilton County, Ohio Court and Other Records*, Vol. 2, p. 159-160.
[22]*Plat Book 2*, 1846, p. 19; *Plat Book 3*, 1868, p. 52; *Road Record Book, 1793-1810*, p. 395-396; *Road Record Book 1, 1793-1850*, p. 92, Hamilton County Engineer's Office, Road Records Division.
[23]Narrative of General Taylor, p. 45.
[24]Ferris, *Early Settlement*, p. 291-292.
[25]Spencer, *Indian Captivity of O. M. Spencer*, p. 32.
[26]Narrative of General Taylor, p. 45; *Year Book, Revolutionary Ancestors of the Sons of the Revolution in the State of Ohio*, 1895, p. 16.
[27]Ferris, *Early Settlement*, p. 275; Olden, *Historical Sketches*, p. 64.

Gregory's Station circa 1791

A stockaded station was built possibly as early as 1791 on a site currently occupied by the LeSourdsville Village Mobile Home Park, 5300 Hamilton-Middletown Road. This site is located in Fractional Section 5, Township 2, Range 3 in present Lemon Township, Butler County.[1]

David Gregory, one of the earliest settlers in present Butler County, was the founder of the station, which stood near a creek bearing the family name.[2] Daniel Doty, who had a temporary residence in 1791 near present day Middletown, reportedly passed by Gregory's Station in 1796 and remembered the small military outpost from his first trip past that site in 1791.[3] The few soldiers reported to have been assigned to the station probably would have been sent from Fort Hamilton.[4] At the station site, the following epitaph is inscribed on the tombstone of David Gregory's wife, Margaret:

> *Here lies the woman, the first save one, who settled on the Miami above Fort Hamilton. Her table was spread, and that of the best, and Anthony Wayne was often her guest.*[5]

David Gregory purchased at least two tracts of land from Jonathan Dayton. The deed for the 412 acres on which his station stood was signed April 1, 1795 and was not recorded until February 28, 1797.[6]

Gregory's Station was located between Bruce's Station (in South Hamilton) and Morrell's Station (on the west side of Excello). A road surveyed from Fort Hamilton through Gregory's Station to Morrell's Station establishes their existence and their actual location. Surveyed and established in 1796, this road ran east from Fort Hamilton passing through Gregory's Station, then turned in a northerly direction and finally veered west to its terminus at Morrell's Station. The road, probably established on a trail used by the army since 1791, was cut 66 feet wide and became the precursor of the present Hamilton-Middletown Road.[7]

In 1800 Butler County was still part of Hamilton County. During January of that year, David Gregory was among 66 petitioners to Congress on behalf of Abraham Freeman. The petitioners asked Congress to pass an act allowing

Freeman to purchase part of reserved Section 26 in Range 4 on Dick's Creek for a much-needed mill site.[8]

Gregory died July 9, 1802 at the age of 34 and was buried on the station site which, by the latter part of the nineteenth century, became the property of Peter W. Shepherd.[9]

Notes

[1] L. H. Everts, *Combination Atlas Map of Butler County, Ohio*, Philadelphia, 1875, p. 83; *Butler Coounty, Ohio Atlas and Pictorial Review*, Hamilton, 1914, p. 45; *The County of Butler: Imperial Atlas and Art Folio of Bulter County, Ohio*, Richmond, Indiana, 1895, p. 33; *Road Record Book Vol. 1 1793-1850*, p. 127, Hamilton County Engineer's Office, Road Records Division; *Middletown U. S. A., All American City*, Ed. George C. Crout, Middletown, 1960, p. 16-17; Map of Butler County, Ohio, James McBride, 1836.
[2] Ibid.
[3] *Middletown U. S. A.*, p. 16-17.
[4] Alta Harvey Heiser, *West to Ohio*, Chap. 1, p. 12.
[5] Personal survey of the burial plots; Stephen D. Cone, *A Concise History of Hamilton, Ohio*, Middletown, 1901, p. 31.
[6] *Index to Transcript Records*, p. 132, Butler County Recorder's Office; *Deed Book A*, p. 300-301, 534-535, Hamilton County Recorder's Office.
[7] Everts, *Combination Atlas*, p. 83; *Butler County, Ohio Atlas and Pictorial Review*, p. 45; *The County of Butler, Ohio: Imperial Atlas*, p. 33, 127; McBride, Map of Butler County, 1836; *Road Record Book, Vol 1. 1793-1850*, p. 127, Hamilton County Engineer's Office, Road Records Division; Highway Map of Butler County, Ohio, 1984.
[8] "United States Territorial Papers," quoted in Alta Harvey Heiser, *Hamilton in the Making*, Oxford,, Ohio, 1941, p. 91-94.
[9] *A Concise History of Hamilton, Ohio*, p. 30.

Griffin's Station circa 1792

On July 23, 1792 Lieutenant Daniel Griffin entered warrant 147 for entire Section 7, Township 3, Range 1 in present Springfield Township.[1] He had served as a private during the Revolutionary War, and after immigrating to present Hamilton County was commissioned a Lieutenant in the 1st Regiment of local militia on December 10, 1791. He was promoted to Captain on August 22, 1797.[2]

Lieutenant Griffin established a station about one half mile west of Captain White's Station and two miles southwest of a large salt lick, located near the present intersection of Galbraith Road and Cross County Highway.[3]

Daniel Griffin was joined by his brother Robert, also a veteran of the Revolutionary War in which he served as Sergeant.[4] Daniel and Jacob Vorhis (Voorhees) and the Robert Caldwell family built their cabins near the Griffin brothers on the south bank of Mill Creek approximately where it is crossed by present Springfield Pike.[5] Daniel Seward, James McCashen and other families built their cabins on the north side of Mill Creek.

Griffin's Station, like White's Station, was a scattered settlement, the buildings being strung out from the banks of Mill Creek west of the present location of the Carthage Fairgrounds north to Caldwell Road.[6]

Samuel and James Caldwell built and operated a saw and grist mill and a distillery on Mill Creek below the station. Their entire enterprise was swept away by a flash flood about 1806.[7]

Although Daniel Griffin entered his warrant for his station site in 1792 most local historians theorize that the station was not established until after the attack on White's Station in October of 1793. Contemporary accounts of that attack do not mention Griffin's Station.[8] However, an advertisement in *The Centinel of the North-Western Territory* establishes the station's existence in 1793:

> *Two Dollars Reward. Lost between Griffin's Station and Fort Washington, one coat and several small articles enclosed therein; to wit, one shirt, one pair of small clothes, one muslin neck cloth, and sundry papers. Whoever will deliver the same to the printer hereof, shall*

receive the above reward. Cincinnati, November 20, 1793.[9]

The station probably existed in the fall of 1792 or spring of 1793 despite inferences to the contrary. The fact that there is no record of Griffin's Station offering assistance to White's Station during the attack on that settlement only indicates that Griffin's Station was unoccupied at the time or that the residents were not alarmed by what little gunfire they might have heard.[10]

On May 13, 1794 John Johnston and Daniel Comer accompanied a large supply train dispatched to Fort Greenville. The caravan consisted of pack horses and wagons pulled by oxen, escorted by foot soldiers and mounted dragoons under the command of Major William Winston.[11] The supply party was strung out as it passed by Griffin's Station and for some unknown reason the commanding officer of the dragoons detained his troops at the station.

The Indians, who had been watching the movement of the supply party and its escort, took advantage of the situation and attacked the front of the supply train several miles north of Griffin's Station. Members of the escort and wagoneers were killed in the well executed attack before the troops lingering at the station were even aware of the incident.[12]

The Griffin Station location is confirmed by official road surveys of 1794-96, prior to major changes in Mill Creek and the old traces.[13] There apparently were no Indian attacks on this station.

Notes
[1] *Symmes Purchase Records*, p. 59, 73; Teetor, *Past and Present of the Mill Creek Valley*, p. 41.
[2] *Official Roster of Revolutionary Soldiers Buried in the State of Ohio*, Vol. 1, p. 165; *The Territorial Papers of the United States*, Vol. 3, p. 481.
[3] Teetor, *Past and Present of the Mill Creek Valley*, p. 40-41; Map of Hamilton County, Ohio, Wm. D. Emerson, Cincinnati, 1847; U. S. Geological Survey Map, Cincinnati, East Quad. 7.5' series; Greve, *Centennial History of Cincinnati*, Vol. 1, p. 292; Olden, *Historical Sketches*, p. 111.
[4] *Official Roster of Revolutionary Soldiers Buried in the State of Ohio*, Vol. 1, p. 165.
[5] Teetor, *Past and Present of the Mill Creek Valley*, p. 41-42; Greve, *Centennial History of Cincinnati*, Vol. 1, p. 292; Olden, *Historical Sketches*, p. 111.
[6] Ibid.
[7] Olden, *Historical Sketches*, p. 111-112.
[8] Teetor, *Past and Present of the Mill Creek Valley*, p. 41-42; Greve, *Centennial History of Cincinnati*, Vol. 1, p. 292; Olden, *Historical Sketches*, p. 111.
[9] *Centinel of the North-Western Territory*.
[10] Ibid., Nov. 9, 1793, April 26, 1794, May 3, 1794; Jacob Burnet, *Notes on the Early Settlement of the North-Western Territory*, p. 110-111.
[11] John Johnston, *Recollections of Sixty Years*, Ed. Charlotte Reeve Conover, Piqua, Ohio, 1957, p. 151.
[12] Ibid.
[13] *Road Record Book, Vol. 1-1B, 1793-1850*, p. 113, 125, Hamilton County Enginner's Office, Road Records Division; Olden, *Historical Sketches*, p. 139-143.

Hayes' Station
1791

Joseph Hayes was born on December 16, 1732 in Chester County, Pennsylvania. At the age of 44 he formed a company of cavalry which he equipped at his own expense and, with the rank of Captain, led during the Revolutionary War.[1] Like many other veterans of the war, Captain Hayes was paid for his services in worthless Continental currency and this forced him into bankruptcy.[2]

Following foreclosure of his property, Hayes and his family left Pennsylvania. They traveled via the Monongahela and Ohio Rivers and after many delays arrived at North Bend in the spring of 1791.[3] Traveling with Hayes were his sons-in-law Thomas Miller, Sr. and James Bennett and their families. Also in the party were the families of Benjamin Walker, Isaac Polk, Garrett Vanness, John White, David Brokaw and Joseph Kitchell.[4]

Although the party took up residence at North Bend, some time later in the year Hayes, Alexander Guard and others began clearing land on the Great Miami River. They built fortified cabins there and referred to the area as Hayes Point.[5] But they retained their cabins at North Bend as primary residences. They continued to improve the Hayes Point property and negotiated a lease for it with Judge John Cleves Symmes.[6]

It is apparent that Captain Hayes' settlement on the Great Miami was not made permanent until the spring of 1793, when North Bend was partially inundated by the rising waters of an Ohio River flood. It was at this time that the Hayes party moved to the site which they had begun clearing almost two years earlier. Historian Samuel Morrison had this to say about the Hayes settlement of 1793:

> *Nearly the whole colony removed having been driven out of their cabins by the Great flood of that year. At this place they had previously erected their cabins in the form of blockhouses.*[7]

At the time it was established the settlement was called Hayes' Station but later was referred to as the Goose Pond Farm.[8]

The Great Miami River was still high and running fast when Alexander

Guard and his family joined the settlement in the spring of 1793. Guard and Hayes nearly drowned trying to maneuver Guard's piroques into the Miami from the Ohio River.[9]

It was probably shortly after this incident that Captain Hugh Dunn's party reached a point on the Great Miami within sight of the Hayes settlement.[10] The Dunn party landed at Hayes' Station where they remained until that fall. Isaac Dunn, son of the founder and a member of Dunn's Station, later described Hayes' Station:

> *Although this little settlement was in a very exposed situation, not being more than 2 1/2 miles above Tanner's Creek one of the great crossings of the Indians in their route to make depradations on the citizens of Kentucky; yet was no fort built for the protection of the settlers. The cabins erected where we landed were so arranged as to afford protection to each other.*[11]

The Hayes settlement consisted of possibly ten families. Isaac Polk, one of the founders, taught school at the station from 1793 to 1796. Although Captain Hayes left the settlement in 1796, it was not abandoned and Joseph Hayes, Jr. continued to live at this Goose Pond Farm until 1801.[12]

In making their initial move to their temporary settlement southwest of the Goose Pond in 1791, the Hayes, Guard and Miller families were following in the footsteps of some of the original settlers of North Bend. Encouraged by a false sense of security in 1789 they had taken up residence on their outlots or established independent settlements west of the village.[13]

Confusion has been propagated over the years concerning the actual location, or definition, of Miami Point. In the most limited terms it would represent the peninsula at the confluence of the Ohio and Great Miami Rivers which prior to November 23, 1847 extended into present Lawrenceburg Township, Dearborn County, Indiana.[14] However, there have been various names and boundaries applied to this peninsula. Joseph Hayes and the families of John Cleves Symmes and William H. Harrison popularized such names as Haye's Point, Point Farm, Longview, Miami Point and Symmes' Point Farm.[15]

An advertisement concerning lease options on the land of John Cleves Symmes clearly indicates that in 1809 the Goose Pond and The Point were thought of as separate geographic entities.[16]

The southern end of Goose Pond intersected the division line of Section 31, in Fractional Range 2 East, Township 1, and Section 36 in Fractional Range 1 East, Township 2, Miami Township, east of Fractional Range 6 and

Guard's Island. This area is near the present site of the Hamilton County public boat ramp in Shawnee Lookout Park west of Brower Road. Miami Point could be considered an extension of the flood plain, reaching from the west terminus of Fort Hill to the east bank of the Great Miami River.[17] Prior to any temporary or permanent settlements at either Miami Point or the Goose Pond, both areas had been surveyed by the Miami Land Company office and by military personnel.[18]

Captain Hugh Dunn's party settled temporarily at Hayes' Station prior to moving to their own settlement in the fall of 1793. Once Dunn's Station was established, there was daily interaction between these two settlements, and many of their inhabitants were related by lineage or marriage. As more settlers joined the two stations their aggregate population began to resemble one extended community.[19]

On Friday, August 22, 1794, acting Territorial Governor Winthrop Sargent arrived at the Great Miami River, viewed the settlers' vast cornfields, and noted that the settlement was large but very scattered.[20]

Despite the fact that Major Byrd's military stockade was within one and one half miles of Hayes' Station, and that vigilance was a part of daily routine at Hayes' and Dunn's Stations, two horses were stolen from the settlement by Indians on Saturday, September 6, 1794.[21]

The available contemporary and secondary information indicates that Captain Hayes' Station stood east of the Great Miami River at the west end of Fort Hill. The station stood on the flood plain in Section 5, Fractional Range 1 East, Township 1, in present Miami Township. Although in the flood plain, the station stood on an elevated terrace out of reach of the flood waters of 1793. It was near Brower Road and northwest of the site of the former John Scott Harrison home. Both sites are now the property of the Cincinnati Gas and Electric Company.[22]

Notes
[1] *The Hayes Family, Origins, History and Genealogy*, p. 60-62, 64, 90.
[2] Ibid., p. 64.
[3] Ibid., p. 64; Shaw, *History of Dearborn County*, p. 109-110; Fletcher, *Dearborn and Ohio Counties*, p. 57.
[4] Ibid.; Narrative of Isaac Dunn, quoted in John Stites Gano Papers, Vol. 3, p. 164-165, Cincinnati Historical Society.
[5] *The Hayes Family*, p. 65, 90, 132, 138; Shaw, *Dearborn County*, p. 110.
[6] *The Hayes Family*, p. 193-194; Shaw, *Dearborn County*, p. 184; Fletcher, *Dearborn and Ohio Counties*, p. 47; The Harrison Papers, Memorabilia, James A. Green Collection, Cincinnati Historical Society.
[7] *The Hayes Family*, p. 64, 90, 193-194, 365; Shaw, *Dearborn County*, p. 109-110, 130, 697-698; Fletcher, *Dearborn and Ohio Counties*, p. 96-97; John Scott Harrison, "Pioneer Life at North Bend," an address to the Whitewater and Miami Valley Pioneer Association at Cleves, Ohio, Sept. 8, 1886; Ferris, *Early Settlement*, p. 359-360.

[8]*The Hayes Family*, p. 132, 138; Shaw, *Dearborn County*, p. 108, 184; Fletcher, *Dearborn and Ohio Counties*, p. 97, 698.
[9]Ibid., p. 97.
[10]Ibid., p. 698.
[11]Narrative of Isaac Dunn, quoted in John S. Gano Papers, Vol. 3, p. 164-165, Cincinnati Historical Society.
[12]*The Hayes Family*, p. 70, 365; Shaw, *Dearborn County*, p. 108, 184.
[13]Henry Howe, *Historical Collections of Ohio*, Cincinnati, 1847, p. 236-237; Letter of John Cleves Symmes to Jonathan Dayton, May 18-20, 1789, Symmes Correspondence, Cincinnati Historical Society.
[14]Narrative of Ezra Hayes, included in the William H. Harrison Papers, Albert J. Green Collection, Cincinnati Historical Society; Maps of Hamilton County by S. Morrison and J. Williams, 1835; Wm. D. Emerson, 1847; Copy of Field Notes of Benjamin Chambers and Wm. Ludlow, Survey of the Great Miami, 1839, Township 5, Range 1 West, Dearborn County Engineer's Office.
[15]*The Hayes Family*, p. 90, 98-99; *The Correspondence of John Cleves Symmes*, Ed. Beverly W. Bond, Jr., Cincinnati, 1926, p. 132; *The Intimate Letters of John Cleves Symmes and His Family*, Ed. Beverly W. Bond, Jr., Cincinnati, 1956, p. 166-167; *Road Record Book 1793-1810*, p. 185-191, Hamilton County Engineer's Office, Road Records Division.
[16]*The Intimate Letters of John Cleves Symmes*, p. 134.
[17]*Survey Book 3*, p. 221-236 and *The Restored Records, Decrees & Plats Affecting Real Estate, 1798-1863, Vol. 1*, p. 27, Hamilton County Engineer's Office, Road Records Division; Maps of Hamilton County by S. Morrison and J. Williams, 1835; Wm. D. Emerson, 1847; A. W. Gilbert, 1848; *Titus' Atlas of Hamilton County*, p. 9; Atlas of Hamilton County, Ohio, 1884, p. 9.
[18]Victor Collot, *A Voyage in North America*, Paris, 1826, Reprints of Americana, New York, 1974, p. 135-136; Journal of General Richard Butler, in *The Olden Time*, Ed. Neville B. Craig, Pittsburgh, 1846-1848, Reprinted Cincinnati, 1876, Vol. 2, No. 2, p. 454-457.
[19]Fletcher, *Dearborn and Ohio Counties*, p. 97, 698, 847; *The Hayes Family*, p. 62, 64, 71-431; Shaw, *Dearborn County*, p. 109- 110, 129-130, 184, 226; Ferris, *Early Settlement*, p. 359-360.
[20]Copy of *Diary of Major Winthrop Sargent, Number 2*, commencing at New York, Oct. 1, 1793 and ending in Philadelphia, Jan. 1, 1796, entry of Friday, Aug. 22, 1794, Cincinnati Historical Society.
[21]Ibid., entry of Thursday, Sept. 11, 1794.
[22]Ibid., Maps and Atlases of Hamilton County as in Footnote 17; Field Notes of Benjamin Chambers and Wm. Ludlow, Survey of the Great Miami, 1839, Dearborn County Engineer's Office; William H. Harrison Papers, Albert J. Green Collection, Cincinnati Historical Society; *Hamilton County Survey and Plat Books*, Book 2, p. 175; Book 3, p. 221-236; Book 6, p. 335; Book 7, p. 154; Book 9, p. 68 and City of Cincinnati and Hamilton County Metropolitan Topographical Survey Maps and Overlays, Hamilton County Engineer's Office, Road Records Division; U. S. Geological Survey Maps, 1914-1970, Hooven and Lawrenceburg, Indiana, Kentucky, Ohio Quad., 7.5' series; "Survey of the Reserved Township Between the Ohio River and the Big Miami," 1795, Short Family Papers, Manuscript Collection of the Cincinnati Historical Society; Copy of John Cleves Symmes survey between the Miami Rivers, drawn by Charles M. Heaton, Sept. 5, 1824, Manuscript Collection of the Cincinnati Historical Society; *The Hayes Family*, p. 70, 132, 365; Shaw, *Dearborn County*, p. 116-117, 184; Autobiography of Joseph Hayes, Jr., courtesy of Mrs. Ina Rix, Manuscript Collection of Westchester, Pennsylvania Historical Society; Narrative of Isaac Dunn, quoted in John S. Gano Papers, Vol. 3, p. 164-165, Cincinnati Historical Society.

The Daniel Gebhart Tavern still stands along old Main Street in Miamisburg, Ohio, site of Hole's Station in 1795.

Holes' Station
1795

In May of 1795 John Cleves Symmes entered into a contract with Zachariah Hole of the Passaic Valley, New Jersey for one hundred acres of land in the sixth entire range of townships in the Miami Purchase. The site was considerably north of the actual boundaries of the Purchase as finally determined by Congress in 1794.[1]

The contract offers an interesting example of the terms that Symmes offered to promote settlement in this northern area at the time. It also shows that bitter experience had taught Symmes to insist on a minimum number of armed men to protect the station. The contract reads:

> *These may testify to all concerned that upon the express condition of Zachariah Hole and his companions or associates actually settling and finally establishing a Station of cabins or houses, clearing land, cultivating the earth and Maintaining a Station as aforesaid in the sixth entire range of townships in the Miami Purchase on any land not already located and entered on the map or record, and that within the following periods of time, viz.—ten Cabins shall be raised and covered with Clabboards or punchions by Christmas day next, and thirty acres of land shall be well cleared (Ms. indecipherable) by the first of June 1796, and the Station shall be settled and protected by at least ten men who shall be more than sixteen years of age, and each Man well provided with a good gun, powder and lead for defence in case of danger—Then in such case and not otherwise, the said John Cleves Symmes will bestow free gratis on the men so settling the Station, whether ten men or more, one hundred acres of land to be divided equally between them, wherever they may build such Station in said Sixth Range not on lands already located—and the said John Cleves Symmes will also sell unto the said Zachariah Hole & to each other man who may assist and join in making such Station as much land contiguous to and adjoining*

round that Station as the said Zachariah Hole or any of his company shall chuse to purchase and may be able to pay for, at the current price, not exceeding one and a half dollars per acre, by next New Year's day, and if any of the Settlers shall desire longer time for payment, they shall have any time not exceeding three years, but the land must remain as security, and as all other credited lands are in the purchase subject to the rising price, or such prices as other wood lands in that neighborhood shall sell at when they pay for the same.

(signed) John Cleves Symmes
Northbend, May 21st 1795[2]

The entire Hole family apparently had a strong interest in western land speculation, since Zachariah Hole and his brothers—John, William and Daniel—were among original lot owners in Losantiville in 1789. The Hole brothers also were among the founders of Ludlow's Station or Mill Creek Village in the spring of 1790.[3]

John Hole had served as a surgeon in the Continental Army during the Revolutionary War and was one of the first practicing physicians to reside in Cincinnati. He eventually owned many parcels of land in and around the village. Dr. Hole left Cincinnati for Kentucky in 1790 because his wife Massee (a cousin of Israel Ludlow) became alarmed at the frequent Indian raids in the vicinity. He returned by the fall of 1793, however, and was instrumental in controlling a smallpox epidemic raging in Cincinnati by using inoculation to prevent spread of the disease.[4]

Zachariah Hole's station was founded, probably, in the fall of 1795 during a period when several of the Hole family's relatives and friends from New Jersey were also building cabins and settlements north of the actual boundaries of the Miami Purchase. At the time, they believed that John Cleves Symmes' claims to the land, and thus their own land titles, were secure. When Symmes failed to raise enough money to pay the Treasury for the land, Congress repossessed this northern section. The settlers were forced to present several petitions to Congress in 1799 asking for preferential treatment in securing clear title to lands they had paid for and improved. Zachariah, William and Daniel Hole were among these petitioners. who were allowed to rebuy their land at very low prices.[5]

The settlers at Hole's Station, besides Zachariah and his wife Hannah, possibly included his brothers John, Daniel and William.[6] A short time later, Dr. John Hole settled on land east of the station along Silver Creek, now known as Hole's Creek, where he later built two sawmills.[7]

Although a small stockade may have been constructed at Hole's Station according to the terms of settlement, the first blockhouse there apparently was built about 1798 in response to rumors of an Indian uprising. The Reverend John Kobler, a Methodist circuit-riding minister, preached for the people of Hole's Station on his first circuit in August of 1798. According to Reverend Kobler, the blockhouse may already have been built by that time although other historians date the construction in 1799. He described the station's inhabitants as "truly poverty stricken."

The building of the blockhouse was reportedly supervised by George Adams, a Virginian and Revolutionary War veteran who had been seriously wounded during General Harmar's disastrous campaign of 1790.[8] The blockhouse was replaced in the early 1800s by a two story hewn-log building known as Gebhart's Tavern which is still standing. An 1810 survey of the state road between Dayton and Cincinnati seemingly places Hole's Station between Linden and Lock Streets along Old Main Street in downtown Miamisburg.[9]

Zachariah Hole sued Symmes in 1801 to gain compensation for his landtitle expenses. The suit was finally settled in 1803 when several sections of Symmes' land were seized by the sheriff and sold to repay Hole. Symmes' entire fortune eventually was lost through similar suits.[10]

By about 1810, Zachariah had moved to Preble County where he founded Lewisburg and built the area's first mill. John and William continued to live in the vicinity of Hole's Station while Daniel moved to Warren County to live with his wife Mary's family, the Beedles of Beedle's Station.[11]

Notes
[1] R. Pierce Beaver, "The Miami Purchase of John Cleves Symmes," p. 314-320.
[2] *Correspondence of John Cleves Symmes*, p. 285-286.
[3] *Early Roster of Cincinnati and Hamilton County*, p. 9; Petition of inhabitants of Mill Creek Village to General Harmar, April 29, 1790, "Transcriptions from the Harmar Papers," Raymond C. Knopf, Anthony Wayne Parkway Board, 1954, Ohio Historical Society Library.
[4] Drake, "Memoir of the Miami Country," p. 76; Houser, *Wilderness Doctor*, p. 9-13; although it has been stated that Dr. John Hole was Cincinnati's first physician, apparently Army surgeon Richard Allison and Dr. Calvin Morrell were both in Cincinnati at least as early as Dr. Hole, if not before. See Virginius C. Hall, "Richard Allison - Surgeon to the Legion, part 1," *The Ohio State Medical Journal*, Vol. 48 (1952) p. 840-841; *Early Rosters of Cincinnati and Hamilton County*, p. 9, 13.
[5] *Genealogical Index of Pioneers in the Miami Valley*, p. 70.
[6] *Wilderness Doctor*. p. 13-14, 16-17, 21-22.
[7] *History of Warren County, Ohio*, 1882, p. 264; John F. Edgar, *Pioneer Life in Dayton and Vicinity, 1796-1840*, Dayton, Ohio, 1896, p. 56-57.
[8] *Dayton and Montgomery County, Resources and People*, Ed. Charlotte Reeve Conover, New York, 1932, Vol. 2, p. 818-819.
[9] *Early Rosters of Cincinnati and Hamilton County*, p. 166.
[10] Lytle Papers, Cincinnati Historical Society, Box 19, Letter 43; Beaver, "The Miami Purchase," p. 321, 338.
[11] *Wilderness Doctor*, p. 16; *Genealogical Index of Pioneers in the Miami Valley*, p. 70.

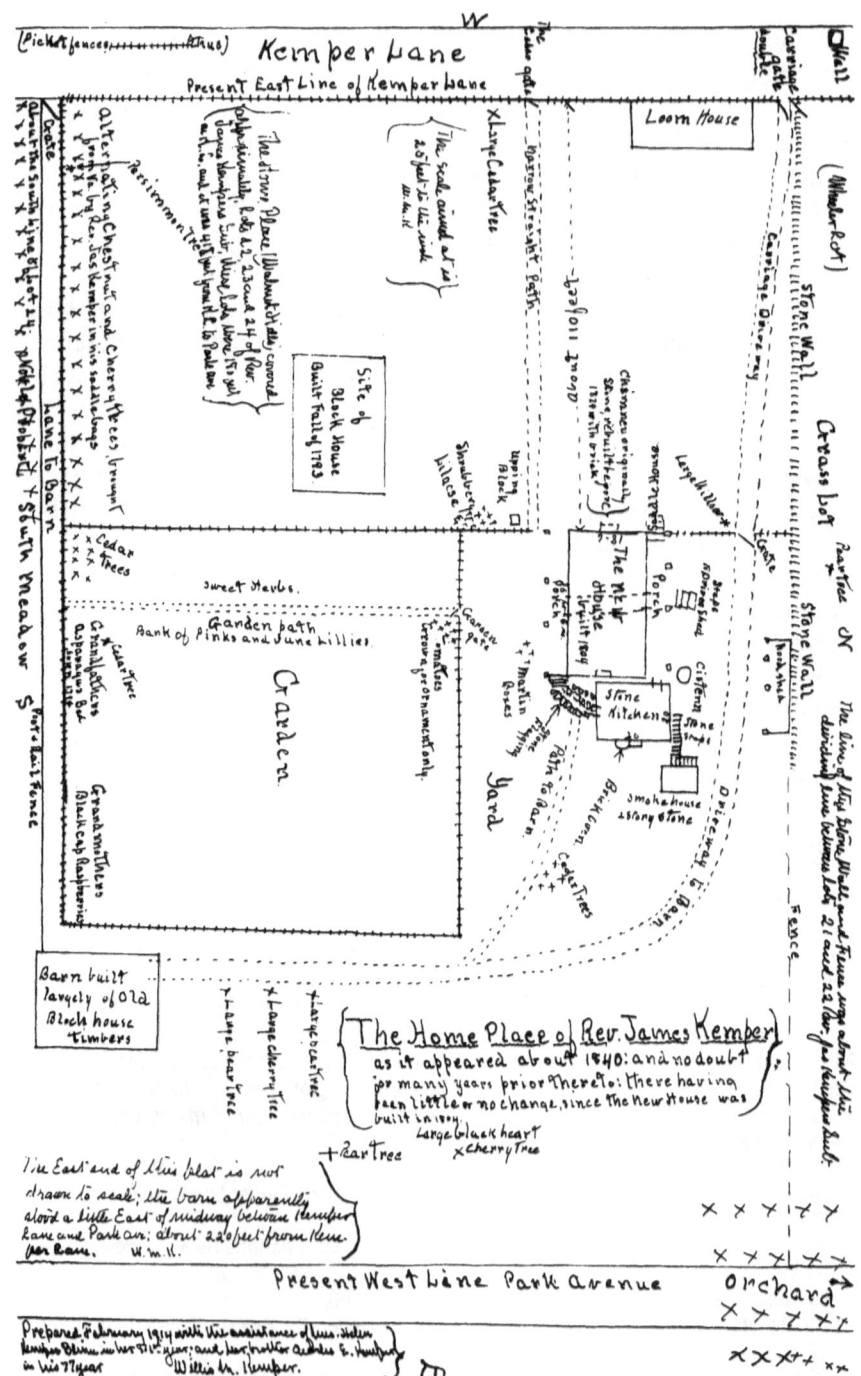

James Kemper Blockhouse
1793

James Kemper was a minister, fully licensed by the Transylvania Presbytery. During a visit to Cincinnati in June 1791 he entered into an agreement with the local Presbyterian organization to attend that congregation for one year. The congregation, the agreement specified, would supply pack horses and guides to assist in moving his wife, ten children and all their household effects from the Danville, Kentucky area near the Dix River.[1]

Daniel Doty and a Mr. French were sent to escort the Kemper family. They took an old ridge trail some sixty miles through Georgetown, Kentucky and then to Lexington where they bought pack horses from an army contractor. On the return trip, the assemblage traveled by way of the old Wilderness Trace to Maysville, Kentucky and then by flatboat down the Ohio River. In those times the only overland routes from Lexington to Cincinnati were perilous narrow Indian trails, unsuitable for transporting cumbersome articles.[2]

The party landed at the foot of Main Street and was lodged temporarily by Jonathan Ludlow. Kemper eventually acquired what may have been a donation lot or perhaps he only held a certificate of purchase from John Cleves Symmes for he never acquired a deed for lot 65 on the west side of Sycamore Street, north of Fourth Street.[3] The family resided there until the fall of 1793 when Kemper, against the advice of General James Wilkinson, the commandant at Fort Washington, decided to move his family to the forested hills northeast of that fort.

A comment attributed to General Anthony Wayne referred to the Kemper settlement as his "out pickett," and that at the sounding of any alarm an armed guard was to be sent to its aid. The government also reportedly supplied the Kemper family with firearms.[4]

Kemper purchased his land in two tracts. The first was in the northeast corner of Section 7, Millcreek Township, and may have been a forfeiture,

---

Sketch of where the James Kemper blockhouse stood in 1793; it also locates in detail the site of one of the pioneer farms, circa 1840, which stood within the present limits of Cincinnati. Drawn in February, 1914 by Willis M. Kemper, Charles E. Kemper and Mrs. Helen Kemper Blinn. *(Manuscript Collection, Cincinnati Historical Society)*

a common occurrence in the Miami Purchase prior to 1795.[5] One deed was for 130 acres and the other for 50 acres, and both were dated August 1795. (Kemper probably held certificates of purchase from Symmes until the deeds were drawn up). The area in question includes present Kemper Lane, Park Avenue, Windsor Street, Cross Lane and Nassau Street.[6]

It may be only a short drive today from Third and Broadway to Kemper Lane or Windsor Street, but in 1793 it was a laborious and dangerous trip. The fact that this intrepid pioneer family survived intact during those uncertain times, despite their isolation, is a credit to their resourcefulness.

After picking a site with the highest elevation in his chosen lots, the minister built a two story log blockhouse for use as a temporary protective home. It was built in military fashion with the second floor projecting over the lower floor to give a better line of fire. Water was drawn from a spring near today's Park Avenue at the east end of Lot 18. (Later a sweep operated well was dug, and a cistern.) One family member always acted as an armed guard while the water was collected. Another spring at the present intersection of Kemper Lane and Nassau Street was considered too far removed to be used safely at that time.[7]

By 1804 Kemper had erected a new two story log house on lots 22 and 23 and it became his permanent residence. This home may be viewed today at the Sharon Woods Historic Village. The blockhouse stood about sixty feet southwest of the west end of the new house and approximately fifty feet from the east side of present Kemper Lane.[8] Three Kemper children were born in the blockhouse between 1795 and 1804.[9]

James Kemper was replaced at his first church by the Reverend John Davies. However, Davies' health failed and he died, leaving his widow, Rhoda Lockwood Davies, and a young son. Mrs. Davies was befriended by several members of her late husband's congregation, including the Kemper family, who were living in their new home at that time. The widow moved into the blockhouse with her son, and probably lived there until her marriage to Peter H. Kemper, January 31, 1809.[10]

The blockhouse was dismantled, possibly prior to 1829, and the timbers used in the construction of the first Kemper barn, which was still in use in 1852. There is some difference of opinion concerning the demise of the blockhouse. The James Kemper family was industrious, frugal and practical as can be seen in the improvements of their original subdivision.[11] They erected a two story stone smoke house and added a beehive oven to a stone kitchen addition, an ambitious endeavor.[12] It is highly unlikely that the Kempers would discard valuable logs which had been hewn for the blockhouse some thirty years prior to the building of the barn.

There do not appear to be any recorded skirmishes with the Indians at this blockhouse. However, prior to 1795 Reverend Kemper often used the dangerous ridge trail along present Grandin Road when commuting to the Columbia congregation and some of the more remote settlements.[13]

During those perilous times every able-bodied man was expected to attend religious services carrying a firearm for protection of all. In 1792 John Wallace, a member of Kemper's Cincinnati congregation, was fined 75 cents for attending a service unarmed.[14] On another occasion, several settlers were killed and scalped by Indians while Kemper held services nearby for the unsuspecting inhabitants of Covalt and Round Bottom Stations.[15]

Between the years of 1789 and 1795 many settlers were accosted by Indians along the original Ohio River road between Cincinnati and Columbia, but James Kemper was wily enough not to have been one of those victims.[16]

In December 1799 Kemper moved his large family to Beedle Station in present Warren County and took charge of the Turtle Creek Presbyterian Church located there in Section 28, Range 3, Township 4, Turtle Creek Township, approximately five miles southwest of Lebanon. A deed to James Kemper for 100 acres of land in that section was recorded on December 19, 1814.[17]

Kemper's tenure at Beedle's Station apparently was not a pleasant experience for his family. The settlement was primitive compared to their former residence at Cincinnati and this difference in lifestyle disenchanted his wife and children. Mrs. Kemper's fashionable bonnets seemed to disturb the women in the congregation and William Beedle raised Kemper's ire in a dispute over property lines.[18]

The Kemper family returned to Cincinnati probably in January 1801 and in the spring of 1802 the Turtle Creek congregation was led by an inspired Presbyterian minister and revivalist named Richard McNemar. Prior to being ordained, McNemar had preached at Cincinnati, Columbia, Covalt Station and Round Bottom from April to July 1792.[19] On April 24, 1805 McNemar converted to Shakerism as did most of the Turtle Creek congregation, who followed McNemar to the Shaker community at Union Village.[20]

Notes
[1]Extracts from the diaries of James and Frederick A. Kemper quoted in "Recollections" by Mrs. Helen Kemper Blinn; Willis Kemper, "A Description of the James Kemper House location and life of James Kemper," included in the Kemper Papers, Manuscript Collection of the Cincinnati Historical Society.
[2]James McBride, *Pioneer Biography*, Vol. 2, p. 184-185.
[3]Kemper Papers; see especially Blinn and Willis Kemper manuscripts.
[4]"Memoirs of James Spring Kemper, D. D.," Cincinnati, 1896, p. 1.
[5]*Symmes Purchase Records*, p. 60, 62.
[6]Kemper Papers; see especially Blinn and Willis Kemper manuscripts; *Deed Book 34*, p. 24, Sept. 23, 1830, Hamilton County Recorder's Office.

[7]Kemper Papers; see Blinn and Willis Kemper manuscripts.
[8]Ibid.,
[9]Ibid.,
[10]"Memoirs of James Spring Kemper," p. 1-2; Kemper Papers; "Family Register of the Ancestors, Connections, and Descendants of Rev. James Kemper," comp. David Kemper, Manuscript Collection Cincinnati Historical Society, p. 26, entry no. 5.
[11]Kemper Papers; "Memoirs of James Spring Kemper," p. 1-2.
[12]Ibid.,
[13]Ibid., page 2.
[14]Cist, Cincinnati in 1859, p. 138.
[15]"Memoirs of James Spring Kemper," p. 2.
[16]Ferris, Early Settlement, p. 264, 312, 314-315, 322-324, 338-340.
[17]Cist's Weekly Advertiser, April 11, 1848; Phillips, Richard the Shaker, p. 20; Deed Book E, p. 30; Deed Book 5, p. 30C, Warren County Recorder's Office.
[18]Johnson, 175 Years at the Lebanon Presbyterian Church 1806-1981, p. 3; Phillips, Richard the Shaker, p. 35.
[19]Ibid., p. 13, 20, 35; Cist's Weekly Advertiser, April 11, 1848.
[20]Phillips, Richard the Shaker, p. 47-48; Johnson, 175 Years at the Lebanon Presbyterian Church, p. 5.

Ludlow's Station or Mill Creek Village 1790

Israel Ludlow was born at Long Hill, near Morristown, New Jersey in 1765. Following his formal education, on orders from Thomas Hutchins, Surveyor General of the United States, Ludlow traveled to the Northwest Territory in 1787 to assist John Cleves Symmes in surveying the Miami Purchase.[1]

In January 1788 Mathias Denman bought from Symmes land opposite the mouth of the Licking River with the intention of founding a city to be called Losantiville or Losantiburg which, of course, eventually became Cincinnati. On August 25, 1788 Denman sold an interest in his purchase to Colonel Robert Patterson and John Filson of Lexington, Kentucky.[2] Filson, a surveyor, was to lay out the proposed city and act as general agent for the developers.[3] However, Filson disappeared while on a survey trip with Symmes and seventy other men in late September 1788.[4]

Denman and Patterson took in Ludlow as a partner to replace Filson. On December 24, 1788 Patterson and Ludlow left Limestone (Maysville), Kentucky with about twelve settlers to establish their new city.[5] Ludlow and other surveyors completed a partial survey of Losantiville on January 7, 1789.[6]

Although his interests with Denman and Patterson plus his survey work in the Miami Purchase kept him busy, Ludlow decided to found his own settlement. On March 9, 1790 he entered land warrant numbers 83 and 84 in the west half of Section 22, Township 3, Fractional Range 2, which later became part of Cumminsville, Millcreek Township. The existing official records show that on January 21, 1793, Ludlow also presented for entry warrant numbers 138 and 139 for one hundred sixty acres in the east half of Section 22, Township 3, Range 2.[7]

Ludlow established his station west of Mill Creek between two much-used fording places.[8] At the time of initial settlement, late spring of 1790, possibly ten families occupied cabins and the blockhouse. The founder, however, chose to live in Cincinnati.

The settlers at Ludlow's Station were understandably nervous about the threat of Indian attack, especially when their numbers were severely reduced after half the men were sent to bring the pioneers' families to the station. They petitioned General Harmar for a corporal's guard to protect the settlement:

> *To General Josiah Harmar*
> *Commandant at Fort Washington*
> *Your memorialists inhabitants of Mill Creek Village beg leave to acquaint General Harmar with some circumstances which we flatter ourselves will justify our troubling him with the present address.*
> *First. Upwards of half our settlers are necessarily called away to bring their families to this Country which renders our Station weak & vulnerable by few of the savages and it is expected a period of two months will expire before they return & secondly we fear in every part of our settlements detatched & weak parties are liable to be made & are easy prey of by our enemy who we have reason to believe daily watch & lurk around us—It is therefore prayed that General Harmar would grant us some assistance during the above period of two months—We have two sufficient block houses erected, one of which shall be ready for the reception of the party not doubting but the permanent assistance of six or eight men would effectually secure our safety, the granting of which will confer a particular favour on your humble petitioners.*
> *Cincinnati, May 29th, 1790*
>
> | | |
> |---|---|
> | Zach. Hole | Jd Miller |
> | Jeremiah Ludlow | John Hole |
> | Thomas Eton | Daniel Hole |
> | Peter Cox | Asa Peck |

The Ludlow Station settlers had good reason to be apprehensive. Soon after they petitioned General Harmar for protection, Peter Cox was killed by Indians. The petition to General Harmar reveals that among the station's earliest settlers were John, Daniel and Zachariah Hole, who later founded their own fortified settlement, Hole's Station, within today's Miamisburg. Their presence at Ludlow's Station is logical since Dr. John Hole's wife Massee was a cousin of Israel and Jeremiah Ludlow.[9]

The station's blockhouse stood near the present intersection of Knowlton and Mad Anthony Streets and on the Baltimore and Ohio Railroad right of way. The property was deeded to the Cumminsville Christian Church in 1832 and the blockhouse was dismantled when the tracks were laid for the Cincinnati, Hamilton and Dayton Railroad about 1855.[10]

John Cleves Symmes noted the station's founding in a letter to his friend Jonathan Dayton in April 1790, stating:

> *We have established three new stations some distance up in the country. One is twelve miles up the Big Miami (Dunlop's), the second is five miles up Mill Creek (Ludlow's), the third is nine miles back in the country from Columbia (Covalt's). These all flourish well. A lad looking for cows, was captivated by the Indians a few weeks ago at the Mill Creek Station; otherwise not the smallest mischief has been done to any.*[11]

Despite Symmes' observation, open hostilities between the northwestern Indian tribes and the government of the United States soon began. Some of the most notable events at Ludlow's Station concerned the Indians and the Federal Army although no attacks were mounted against the blockhouse.

An interesting letter from Symmes to Dayton dated November 4, 1790, following General Josiah Harmar's defeat, mentions Symmes' attempt to travel from North Bend to Ludlow's Station. Symmes wandered around in the woods for two days before ending up at Dunlap's Station, not his original destination.[12]

On August 7, 1791 General Arthur St. Clair organized his army at Fort Washington, moved up the Mill Creek Valley to Ludlow's Station and encamped there until September 17 when the army moved northwest to a disastrous defeat in November.[13] Part of the army which escaped from the battlefield fled to Fort Washington. Their return brought them to Ludlow's Station, which had been abandoned,[14] and they camped here before continuing their flight to Cincinnati. The troops were in a state of shock, and not surprisingly, the accidental discharge of a musket led to a panic during which "the officers from the blockhouse and the various neighboring parties could be heard jumping, one after another, into the creek, to make their way to Cincinnati."[15]

From this contemporary account of William Wiseman it is certain that there was at least one fortified blockhouse at Ludlow's Station.

The importance of the station as a storage depot for St. Clair's army is emphasized by a journal kept by Captain Samuel Newman of the 2nd U. S. Infantry Regiment during the 1791 campaign. Newman noted on September 27, 1791 that the Indians had stolen 56 government pack horses from Ludlow's

Station two days earlier. He also noted that the station was fourteen miles from the army's camp at Fort Hamilton and seven miles from Fort Washington. Newman observed that the Indians were effectively preventing the movement of the army's supplies by stealing many of the pack horses.

The supplying of General Anthony Wayne's army during the campaigns of 1793 and 1794 was handled in a much more efficient manner. Elliot and Williams, supply contractors for Wayne's army, reported on July 28, 1793 that they were preparing to send one hundred twenty pack horses from Ludlow's Station on the following day to join another convoy traveling from Fort Hamilton to Fort Jefferson. This shipment brought to 250,000 the number of rations available at Fort Jefferson. Winthrop Sargent also noted in his diary at the same time that a division of Kentucky volunteers had left Ludlow's Station that morning to join the regular army.[16]

In 1794 an Indian attack on a party of four government packhorsemen near Ludlow's Station left one rider dead and another mortally wounded. The dead man was found lying in a nearby creek which then acquired the name of Bloody Run. The wounded man was taken to the cabin of Abner Boston, near the station, where he died several days later.[17]

Two important military roads converged near Ludlow's Station, meeting at McHenry's Ford, a much-utilized crossing with a stable limestone floor. The two traces came up Mill Creek from Cincinnati to the ford practically as one at an early date but after crossing Mill Creek, St. Clair's trace veered to the northwest and Wayne's trace, or the Great Road, ran north through today's Carthage.[18]

Ludlow did not move from Cincinnati to his station site until after the signing of the Greenville Peace Treaty in 1795. Prior to moving, he had laid out the town of Fairfield (Hamilton) on December 17, 1794 and on August 20, 1795, with three other investors, purchased from Symmes the future site of Dayton.[19]

When Ludlow returned to his station, he and his brother John had a large log house built near Ludlow's Ford, north of the blockhouse, which became known as the Ludlow Station Farm. Israel resided at Station Farm until dying there on January 21, 1804.[20]

One of the most interesting episodes in the Station Farm's history occurred after the death of its founder. In 1803 President Thomas Jefferson decided to replace General Rufus Putnam of Massachusetts, a founder of Marietta, Ohio in 1788, as Surveyor General of the United States. General Putnam, a Federalist, was a political opponent of Jefferson and the President also considered him incompetent.[21]

In Putnam's stead, Jefferson appointed 45 year old Jared Mansfield, a distinguished mathematician and graduate of Yale College. After spending about a year in Marietta familiarizing himself with the job and taking over his duties, Mansfield decided to move to the Cincinnati area, closer to major surveys being undertaken to the west in today's Indiana and Illinois.[22]

Rather than live in the noisy, muddy and unhealthy village of Cincinnati, Mansfield established his headquarters in one of the wings of the Ludlow Station Farm mansion house. He set up his office in October of 1805 in this beautiful country setting, near the clear, tree-lined Mill Creek.[23]

While settling in, Mansfield impatiently awaited the arrival of a set of astronomical and surveying instruments with which he hoped to begin a new, more accurate surveying system. These instruments, made in England, were among the most advanced in the world and had been paid for by the President out of Jefferson's own contingency fund.[24]

After the arrival of the new instruments, which included a powerful telescope and an astronomical pendulum clock, Mansfield set up at Ludlow's Station what was probably the first astronomical observatory west of the Alleghenies. Using his new system, he then established a meridian line in southern Indiana which provided a base line for the survey in that state and in part of Illinois.[25] The system proved such a notable success that it was used to survey the remainder of the Northwest Territory and most of the states west of the Mississippi.[26]

Among the visitors at Mansfield's Ludlow Station office were his deputy surveyors who included future Ohio and Michigan governors Thomas Worthington, Ethan Allan Brown and Lewis Cass. Notable Indian chiefs who also visited the office to discuss boundary lines for Indian lands included Little Turtle of the Miamis and the Delaware, Buckongahela.[27]

Mansfield and his family lived at Ludlow Station Farm for about four years before moving to a home called Bates' Place, a few miles closer to Cincinnati. He resigned his post as Surveyor General in 1812 and taught mathematics at the U. S. Military Academy at West Point from 1814 to 1828. He then retired, and with his wife Elizabeth, returned to Cincinnati to live. Mansfield died while on a visit to New Haven, Connecticut in 1830.[28] Mansfield, Ohio is named after him.

Notes
[1]Henry B. Teetor, *Life and Times of Israel Ludlow*, Cincinnati, 1885, p. 7; Olden, *Historical Sketches*, p. 93; Hon. Geo. W. Hook, et. al., *History of Dayton, Ohio*, p. 35; Jones, *Extracts from the History of Cincinnati*, p. 24.
[2]Ibid., p. 20, 21; Teetor, *Israel Ludlow*, p. 11.
[3]Jones, *Extracts*, p. 25.
[4]Ibid., p. 24; Letter of John Cleves Symmes to Jonathan Dayton, May 18- 20, 1789, Symmes Correspondence, Cincinnati Historical Society.
[5]Ibid., Jones, *Extracts*, p. 24.
[6]Greve, *Centennial History of Cincinnati*, Vol. 1, p. 186.

7 Ibid., p. 281; Olden, *Historical Sketches*, p. 93; *Symmes Purchase Records*, p. 65.
8 Drake, "Memoir of the Miami Country," p. 85; Greve, *Centennial History*, Vol. 1, p. 281.
9 Ibid.; Teetor, *Israel Ludlow*, p. 34; Drake, "Memoir," p. 97; Petition to General Harmar from inhabitants of Mill Creek Village, May 29, 1790, "Transcriptions from the Harmar Papers," Richard C. Knopf, Anthony Wayne Parkway Board, 1954, Ohio Historical Society Library.
10 Greve, *Centennial History*, Vol. 1, p. 281-283; Teetor, *Israel Ludlow*, p. 34.
11 Letter of John Cleves Symmes to Jonathan Dayton, April 30, 1790, Symmes Correspondence, Cincinnati Historical Society.
12 Letter of John Cleves Symmes to Jonathan Dayton, Nov. 4, 1790, Symmes Correspondence, Cincinnati Historical Society.
13 Olden, *Historical Sketches*, p. 122-124; Teetor, *Israel Ludlow*, p. 34-35; Teetor, *Mill Creek Valley*, p. 22.
14 Ferris, *Early Settlement*, p. 329; Cist, *Cincinnati in 1859*, p. 101-102.
15 Ibid.
16 Milo H. Quaife, "A Picture of the First United States Army," *Wisconsin Magazine of History*, Vol. 2 (1918-1919), p. 65; Letter of Robert Elliott and Elie Williams to General Anthony Wayne, July 28, 1793, Cincinnati Historical Society; Copy of *Diary of Major Winthrop Sargent, Number 2*, Cincinnati Historical Society.
17 Teetor, *Mill Creek Valley*, p. 62-64.
18 Olden, *Historical Sketches*, p. 122-123, 136-137.
19 Ibid; *History of Dayton, Ohio*, p. 34; "Memoirs of Benjmain Van Cleve," *Quarterly Publication of the Historical and Philosophical Society of Ohio*, Vol. 17 (1922), p. 55; Teetor, *Israel Ludlow*, p. 35.
20 Ibid., p. 9, 34; John Day Caldwell Collection, Book A, p. 3, Cincinnati Historical Society; Letter of John Cleves Symmes to John Cleves Short, January, 1804, quoted in *Intimate Letters of John Cleves Symmes*, p. 6; Greve, *Centennial History*, Vol. 1, p. 282.
21 Charlotte W. Dudley, "Jared Mansfield: United States Survyeor General," *Ohio History*, Vol. 85 (1976) p. 234-237.
22 Ibid., p. 236-237.
23 Ibid., p. 237-239.
24 Edward Mansfield, "The Annual Address Delivered Before the Cincinnati Astronomical Society," Cincinnati, 1845, p. 15-16, 30-31.
25 Dudley, "Jared Mansfield," p. 239-240.
26 Ibid., p. 239.
27 Ibid., p. 241; Greve, *Centennial History*, Vol. 1, p. 281-283.
28 Dudley, "Jared Mansfield," p. 243.

McFarland Station
1794 or 1795

On February 7, 1793 two sections of land were transferred to Colonel John McFarland and John S. Gano by the Miami Land Company.

In the final transaction McFarland received a deed to the east half of Section 30 and the entire Section 24, totaling 960 acres. The land is in the fourth township in Fractional Range 2 in present Columbia Township. (In the final deed McFarland's name was spelled McFarling.[1])

Local historians date this purchase in the spring of 1795 and McFarland as emigrating from Fayette County, Pennsylvania.[2]

Actual date of construction of the station and activities there are not known to the authors. A road survey from Captain Benham's in Cincinnati past McFarland's Station in 1797 places the station between present Ravenwood and Zinsle Avenues, west of Kennedy Avenue in Kennedy Heights Park, Pleasant Ridge. There were no reported Indian attacks at this station.[3]

Notes
[1] *Symmes Purchase Records*, p. 63-63, 71.
[2] Olden, *Historical Sketches*, p. 126; Greve, *Centennial History of Cincinnati*, Vol. 1, p. 292.
[3] *Road Record Book, Vol. 1-1B, 1790-1850*, p. 63, 150-153; Hamilton County Engineer's Office, Road Records Division; Map of Hamilton County by Wm. Emerson, 1847; *Titus' Atlas of Hamilton County*, p. 39; Atlas of Hamilton County, Ohio, 1884, p. 2; U. S. Geological Survey, Cincinnati East Quad, 7.5' series.

McHenry's Blockhouse 1790

On January 22, 1790 Israel Ludlow, on behalf of Joseph McHenry, a volunteer settler, made an application for an entry of one hundred six acres in the northeast portion of Section 27, Township 3, Fractional Range 2. The land belonged to Isaac Winans and the entry was made under the forfeiture clause in the Miami Land Company contract.[1]

A letter dated May 31, 1845, from Thomas Irwin to Charles Cist states that "Mr. McHenry had a large family, two sons and two daughters, young men and young women. They lived a number of years where the Hamilton road crossed the Millcreek, perhaps four or five miles from the city" at McHenry's Ford.[2]

In his *History of College Hill and Vicinity*, General Samuel F. Cary placed McHenry's blockhouse on the east side of Spring Grove Avenue at Cumminsville, "near barn #3 for the horse drawn trolley car."[3]

The crossing of Mill Creek mentioned by Irwin places the blockhouse properly considering the location of the entry, the placement of other early blockhouses in relation to Mill Creek and the early road surveys to and from that site. One of those early roads was a survey from McHenry's past Goudy's Mill to Ludlow's Ford in 1798.

In 1810 a road was surveyed from widow McHenry's to the Colerain Road. By 1827, we find two surveys which include McHenry's Ford. One is an alteration to the road surveyed in 1798. The other started at Phebe Roll's barn west of McHenry in Section 27 to the state road below Gano's bridge on Mill Creek. The earliest surveys, of course, show only one main road from Cincinnati crossing at McHenry's Ford and then immediately branching off in varying directions, one being the old Hamilton Road.

Today the blockhouse would be east of Colerain and Spring Grove Avenues near the end of old Ford Street on the west side of Mill Creek in Mill Creek Township.[4]

Notes
[1] *Symmes Purchase Records*, p. 20.
[2] Cist, *The Cincinnati Miscellany*, Vol. 2, p. 22-23.
[3] Samuel F. cary, *History of College Hill and Vicinity*, College Hill, 1886, p. 13-14.
[4] *Road Record Book, Vol. 1-1B 1790-1850*, p. 157-158, 225; *Road Record Book, 1825-1830*, p. 235. (Plat Illustration), Hamilton County Engineer's Office, Road Records Division; Maps of Hamilton County by S. Morrison and J. Williams, 1835; Wm. Emerson, 1847; A. W. Gilbert, 1848; C. S. Mendenhall, ca. 1877; *Titus' Atlas of Hamilton County, Ohio*, p. 50-51; Atlas of Hamilton County, Ohio, 1884, p. 1.

Mercer's Station or Mercersburg 1792

Aaron Mercer, born in Ireland in 1746, emigrated to America sometime prior to the Revolutionary War and settled in Frederick County, Virginia. A relative of General Hugh Mercer, Aaron served in the Frederick County militia during the Revolution, apparently attaining the rank of Captain.

Like many other veterans of the Revolution who later moved to the Miami Country, Mercer reportedly was bankrupted by supporting the war effort. He left his home in Winchester, Virginia in 1790, reaching Columbia as the demoralized Federal Regulars and local militia were returning from the scene of General Harmar's defeat.[1]

During the following two years he apparently had his son-in-law, Ichabod Benton Miller, survey and lay out the plan of a town with inlots and outlots located near several active perennial springs.[2] Mercer was a participant in the common practice of squatting on another person's property. The land he chose belonged to Nathaniel Massie, deputy surveyor of the Virginia Military District, and was within the boundaries of that district in Survey Number 2276.[3]

Mercer began building a strong stockade in the spring of 1792 even though the land was not legally conveyed from Massie to Mercer until the spring of 1796.[4] The inhabitants of Mercersburgh probably resided within the confines of the stockade until the Indian problems were resolved. They were not subjected to the attacks or isolated violent fatalities experienced by neighboring settlements.

Dwellings outside the garrison prior to the Greenville Treaty were few. If Captain Mercer had encountered Indians representing in number their prehistoric counterparts who had occupied the Newtown area, his settlement could have been short lived.[5]

Several early road surveys help strengthen the validity of the Mercersburgh plat. A road was surveyed in 1794 from Columbia to Garrard's Town to Round Bottom. In 1793 a road was surveyed from the garrison at Mercersburgh to the Little Miami in Round Bottom, the distance being three miles, thirty six poles. In 1796 a road was surveyed and laid out from Newtown to Beasley's Mill, one mile and sixteen poles north.

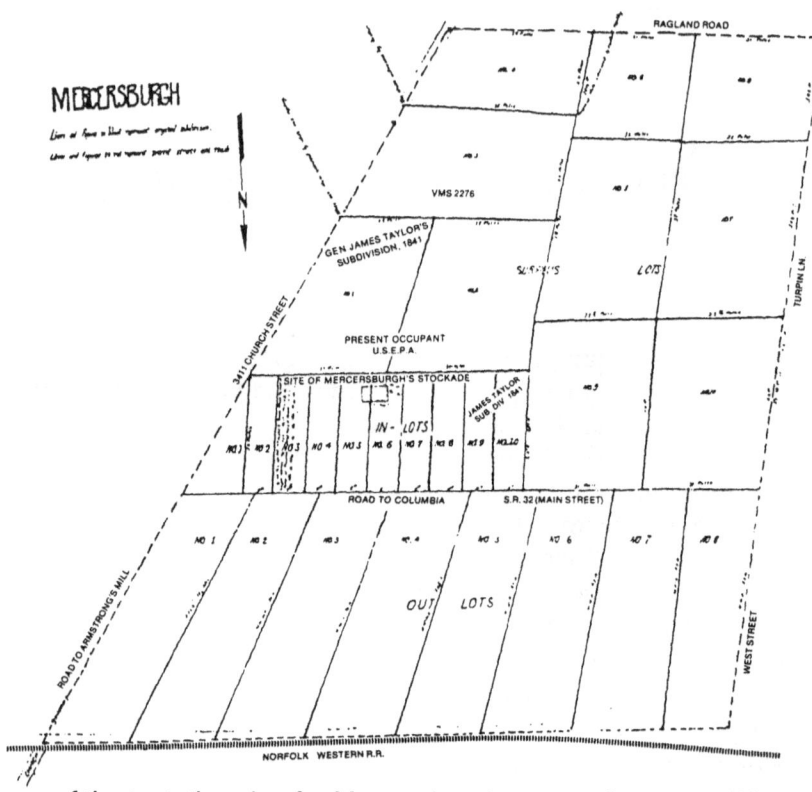

A copy of the tentative plan for Mercersburgh reportedly surveyed in 1790 and attributed to the founder's son-in-law, Ichabod Benton Miller. The fort stood approximately 500 feet west and 400 feet south of two pre-historic trails which evolved into early historic traces. *(Courtesy Anderson Township Historical Society; contemporary titles added by the authors.)*

The stockaded station was on property now owned by the United States government and utilized as a fish hatchery and experimental station. It lies near the intersection of Church Street and State Route 32 in Anderson Township. The plaque set by the Mariemont Chapter of the D. A. R. is well placed.[6]

Notes
[1]*History of Cincinnati and Hamilton County, Ohio*, Cincinnati, 1894, p. 40-41; Robert Craig, *Revolutionary Soldiers in Hamilton County, Ohio*, p. 25; J. T. McAllister, *List of the Virginia Militia in the Revolutionary War*, Hot Springs, Virginia, 1913, p. 203.
[2]Plat of Mercersburgh attributed to Ichabod Benton Miller, original is the property of Mrs. C. P. Sticksel, Newtown, Ohio (copy courtesy of Mrs. Jean Williamson, Anderson Township Historical Society); Samuel Durham, *The Pioneer Settlers of the Lower Little Miami Valley*, privately printed, 1897, p. 7, 14.

[3]*Survey Book 11, Virginia Military Surveys*, Hamilton County Engineer's Office, Road Records Division; Howe, *Historical Collections of Ohio*, Columbus, 1890, Vol. 1, p. 224; Greve, *Centennial History of Cincinnati*, Vol. 1, p. 293.
[4]Land records of Hamilton County, Hamilton County Recorder's Office, transfers dated April 2, 1796, witnessed May 19, 1796, N. Massie to Capt. A. Mercer, 139 acres; April 2, 1796, witnessed June 13, 1796, N. Massie to I. B. Miller, 440 acres.
[5]Mills, *Archaeological Atlas of Ohio*, p. 31; S. F. Starr, "The Archaeology of Hamilton County," p. 18-20, 28-29, 35-36, 50-61.
[6]*Road Record Book, Vol. 1-1B, 1790-1850*, p. 92, 106-108, 112-114, Hamilton County Engineer's Office, Road Records Division; maps of Hamilton County by S. Morrison and J. Williams, 1835; Wm. Emerson, 1847; A. W. Gilbert, 1848; C. S. Mendenhall, ca. 1877; *Titus' Atlas of Hamilton County, Ohio*, p. 43; Atlas of Hamilton County, Ohio, p. 3; U. S. Geological Survey, Withamsville, Ohio-Kentucky Quad. 7.5' series.

Morrell's Station
1795

During 1791 Daniel Doty, a colorful pioneer, built a log cabin on the east bank of the Great Miami River in Fractional Section 34 in present Lemon Township. Butler County. The cabin stood in the midst of a large prairie which extended along the river to present day Middletown.[1]

In Daniel Doty's biography there is mention of a blockhouse within pickets and a few cabins on the south side of the prairie near Dick's Creek, a little west of the crossroads south of his cabin. Doty did not identify the members of this station nor did he give it a more precise location.[2]

The founder of that station was Dr. Calvin Morrell, M. D., a native of New Jersey and Revolutionary War veteran.[3] The stockade stood at the present site of Excello, approximately one thousand feet west of the old Hamilton-Middletown Road (Main Street) and south of State Route 63. Excello is located in Section 32, Township 2, Range 4, Lemon Township, Butler County, near Dick's Creek.[4]

Morrell was one of the early lot owners (lot number 7) of Losantiville and was among inhabitants listed in a short census there in 1790.[5] His household consisted of five family members.[6]

On July 5, 1791 Morrell applied for one hundred six acres in the northeast corner of Section 32, Township 4, Range 2. He entered for the land by reason

The road surveyed in 1796 from Fort Hamilton to Morrell's Station was the precursor to the Hamilton-Middletown Road. (Hamilton County Engineer's Office, Road Records Division)

of non-settlement by John Carpenter.[7] Although Morrell was acquiring various land holdings in the Miami Purchase in 1790 - 1791, including apple orchards, he probably spent most of his time through 1794 at Columbia. There, in 1792 he was a private in Captain James Flinn's company of volunteer militia. In 1793 he spent a short term in the Cincinnati jail for refusing to pay for drinks in Captain George Gordon's City Inn. In Cincinnati on December 27, 1794, Morrell was appointed an officer of the newly organized Nova Caesarea Harmony Masonic Lodge No. 2.[8]

It is not known how many land transactions Morrell entered into with John Cleves Symmes and Jonathan Dayton; however, he was one of many settlers who unwittingly purchased land from the Miami Land Company north of its Patent Line.[9] One such purchase was the site of Morrell's stockade settlement. In a letter to Robert Morris dated August 22, 1795, Symmes wrote:

> *I enclose you a draught on Wheelan and Miller for*
> *one thousand dollars, draw this money and out of it pay*

> to Jonathan Dayton Esqr the balance due him on a bond he has against Doct-Calvin Morrel & Doct-Budd, for land sold by Capt Dayton to Morrel, I have given Morrel his deed therefor & have pledged myself to, Capt Dayton for the payment of Morrel's money it differs not much of the three hundred 20 or 40 dolrs the residue of the above 1000 dollars after Morrels bond is paid.[10]

In 1799 and 1800 Morrell was among those petitioning Congress to rebuy at specially low prices land sold them by Symmes north of the Miami Purchase boundary line.[11] In 1802 he advertised for sale his station property, including part of the large prairie.[12] One of his property titles in Range 4 was challenged in court by James Brady.[13]

Morrell apparently sold his properties by the early part of 1805 and by late spring of that year joined a Shaker community[14] known as Union Village or Shaker Village, located west of Lebanon and north of Beedle's Staton.[15] Much resentment and harassment was displayed towards the Union Village Shakers by the settlers at Lebanon and Beedle's Station, erupting into mob violence in 1810, 1813 and 1819.[16]

On Monday, August 9, 1819, two hundred persons attacked the Shakers' South House; Morrell was knocked down and nearly beaten to death.[17] He recovered and during 1820 and 1824 was active in bringing the Shaker settlers at Darby Plains, Union County, Ohio to the Whitewater Valley where they formed the Whitewater Shaker Community. Morrell remained at the Whitewater settlement until returning to Union Village in 1832.[18]

Notes
[1]*Centennial History of Butler County, Ohio*, p. 6, 285, 910.
[2]McBride, *Pioneer Biography*, Vol. 1, p. 189.
[3]*Official Roster of Soldiers of the American Revolution Buried in the State of Ohio*, Vol. 1, p. 263.
[4]*Road Record Book, Vol. 1-1B, 1790-1850*, p. 92, 106-108, 112-114, Hamilton County Engineer's Office, Road Records Division; U. S. Geological Survey Map, Hamilton, Ohio Quad., 7.5' series; road maps of Butler County; Everts, *Combination Atlas Map of Butler County, Ohio*, p. 83; *Butler County, Ohio Atlas and Pictorial Review*, Hamilton, 1914, p. 45; *The County of Butler, Ohio*, p. 33; map of Butler County, Ohio, James McBride, 1836.
[5]*Early Rosters of Cincinnati and Hamilton County*, p. 9, 13; Jones, *Extracts from the History of Cincinnati*, p. 50.
[6]*Early Rosters of Cincinnati and Hamilton County*, p. 13.
[7]*Symmes Purchase Records*, p. 50.
[8]Greve, *Centennial History*, Vol. 1, p. 366, 371; *Centinel of the North-Western Territory*, Feb. 1, 1794; The Torrence Papers, Cincinnati Historical Society, Box 45, Folders 1-15.
[9]*Early Rosters of Cincinnati and Hamilton County*, p. 160, 166.
[10]Letter of John Cleves Symmes to Robert Morris, Aug. 22, 1795, Symmes Correspondence, Cincinnati Historical Society.
[11]*Early Rosters of Cincinnati and Hamilton County*, p. 160, 166.

[12]*Western Spy & Hamilton Gazette*, March 20, 1802.
[13]Ibid., July 20, 1803.
[14]J. P. Maclean, "Mobbing the Shakers of Union Village," *Ohio Archaeological and Historical Society Publication*, Vol. 11 (1903) p. 110.
[15]*Centennial Atlas of Warren County, Ohio*, Lebanon, Ohio, 1903, p. 13.
[16]Maclean, "Mobbing the Shakers of Union Village," p. 110-129.
[17]Ibid., p. 129.
[18]J. P. Maclean, "Origin, Rise, Progress and Decline of the Whitewater Community of Shakers," *Ohio Archaeological and Historical Society Publication*, Vol. 13 (1904) p. 403-408, 411, 414, 418.

Mounts' Station 1795

In October of 1795, William Mounts, with his own and five other families, setttled on a tract of land in the Virginia Military District in today's Hamilton Township, Warren County. Among those at the settlement in addition to Mounts, his wife Catherine and their six children, were the families of Thomas Forsha, Thomas Leonard and Thomas Watson.[1]

Mounts, a native of Fayette County, Pennsylvania, was a veteran of the Revolutionary War who had served both in the Continental Army and in the Westmoreland County Militia.[2]

He and Martin Varner jointly purchased 1200 acres along the Little Miami River from Robert Todd in October of 1791.[3] The settlement was on the south side of the river, approximately two miles from the mouth of Todd's Fork, between today's Morrow and South Lebanon.[4]

The site is located on a farm, later owned by William P. Morris, in Survey No. 1546 west of Stubbs Mills Road and south of Morrow-Millgrove Road, in a dedicated park area.[5] An early road was laid out from Mounts' Mill to the Pisgah Mill and another road from Zoar, south of Mounts' Station to Goshen.[6]

Although there was no blockhouse or stockade per se at Mounts' Station, the settlement was laid out in a most practical manner. The cabins were arranged in a defensive circle around a large spring which provided the settlement's water supply.[7] The people of Mounts' Station were not endangered by the Indians since the settlement was founded after the signing of the Treaty of Greenville in August of 1795.

Notes
[1] *History of Warren County*, p. 606; *Genealogical Index of Miami Valley Pioneers*, p. 128.
[2] Ibid., p. 128.
[3] *History of Warren County*, p. 606.
[4] *Centennial Atlas of Warren County, Ohio*, p. 13; Bone, *Complete Atlas of Warren County*, p. 5.
[5] Ibid., p. 5; *Warren County Commissioners' Journals*, Vol. 1, p. 176, Vol. 3, p. 283.
[6] Ibid., Vol 2, p. 81, 87, 89-90, Vol 8, p. 35, 50, 63.
[7] Bone, *Complete Atlas of Warren County*, p. 5; *History of Warren County*, p. 606.

Nelson's Station circa 1792

Nelson's Station consisted of two log cabins aligned east to west forty feet apart and enclosed by a palisade. The enclosure was covered with a crude roof to protect livestock at night. The pickets consisted partly of saplings with one gateway on the south side of the palisade.[1]

Two springs supplied the station with fresh water. One flowed near the later residence of John C. Ward. The other originated on property later occupied by Wood's ice plant.[2] The station stood near today's Madison Road between Stewart and Ebersole Avenues in Section 16, Township 4, Fractional Range 2, in Columbia Township.[3]

Two Nelson brothers and their brother-in-law squatted on the station site although they had no legal rights to the land by purchase. They probably constructed the stockade station in 1792, west of the later settlement of Madison (Madisonville) and one quarter mile south of a contemporaneous station referred to as the Red Bank Station[4] Robert Winslow was fourteen years old when he arrived at the Red Bank Station in February 1793.[5]

The Nelson brothers were considered by some neighbors as rather wealthy since they owned several horses and two cows.[6] Fifty two years later Winslow, Wilson Griffin and other early settlers of Columbia Township met to reminisce about the pioneer adventures in the Miami Purchase.[7]

There was much hostile Indian activity with the settlements below Nelson's Station from 1789 to 1795. In May 1794 an advertisement appeared in a Cincinnati newspaper offering a bounty of $136 for each Indian scalp presented to the proper authorities.[8]

Paying rewards by public subscription, or privately, was an accepted practice in the early settlements in the Miami Purchase.[9] If one or more persons found a lost item or recovered one which had been stolen, those persons were entitled to compensation for the return of the item to its owner, or they could retain the object if they wished.[10]

On the evening of Saturday, May 17, 1794 Benjamin Orcutt, a constable in Columbia Township, stopped at the cabin of a friend near Nelson's Station.[11] (Orcutt and Samuel Nelson were members of Captain Brice Virgin's volunteer militia company; Orcutt was a sergeant and Nelson served as a private.)[12]

At some time during the night, two Indians stole the constable's horse and headed for an area now known as Indian Hill. On the following morning a party of men led by Ephriam Kibbbey, a captain of the volunteer militia, pursued the two Indians.

Among the pursuing party were Samuel Nelson, Stephen Shipman, Hudson Hubbs, John Dunlap, a Mr. Gordon, Thomas and Samuel Nutts and Thomas Beasley.[13] The Indians were tracked through an oat field where they had taken down a section of rail fence. When Captain Kibbey and his party first sighted the stolen horse, one Indian was leading the animal while the other rode it side-saddle. The settlers fired on the horse thieves, killing the rider. The other escaped.[14]

The party recovered the constable's horse, which they decided to keep, but also returned with the highly valued Indian scalp plus sundry items taken from him. The $136 bounty was paid in corn by subscription.[15]

There are true and erroneous stories concerning violent death and disappearance of many of the early settlers in the Miami Purchase between 1789 and 1795. Robert Winslow of Red Bank Station made a plausible point of explanation for some of those tragedies: "It is a wonder we were not all killed; we always had our jug of whiskey and frequently no gun, and went singing and hallooing through the woods."[16]

Notes
[1]Charles L. Metz, "Madison Subsequently Named Madisonville and Its Early History," Manuscript Notebook, Charles L. Metz Collection, Cincinnati Historical Society.
[2]Ibid.
[3]Ibid; maps of Hamilton County, Ohio by S. Morrison and J. Williams, 1835; Wm. D. Emerson, 1847; Atlas of Hamilton County, Ohio 1884, p. 2; U. S. Geological Survey Map, Cincinnati East Quad, 7.5' series; *Hamilton County, Ohio Business Directory*, 1911-12, p. 200.
[4]Metz, "Madison Subsequently Named Madisonville;" quoted in *Cist's Daily Advertiser*, Dec. 9, 1847.
[5]Narrative of Robert Winslow, quoted in *Cist's Daily Advertiser*, Dec. 9, 1847.
[6]Metz, "Madison Subsequently Named Madisonville."
[7]Narratives of Robert Winslow and Wilson Griffin quoted in *Cist's Daily Advertiser*, Dec. 9, 1847 and *Cist's Weekly Advertisers*, Dec. 14, 1847.
[8]*Centinel of the North-Western Territory*, May 17, 1794.

[9]Narratives of Robert Winslow and Wilson Griffin quoted in *Cist's Daily Advertiser*, Dec. 9, 1847 and *Cist's Weekly Advertisers*, Dec. 14, 1847.
[10]Ibid.
[11]*Centinel of the North-Western Territory*, May 24, 1794; Narratives of Robert Winslow and Wilson Griffin quoted in *Cist's Daily Advertiser*, Dec. 9, 1847 and *Cist's Weekly Advertisers*, Dec. 14, 1847.
[12]Torrence Papers, Cincinnati Historical Society, Box 45, Folder 1-15.
[13]Ibid., Footnote 11.
[14]Ibid.
[15]Ibid.
[16]Narrative of Robert Winslow and Wilson Griffin quoted in *Cist's Daily Advertiser*, Dec. 9, 1847.

Unsigned sketch of Nelson's Station, possibly by Dr. Charles Metz, included in *Reminiscences of Early Madisonville*. (Metz Collection, Cincinnati Historical Society)

North Bend (Symmes City) and South Bend 1789

John Cleves Symmes was born at Southold, Long Island, July 21, 1742. He served as a militia officer during the Revolutionary War and later became Chief Justice of New Jersey and a Representative to Congress from his state.[1]

During the post-Revolutionary period a group of former officers, most from New York and New Jersey, formed a company of land speculators and purchased a vast tract north of the Ohio River between the Great and Little Miami Rivers known as the Miami Purchase. Judge Symmes was an associate in, and agent for, this Miami Land Company and was responsible for initiating surveys of the tract and administering the company's land transactions.[2]

He and other associates proposed a plan for a city and villages which were intended to develop near the confluence of the Great Miami and Ohio Rivers. Symmes had grand visions of the potential success of Miami Point and felt that after several years of development it might rival in many respects Montauk Point, Long Island.[3]

Symmes planned a temporary settlement three quarters of a mile above the mouth of the Great Miami, on the Ohio River flood plain. His strategy was to occupy Fort Finney, an abandoned military installation, but the vacant fort was inundated by Ohio River flood waters during the winter of 1788-1789. He ordered a landing at an alternate site four and one half miles above the mouth of the Great Miami despite objections from the commander of his military escort.[4]

The pioneer party, with a company of Federal troops, landed on February 2, 1789 at a place later known as both Symmes City and North Bend. In a letter to his friend and associate Jonathan Dayton, a delegate to Congress then meeting in New York, Symmes described the North Bend landing:

> *We landed about three of the clock in the afternoon with Capt Kearsey, and his whole company (45 men) which had joined him at Columbia. That afternoon we raised what in this country is called a camp by setting*

two forks of saplings in the ground, a ridge pole across and leaning boat boards which I had brought from Limestone (Maysville, Kentucky), one end on the ground and the other against the ridge pole, enclosing one end of the camp and leaving the other open to the weather for a door where our fire was made to fend against the cold which was very bitter.[5] (Although Symmes refers to Kearsey as Captain, he actually held the rank of Lieutenant at that time.)

A detailed account of Abraham Lincoln's first home in Indiana coincides with the description of Symmes' camp; this type of shelter was called a half-faced cabin.[6]

Judge Symmes could not forsee the series of events which would determine the destiny of his village as he proceded through the final stages of plotting the lots and public areas of North Bend.[7] He had chosen for himself and two of his nephews three adjoining lots near the Ohio River totalling 198 linear feet. On these lots they erected seven structures of which five were quite elaborate considering the difficulties of obtaining building materials at the time.

The buildings occupied the total linear footage of the three lots, with the five most easterly buildings either adjoining each other or nearly so. The first residence raised was located at the eastern terminus of the property while the fifth building, a smoke house, was attached to the fourth in-line residence, a large log structure containing a two story basement. Connecting these five buildings to the remaining two at the western terminus of the property was an eight foot high fortified gate which was attached to the smoke house and to the sixth in-line residence, a double log cabin.

This gate may have been the first defensive feature applied to any structure at North Bend. A combination barn and stable completed this assortment of buildings, all of which had been aligned across the property east to west in Section 20, Township 1, Fractional Range 2, Miami Township west of Indian Creek. Symmes' house stood south of the present intersection of Washington and Symmes Avenues and adjacent to a spring which originated near that intersection.[8]

Prior to May 1789, North Bend had not experienced any problems with the Indians yet Symmes found it difficult to keep village in-lots occupied. Among the major determents to the growth of the village were the distorted stories of Indian attacks on the Miami settlements propagated by Kentucky land speculators among potential settlers of the Miami Purchase.[9]

Lieutenant William Kearsey, sent by General Harmar to protect the settlements, had intended to occupy old Fort Finney but this was not feasible at

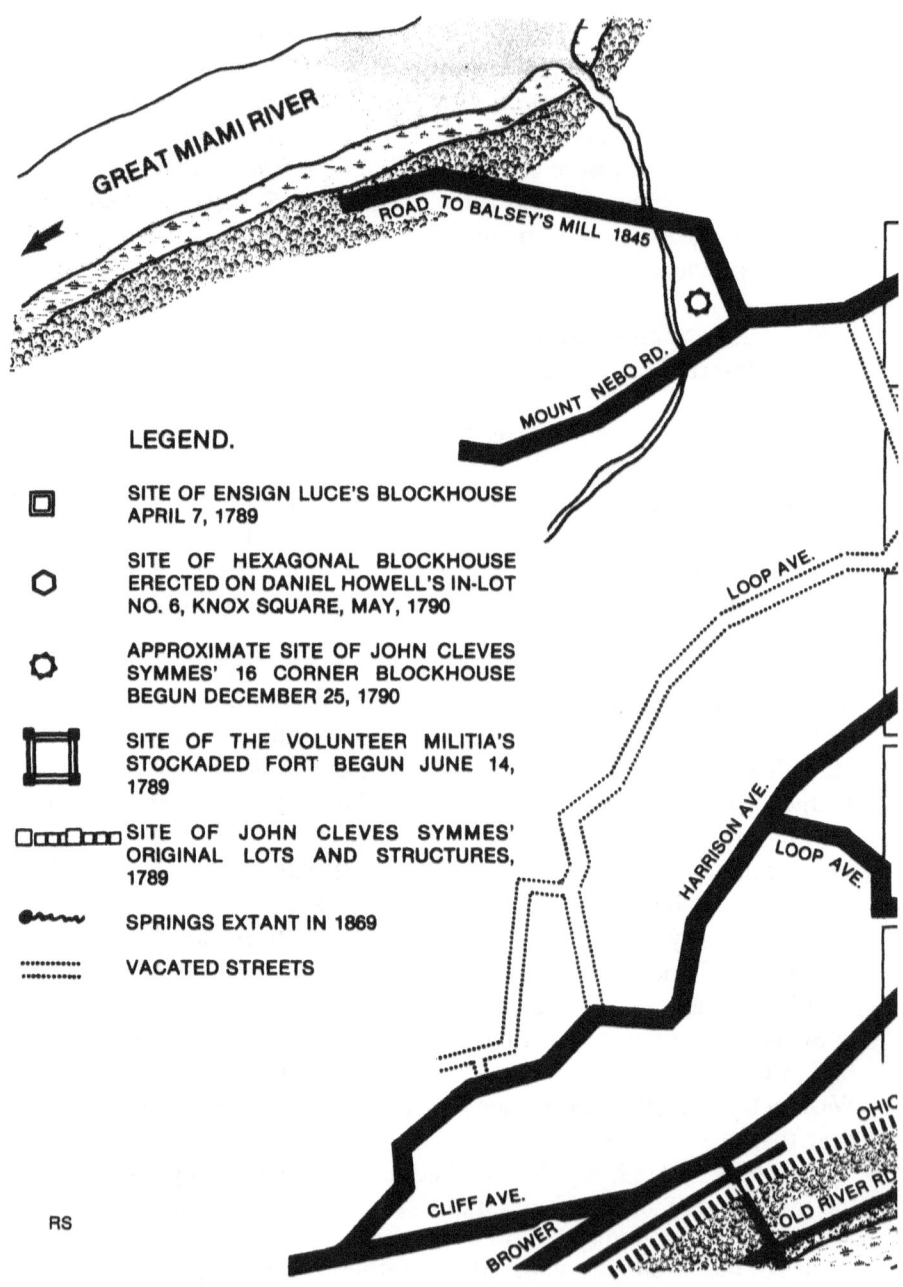

Composite plan of North Bend, Miami Township, founded in 1789 by John Cleves Symmes. (Illustration by Richard Scamyhorn)

the time of the initial landing. Kearsey became belligerent and refused to erect any type of defense at North Bend. On March 8, 1789, when his rations were reduced, Kearsey took the bulk of his troops to Fort Steuben at the Falls of the Ohio River at Louisville, leaving only five men to protect the North Bend inhabitants.[10]

General Harmar had a dual role in mind for the troops he had sent with Symmes and may have ordered Kearsey to occupy Fort Finney, a plan which Symmes discouraged on their arrival. In a letter to Major John P. Wyllys, commandant at the Falls, dated January 22, 1789, Harmar intimated that such a plan might be initiated:

> *Dear Major—It is not improbable but that two companies will be ordered to be station at the mouth of the Great Miami, not only as a better cover for Kentucky, but also as a protection to Judge Symmes in his intended settlement there.*[11]

Symmes was greatly concerned about the conduct of Lt. Kearsey and the possible ramifications resulting from his evacuation to the Falls.[12] Shortly after Kearsey's departure, Maj. Wyllys received a letter from Symmes explaining the precarious position at North Bend and requesting military assistance.[13]

Kearsey's unmilitary conduct did not go unnoticed and on May 7, 1789 Major Wyllys received a letter from General Harmar insisting on a board of inquiry into Kearsey's actions:

> *I am exceedingly displeased with the conduct of Lieut. Kersey, in abandoning Judge Symms' settlement, which he was ordered to protect: very satisfactory reasons indeed must be given, by him, for quitting his post, otherwise he shall certainly be arrested.*[14]

Eighteen soldiers from the 1st U. S. Regiment, under the command of Ensign Francis Luce, arrived at North Bend on March 30 or 31, 1789. They had been sent without government supplies, but with Judge Symmes' help procured enough tools to build a small blockhouse, large enough to accommodate only the troops leaving the civilians to fend for themselves. The blockhouse was erected six hundred feet southwest of the Judge's home and was completed during the first week of April.[15]

Symmes was for the time appeased by Major Wylly's decision to send the small complement of soldiers and that May enthusiastically implied to his colleague Dayton that Ensign Luce had erected a good blockhouse. But by July he was lamenting to Dayton that this blockhouse was small and badly constructed and about General Harmar's lack of cooperation.[16]

Symmes was anxious to start another settlement about seven miles upriver from North Bend at a place called South Bend. This settlement was laid out to extend one mile along the Ohio River, but the proposed plan for the village was abandoned after Symmes examined the ground. A site finally was chosen two miles further west, with the settlement extending along the river bank through Fractional Section 22, into Section 23, Fractional Range 1, Township 3, Delhi Township, west of present Anderson Ferry, Hamilton County.[17]

The developers and future inhabitants of South Bend were living at North Bend and commuting to their building site by boat accompanied by some of Ensign Luce's soldiers.[18] On May 21, while enroute to South Bend, the work party was attacked by a dozen or more Indians firing on the boats from the river bank. One soldier was killed and four others, plus two civilians, were wounded.[19] Symmes related the details and the date of the attack, stating that Ensign Luce had summoned him to come at once to the blockhouse to help in caring for the wounded.[20]

A few days prior to this incident Symmes had sent Isaac Freeman, an Ensign in the volunteer militia, with a guide and interpreter to the Indian towns on the Auglaize River. Their mission was to negotiate the release of prisoners and to ascertain as well the strength and intentions of the Ohio Indian tribes.[21]

Symmes was aware of the detrimental effect that inadequate defenses had on pioneer communities. He also recognized the flaws in his company's land purchase regulations as compared to those of the Ohio Company, whose settlement at Marietta resembled the New England plan of building connected towns and villages, with restricted settlement rules.[22] The problems experienced at North Bend were not confined to that community, as a settlement pattern was evolving in the Miami Purchase with independent stations siphoning off inhabitants from parent settlements.[23]

On June 14 Ensign Luce received word from Major Hamtramck at Post Vincennes that the Miami and Wabash Indians intended to destroy the settlements in the Miami Purchase that fall.[24] This news, combined with the aloofness displayed by General Harmar concerning their position, prompted the inhabitants of North Bend to immediately initiate construction of a stockade.

The location of this defense was noted by Colonel Charles Whittlesey in 1844: "the little fortress stood near the (Ohio) river on the upper side of a (Indian) creek a few yards above General Harrison's late residence." This reference is to Symmes' original log home which was purchased by his son-in-law, future President William Henry Harrison after Harrison resigned his army commission in 1797.[25]

Isaac Freeman completed his mission and returned in July, confirming the possibility of a large scale attack by some seven hundred warriors. Luke Foster, a resident of Columbia and a member of Captain James Flinn's volunteer militia company, stated that upon receipt of Freeman's report Columbia, Cincinnati and North Bend began building new defenses. By the first week of September, he reported, the people of Columbia were living in two strong stockaded works.[26]

Despite Foster's affirmation that the settlements were preparing for the expected attack from Indians of the Northwest Territory, that month of July 1789 was a dismal one for North Bend and the plight of civilians and military was desperate.[27] Ensign Luce sent several of his men to Cincinnati to obtain flour and corn meal. The military's usual methods of making such purchases at the time was to issue vouchers; sometimes these were worthless.

The shopping party approached Francis Kennedy whose boat was tied off at a Cincinnati landing, and after some negotiation threatened to confiscate some of his flour and corn meal if he refused to give it to them willingly. Kennedy stood them off at gun point and it wasn't until Symmes issued a promisory note that the soldiers were able to obtain the supplies.[28] This was only one of many frustrations endured by Ensign Luce and by March 24, 1790 he had resigned his commission.[29]

Of all the original settlements in the Miami Purchase, North Bend probably experienced the most constant vacillation of its inhabitants between 1789 and 1791. In the spring of 1790 many vacant cabins stood on the in-lots and the weary remnant of original settlers joined with the uninitiated newcomers in erecting additional defenses. Daniel and Eunice Howell landed at North Bend about March 18, 1790 and in a letter the following month to their family in New Jersey expressed their disillusionment:

> *We are not in so good a condition at present as I could wish but ware going imedeately to fortify and build a blockhouse tho it is said they will never attack the houses and I don't Expect they will yet we chuse to be as Safe as possible.*[30]

Reverend Benjamin Chidlaw described a hexagonal blockhouse at North Bend in which Eunice Howell is reported to have delivered a child in August of 1790. He gave the approximate location of the structure in relation to certain landmarks as they existed in 1876. The location he described coincides with in-lot number 6, which Eunice and Daniel Howell occupied in Knox Square in 1790.

The blockhouse stood in Section 20, Township 1, Fractional Range 2, Miami Township, west of present Miami Avenue and above the Baltimore and Ohio Railroad tracks. It was built of heavy logs eighteen feet long and it stood ten feet high. The upper section containing portholes extended two feet over the structure's lower areas.[31]

Jacob Parkhurst, a member of the Kentucky volunteer militia, visited his sister at North Bend in the fall of 1790. Her husband Stephen Carter had been killed and scalped by Indians in the village that April, prior to an epidemic throughout the summer which took the lives of some of the original settlers.[32]

Parkhurst returned to Nort Bend that winter to assist his sister and while there he joined Captain Brice Virgin's volunteer militia.[33] On Christmas Day Judge Symmes requested all able bodied men to assist in erecting a fort on the Miami bottom which Parkhurst described as a cabin with sixteen corners. The structure, unique in the area, was noted by Parkhurst as a curiosity and he remarked that:

> *It was a log cabin with 16 corners, which he (Symmes) had planned so as to afford a chance to fire on the enemy from the port holes in every direction, if they should advance to scale the walls or set fire to the building. We did not finish it that day, for the days were short and it was a troublesome building to raise; it took eight cornermen, each of whom was required to carry up two corners. I was one of the cornermen, but we did not cover it that day, and the weather setting in hard, it was not finished when I left North Bend. It was calculated for four fireplaces, and for four families to live. I thought it was an invention of the old Judge to have something curious and exciting to send back to New Jersey, but I never understood that it was invaded by the enemy, as the settlements soon became consolidated up the Miami to Colerain.*[34]

Apparently this odd blockhouse had an almost circular design to offer a clear overlapping field of fire in every direction.

By the summer of 1791 there were many fortified cabins interspersed with the blockhouses and stockades throughout the village and extending to Miami Point.[35]

Judge William Goforth, an early resident at Columbia, noted that there were 80 soldiers stationed at the North Bend garrison during 1791.[36] At that same time there were only eighteen or twenty families at South Bend protected by twenty militiamen stationed in a stockaded fort located there.[37]

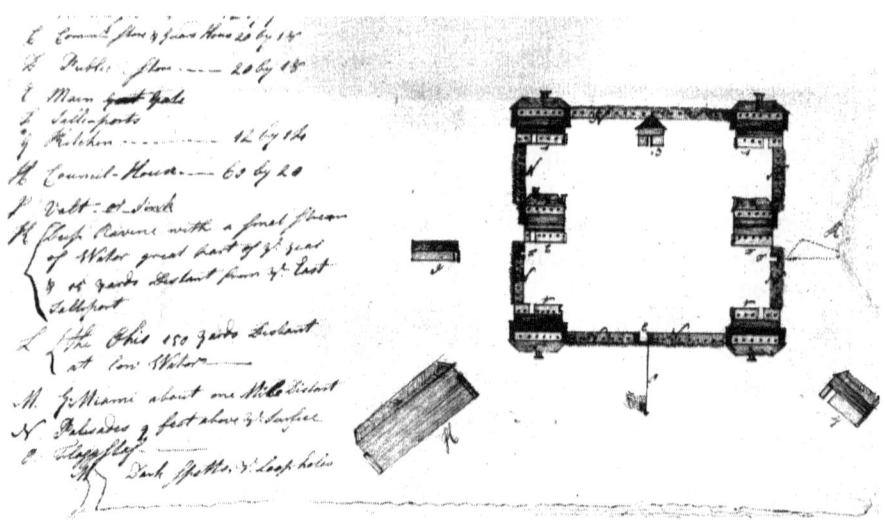

This plan of Fort Finney, located near the mouth of the Great Miami River, was probably drawn in 1785. One of the Fort's blockhouses survived at least until 1866 and was apparently the Sugar Camp blockhouse sketched by Henry Howe in the 1840s. *(Courtesy of the William Henry Smith Library, Indiana Historical Society, Northwest Territory Collection)*

After the Indian attack on Dunlap's Station or Colerain in January 1791, Judge Symmes' frustration at the regular army's inability to protect the Miami Country settlements resulted in an angry and intemperate letter he sent to General Harmar. Harmar's reply, written on January 21, was equally impassioned:

> *Sir: I have received your letter of the 19th instant it is couched in such an improper Style that it requires scarcely an answer. With respect to the distribution of the troops I claim the privilege of being the Only Judge. I do not think it prudent to entrust you with a Fieldpiece. Drums we have none to Spare, nor any of that kind of "apparatus." As the United States promised you protection, you should write to Government to raise more troops. Otherwise it is impossible. Had I received your indelicate letter in time, be assured Sir, that, instead of reinforcing + Strengthening your Station called Coleraine, I should have ordered no troops for that purpose.*[38]

General Harmar was also under considerable strain. Humiliated by his defeat the previous October near the present site of Fort Wayne, Indiana, he would soon undergo an inquiry into his conduct and would be replaced as military commander in the Northwest Territory by Governor St. Clair. In a letter written shortly after his reply to Symmes, Harmar pleaded with Secretary of War Henry Knox for reinforcements and described his inability to protect the region's settlements due to the weakened state of his command.[39]

Like most of the other settlements in the Miami Purchase, North Bend and South Bend unfortunately lost most of their professional soldiers and volunteer militia in the fall of 1791 when they joined General St. Clair's army in its march to the north.

It had been difficult for Symmes to persuade the residents of his city to remain on more than one occasion and this became especially true after St. Clair's disastrous defeat in November. Despite this fact, an observation made in the fall of the following year listed the population of North Bend at between three and four hundred people, with the majority of the inhabitants living on farms (out-lots) while the town remained small.[40] Major Winthrop Sargent visited North Bend in August 1794 and noted in his diary:

> *the place always wretched has fallen off much in thrity months - the time since I was last there - but the country above it has considerably improved - at that date there was not a single intervening house from Cincinnati, excepting at South Bend seven miles of this distance...*[41]

Until 1795 the village population fluctuated rapidly during periods of unrest, but even following the signing of the Greenville Treaty old North Bend never attained the status which Symmes hoped it would. He resided in his original log house until 1797. In a letter to his confidant Robert Morris at New Brunswick, New Jersey, dated December 22, 1795, Symmes related that a new house designed by his wife, Susanna Livingston, was under construction.[42]

Misfortune and poor money management plagued Symmes. Continuing negotiations with Congress and the Treasury Department over the terms of his land purchases resulted in constant frustration. He finally gained clear title to only about one third of the million acre tract for which he had originally negotiated. His belief that he would eventually gain title to the entire area led him to sell large parcels of the land beyond the actual limits of the Miami Purchase. By 1799 and 1800, the angry settlers to whom Symmes had sold this disputed property were petitioning Congress for aid and were suing Symmes to regain their initial investments.

The problems which affected Symmes' personal life and slowly eroded his vast holdings had by 1811 left him and his business affairs in a state of depression. Susanna, his third wife, left him and the profits from his local land holdings were negligible.[43] The large house she had designed was destroyed by arson in 1811 and thereafter Symmes spent most of his time in a cabin he constructed near the mouth of the Great Miami River.[44] He died at Cincinnati on February 26, 1814 and was buried at North Bend.[45]

Notes

[1] *The Intimate Letters of John Cleves Symmes*, Introduction, XVI.
[2] Letter of John Cleves Symmes to Jonathan Dayton, May 18-20, 1789 and letter of John Cleves Symmes to Jonathan Dayton, Daniel Marsh and Matthias Ogden, Jan. 1, 1790, Symmes Correspondence, Cincinnati Historical Society.
[3] Letter of John Cleves Symmes to Jonathan Dayton, May 18-20, 1789, Symmes Correspondence, Cincinnati Historical Society; Plan of Symmes' City (City of Miami) by John Cleves Symmes, Manuscript in Collection of Cincinnati Historical Society.
[4] Letter of John Cleves Symmes to Jonathan Dayton, May 18-20, 1789, Symmes Correspondence, Cincinnati Historical Society.
[5] Charles Cist, *Early Annals and Future Prospects of Cincinnati in 1841*, Cincinnati, 1841, p. 204.
[6] Albert Beveridge, *Abe Lincoln in Indiana*, Boston, 1928, reprinted Fort Wayne, Indiana, 1953, p. 16.
[7] Letter of John Cleves Symmes to Jonathan Dayton, Daniel Marsh and Matthias Ogden, Jan. 1, 1790, Symmes Correspondence, Cincinnati Historical Society.
[8] *Restored Records, Decrees & Plats Affecting Real Estate 1798-1863*, Vol. 1, p. 29, Hamilton County Engineer's Office, Road Records Division; U. S. Geological Survey Map, Addyston, Ohio-Kentucky Quad., 7.5' series; Howe, *Historical Collections of Ohio*, Cincinnati, 1847, p. 230-231.
[9] Letter of John Cleves Symmes to Jonathan Dayton, May 18-20, 1789, Symmes Correspondence, Cincinnati Historical Society.
[10] Ibid.
[11] *Military Journal of Major Ebenezer Denny, an Officer in the Revolutionary and Indian Wars*, Historical Society of Pennsylvania, Philadelphia, 1859, Appendix I, p. 235.
[12] Letter of John Cleves Symmes to Jonathan Dayton, May 18-20, 1789, Symmes Correspondence, Cincinnati Historical Society; Drake, "Memoir of the Miami Country," p. 72-73.
[13] Letter of John Cleves Symmes to Jonathan Dayton, May 18-20, 1789, Symmes Correspondence, Cincinnati Historical Society. [14] Letter of General Josiah Harmar to Major John P. Wyllys, May 7, 1789, Harmar Papers, Letter Book E, Letter 82, William Clements Library, University of Michigan.
[15] Letter of John Cleves Symmes to Jonathan Dayton, May 18-20, May 2 and July 17, 1789, Symmes Correspondence, Cincinnati Historical Society; Letter of Luke Foster to Thomas Clark, May 23, 1819, quoted in Drake, "Memoir of the Miami Country," p. 102-103.
[16] Letter of John Cleves Symmes to Jonathan Dayton, May 18-20, 1789, Symmes Correspondence, Cincinnati Historical Society.
[17] Letter of John Cleves Symmes to Jonathan Dayton, May 18-20, 1789, Symmes Correspondence, Cincinnati Historical Society; Reeder Family Papers, Folder 15, "Reminiscences of Allen L. Reeder," Cincinnati Historical Society; Letter of John Cleves Symmes to Capt. John Stites Gano, May 11, 1789, John S. Gano Papers, Vol. 3, p. 237, Cincinnati Historical Society.
[18] Letter of John Cleves Symmes to Jonathan Dayton, May 18-20, 1789, Symmes Correspondence, Cincinnati Historical Society.
[19] Ibid.
[20] Ibid.
[21] Drake, "Memoir of the Miami Country," p. 103-104; "Selections From The Torrence Papers, VIII," *Quarterly Publication of the Historical and Philosophical Society of Ohio*, Vol. 13 (1918), p. 67.
[22] Letter of John Cleves Symmes to Jonathan Dayton, May 18-20, 1789, Symmes Correspondence, Cincinnati Historical Society.

[23] Ibid.
[24] Letter of Major John Hamtramck to Major John P. Wyllys, May 27, 1789, quoted in *Outpost on the Wabash, 1787-1791*, ed. Gayle Thornbrough, Indiana Historical Publications, Vol. 19, Indianapolis, 1957, p. 171- 173.
[25] Letter of John Cleves Symmes to Jonathan Dayton, May 18-20, 1789, Symmes Correspondence, Cincinnati Historical Society; Letter of William Henry Harrison to John Cleves Short, April 6, 1814, Harrison Papers, Cincinnati Historical Society; Letter of John Cleves Symmes to Robert Morris, Dec. 22, 1795, Symmes Correspondence, Cincinnati Historical Society; James A. Green, *William Henry Harrison, His Life & Times*, Richmond, Virginia, 1941, p. 272, 288-289, 407, 413, 417, 433; James A. Green, "North Bend," p. 5; Whittlesey, "Notices of Hamilton County, Ohio," p. 19, Cincinnati Historical Society; Narrative of Rebecca Reeder, quoted in Cist, *Early Annals and Future Prospects in Cincinnati, 1841*, p. 149.
[26] "Selections From The Torrence Papers, VIII," *Quarterly Publication of the Historical and Philosophical Society of Ohio*, Vol. 13 (1918), p. 98; Drake, "Memoir of the Miami Country," p. 104.
[27] Narrative of Rebecca Reeder, quoted in Cist, *Early Annals and Future Prospects in Cincinnati, 1841*, p. 148-149.
[28] Ibid.
[29] Letter of General Josiah Harmar to General Henry Knox, March 24, 1790, quoted in *Military Journal of Major Ebenezer Denny*, Appendix I, p. 250; Alta Harvey Heiser, *West to Ohio*, p. 12-13.
[30] Letter of Daniel and Eunice Howell to Ezekiel Howell, April 24, 1790, quoted in "News From North Bend," ed. Lee Shepard, *Bulletin of the Historical and Philosophical Society of Ohio*, Vol. 15 (1857), p. 324- 325.
[31] Reverend Benjamin Chidlaw, "Early Times," 1876, quoted in Marjorie Byrnside Burress, *It Happened 'Round North Bend*, Cincinnati, 1970, Ch. 3, p. 1; *Deed Book F-1*, p. 89, Hamilton County Recorder's Office.
[32] "Autobiography of Jacob Parkhurst," quoted in *It Happened 'Round North Bend*, Cincinnati, 1970, Ch. 3, p. 2; Letter of Daniel and Eunice Howell to Ezekiel Howell, April 24, 1790, quoted in "News From North Bend," p. 235.
[33] "Autobiography of Jacob Parkhurst," quoted in *It Happened 'Round North Bend*, Cincinnati, 1970, Ch. 3, p. 2; "Selections From the Torrence Papers, VIII," p. 97.
[34] Jacob Parkhurst, *Sketches of Jacob Parkhurst 1772-1863 by Himself*, Knightstown, Indiana, 1976, p. 9.
[35] "Autobiography of Jacob Parkhurst," quoted in *It Happened 'Round North Bend*, Cincinnati, 1970, Ch. 3, p. 2; Thomas Ashe, Esq., *Travels in America, 1806*, London, reprinted Newburyport, Mass., 1808, p. 231.
[36] Excerpts from the diary of William Goforth, quoted in Greve, *Centennial History of Cincinnati*, Vol. 1, p. 200; *The Western Spy*, May 2, 1817.
[37] Letter from Washington, Kentucky, quoted in "The Early Settlements Around Cincinnati," *Phildelphia Daily General Advertiser*, Oct. 18, 1791, Robert Clarke Collection, Box 1, Folder 3, No. 448, Cincinnati Historical Society; *Diary of Major Winthrop Sargent, Number 2*, entry of Thursday, Aug. 21, 1794.
[38] Letter of General Josiah Harmar to John Cleves Symmes, Jan. 21, 1791, Letter Book I, Harmar Papers, William Clements Library, University of Michigan.
[39] Letter of General Josiah Harmar to General Henry Knox, Jan. 25, 1791, Folio Letter Book A, Harmar Papers, William Clements Library, University of Michigan; Francis Paul Prucha, *The Sword of the Republic, The United States Army on the Frontier, 1783-1846*, Bloomington, Indiana and London, 1977, p. 21-22.
[40] Ibid., *Diary of Major Winthrop Sargent*; John Heckewelder, *A Narrative of the United Brethren Among the Delaware & Mohegan Indians*, p. 76.
[41] Ibid., *Diary of Major Winthrop Sargent*.
[42] Letters of John Cleves Symmes to Robert Morris, Aug. 22, 1795, Dec. 22, 1795 and Feb. 28,

1796, Symmes Correspondence, Cincinnati Historical Society; James A. Green, "North Bend," quoted in *The Ohio Social Science Journal*, Vol. 4 (1932), p. 5; Howe, *Historical Collections of Ohio*, Columbus, 1891, Vol. 2, p. 138-139.
[43]*The Intimate Letters of John Cleves Symmes*, Introduction, XXV-XXVII, XXX, p. 26, 29-30, 134-139; Letter of John Cleves Symmes to Colonel James Henry, July 7, 1811, 1 W.W., Mic. #49, Manuscript Collection, Cincinnati Historical Society.
[44]Letter of John Cleves Symmes to Colonel James Henry, July 7, 1811, 1 W.W., Mic. #49, Manuscript Collection, Cincinnati Historical Society.
[45]Charles H. Winfield, "Life and Public Services of John Cleves Symmes," *Proceedings of the New Jersey Historical Society*, Second Series, Vol. 4 (1875-1877), p. 39.

The Paxton Settlement 1795

Thomas Paxton, a Pennsylvanian born in 1739, was commander of a company of Bedford County Rangers and became Lieutenant Colonel of the Second Battalion of Bedford County Militia during the Revolutionary War.[1]

About 1790 Paxton, his second wife Martha, and his ten children (several of whom were adults with spouses and children of their own) emigrated to Kentucky. The party traveled down the Ohio River from Pittsburgh with other settlers in a flotilla of sixteen flatboats, enduring a severe Indian attack along the way.[2]

Some accounts indicate that the Paxtons settled in Bourbon County (in a section now part of Nicholas County) near present day Carlisle. Another version states that Paxton held large areas of land near today's Covington in Kenton County. Paxton's title to his Covington property reportedly proved defective and in return he was given title bonds to land north of the Ohio River.[3]

Although several Clermont County historians assert that Paxton led the advance guard of General Anthony Wayne's army at the Battle of Fallen Timbers in August 1794, there appears to be little solid evidence to support this claim.[4] However, a remark made by future President James Buchanan many years later supports the assertion that Paxton did serve in some capacity at Fallen Timbers.[5]

Paxton apparently was one of the first settlers in the interior of today's Clermont County. He founded a settlement there sometime in 1795 together with four of his sons-in-law: Owen Todd, John Ramsey, James Smith and Silas Hutchinson. His young son, Samuel, and his five other sons-in-law, John Donnell, Redmond McDonough, Samuel Jack, David Snider and Robert Orr also eventually joined the settlement. Another son, Thomas, was born there in 1799.[6]

The first dwelling at the Paxton settlement, according to reports, was a double log cabin surrounded by a stockade.[7] Though Paxton owned a considerable amount of land in today's Clermont County, the traditional placement of his stockade is on the farm later owned by his son Samuel. This area lies in Miami Township, east of the Little Miami River and thus within the boundaries of the Virginia Military District. It was originally part of Martin Nall's survey number 2194, just west of Ward's Corner Road, about one half to three quarters of a mile south of the present city limits of Loveland, and near a small fishing lake. Paxton was buried near this site in the Ramsey family cemetery in 1813.[8]

Paxton's settlement, described by a traveller in 1797[9] as six or seven miles from Deerfield (today's South Lebanon), was an important local center for religious services and early elections. The large and prosperous Paxton family continued to have considerable influence in Clermont County well into the next century.[10] In his later years, however, Paxton was apparently in ill health and heavily in debt to William Lytle, as illustrated by a letter he wrote Lytle in 1807:

> *January the Eight 1807 Dear Sir*
> *I never was Cast down so much in not standing to my word about that money. I have not been abel to Ride on mile from my hous to Colect the money...*
> *Dear Sir dont get angrey. I have sent a man yesterday up to Mad River to a man that owes me Three Hundred Dolars. I hope to Receve it in a few days. John Cramer within one mile of my hous owes me Three Hundred Dolars and Eight Barels of whiskey. it is one year old, good Proof Licker. I am to Receve it at market price. you can have what you want from me if you will Ride over to my hous and see the Licker. I am to take the Eight Barels at market price. you may have the one half or more*
> *Your Humbel Sarvent*
Thomas Paxton[11]

Notes
[1] *Pennsylvania Archives*, Series 2, Vol. 14, p. 652. 655-656, 661.
[2] *History of Warren County, Ohio*, p. 664-665; Jack Hutchinson, "Colonel Thomas Paxton," Manuscript in Collection of Greater Loveland Historical Society, p. 3-4.
[3] Ibid.; Rockey and Bancroft, *History of Clermont County*, p. 175.
[4] Ibid., p. 175, 486-487; Letters from the Filson Club of Louisville to Edwin E. Smith, Nov. 11, 1981, and to Audrey Gomes, Jan. 7, 1985, concerning Paxton's military service, Greater Loveland Historical Society.
[5] Article in *Clermont Sun*, March 1891, quoted in Elder Herring, "The History of Loveland," *The Loveland Herald*, Oct. 29, 1936.
[6] Rockey and Bancroft, *History of Clermont County*, p. 460-461, 472, 480, 487; Byron Williams, *History of Clermont and Brown Counties, Ohio*, Milford, Ohio, 1913, Vol. 1, p. 205.
[7] Hutchinson, "Colonel Thomas Paxton," p. 6.
[8] Rockey and Bancroft, *History of Clermont County*, p. 460-461; *Atlas of Clermont County, Ohio*, Philadelphia, 1870, p. 7; U. S. Geological Survey, Goshen, Ohio and Madeira, Ohio Quads., 7.5' series.
[9] *History of Warren County*, p. 411-413.
[10] Hutchinson, "Colonel Thomas Paxton," p. 6-7; Rockey and Bancroft, *History of Clermont County*, p. 176, 486-487.
[11] Letter of Thomas Paxton to William Lytle, Jan. 8, 1807, Lytle Papers, Box 9, Letter Number 75, Cincinnati Historical Society.

Pleasant Valley Station 1793

On April 27, 1789 the brothers Luke, Zebulon and Gabriel Foster, natives of New York, arrived at Columbia with James Seward and Jonathan Pittman of New Jersey.[1]

The Fosters resided in Fort Miami at Columbia until that fall when they and others fortified and took up residence in ordinary cabins outside the fort.[2] During that winter, which was prior to the existence of any organized militia, the safety of the community's residents depended on a small guard from Fort Washington, some hired scouts and their own efforts in banding together as Minutemen.[3]

The volunteer militia was organized in the Miami Purchase in 1790 under government military rules and supervision. Luke Foster was commissioned a lieutenant in the militia's 1st Regiment on January 4, 1790 and was among regulars and militia sent by General Harmar to aid Dunlap's Station after an attack there on January 10, 1791. A year later a muster of the Columbia militia under the command of Captain James Flinn was called by Lieutenant Levi Woodward. Luke and Gabriel Foster were listed as privates on this official muster roll.[5]

This was before the Fosters joined Henry Tucker and other Columbia people in the spring of 1792 to start Tucker's Station in present Springfield Township.[6] Before the blockhouse there could even be finished, a bitter dispute over boundary lines arose between the Fosters and Tucker and some members of the new settlement returned to Columbia.[7] During the next winter the dispute was resolved and a party of settlers, including Henry Weaver, John McCashen, James Seward and Ziba Wingent, joined the Fosters in founding the Pleasant Valley Station in the spring of 1793.[8]

The Pleasant Valley settlement was located in fractions of Sections 9 and 10, Township 3, Range 1, in present Springfield Township.[9] In settlement of their dispute, Luke Foster received by forfeit from Henry Tucker ten acres in the southwest corner of Section 4. Tucker also gave Zebulon Foster five acres adjoining Luke's land to the north.[10]

A blockhouse was erected on a site convenient to both the Tucker and Pleasant Valley settlements, situated on a line between Sections 4 and 10, on the west bank of Mill Creek. It was later bisected by a section of road replacing old Hamilton Road, named the Springfield Pike. Had the blockhouse survived, it would now be standing in the middle of Springfield Pike near the intersection of Grove Road, southwest of Tucker Station's original blockhouse.

Pleasant Valley Station was completed in the fall of 1793. Through 1797, the local Presbyterian congregation assembled for services at the blockhouse in Foster's Grove.[11]

In 1792 an extension of the military road leading to Fort Hamilton was made, branching out and running northeast from Ludlow's Station to White's Station.[12] A petition to further extend and improve this branch of the road was presented by Pleasant Valley Station settlers to Hamilton County Court in August of 1794. The inhabitants of White's and Tucker's Stations angrily contested the petition, claiming:

> ...*it could only be calculated for the interest and convenience of three or four discontented individuals...and also extremely inconvenient to those inhabitants who must be called out to work on said road, at the distance from ten to sixteen miles, the inconvenience is too obvious to require explanation.*

> *Your honor's petitioners need not add... how apparently unable are the inhabitants of those stations to secure safety to themselves, their wives, their children, and property, from the inroads and depredations of the Indians.*
>
> *This itself is grievous, but how much more additionally so if they should be called out to work on this unnecessary road, and leave defenseless women, children and property an easy prey to a subtle and a watchful foe. We, therefore, pray your honors to reject the said proposed highway, and dismiss the petition praying for the same.*[13]

Many of the same petitioners signed three other petitions, dated in November 1794, February 1795 and November 1795, to alter and improve the roads leading from White's to Runyon's Station.[14] Perhaps the virtual end of Indian hostilities had finally made it safe to attend to road-building; or perhaps self-interest proved stronger than fear in this case. Tucker's initial protest may have indicated a lingering resentment towards the Fosters.[15]

Luke Foster later was active in Hamilton County's judicial system, becoming one of its early associate justices. He was appointed Justice of the Peace in and for the county on January 15, 1803.[16] Although his official duties often kept him from home, Judge Foster maintained his farm at Pleasant Valley. He was killed by a Cincinnati, Hamilton & Dayton Railroad train there on August 28, 1857.[17]

Notes

[1] Letter of John Reily to Daniel Drake, Dec. 22, 1831, quoted in Drake, "Memoir of the Miami Country," p. 113-114; Letter of Luke Foster to Thomas Clark, May 23, 1819, quoted in Drake, "Memoir of the Miami Country," p. 103-104.
[2] Ibid., p. 103-104.
[3] Ibid.
[4] Manuscript Journal of Official Records, quoted in *The St. Clair Papers*, Vol. 2, p. 131 (footnote); Drake, "Memoir of the Miami Country," p. 111; *The Territorial Papers of the United States*, Vol. 3, p. 295.
[5] The Torrence Papers, Cincinnati Historical Society, Box 45, Folder 1-15.
[6] Olden, *Historical Sketches*, p. 114; Teetor, *Mill Creek Valley*, p. 43; Greve, *Centennial History of Cincinnati*, Vol. 1, p. 118.
[7] Ibid.
[8] Teetor, *Mill Creek Valley*, p. 44-45; Olden, *Historical Sketchs*, p. 114.
[9] Ibid.; map of Hamilton County, Ohio, Wm. D. Emerson, 1847; U. S. Geological Survey, Cincinnati, Ohio East Quad., 7.5' series.
[10] *Plat Book 2*, p. 200, 209, Hamilton County Recorder's Office.
[11] Rev. Wm. H. James, *79th Anniversary of the Presbyterian Church, Springdale, Ohio*, Cincinnati, 1876, p. 5; Teetor, *Mill Creek Valley*, p. 44-45; Greve, *Centennial History*, Vol. 1, p. 292.
[12] Olden, *Historical Sketches*, p. 138.

[13]Ibid., p. 139-141.
[14]bid., p. 142-145; *Road Record Book 1-1B, 1793-1850*, p. 112, Hamilton County Engineer's Office, Road Records Division.
[15]Greve, *Centennial History*, Vol. 1, p. 292.
[16]"A Leaf from Old Records," *Cist's Weekly Advertiser*, Jan. 22, 1845; *The Territorial Papers of the United States*, Vol. 3, p. 535.
[17]*Year Book of the Ohio Society of the Sons of the American Revolution*, Cincinnati, 1895, p. 50; Ford, *History of Hamilton County, Ohio*, p. 364.

Round Bottom or Clements' Station 1789

This settlement has been referred to by historians as Round Bottom, Clemen's, Clemmon's and Clements' Station. Dr. Ezra Ferris stated in 1851 that there was a settlement made at Round Bottom, a short distance below Covalt's and above Newtown (Mercer's Station).[1] A letter from General Harmar at Fort Washington to General Henry Knox, confirms that Round Bottom Station was three quarters of a mile below Covalt's and on the west side of the Little Miami River.[2]

The station was established by Forgerson Clements, his wife Elizabeth and their nine children, along with Isaac Morris, Joseph Beagle and Jonathan Tichenor. A corporal's guard was assigned to the station for added protection.[3] Joseph Martin, one of the original settlers at Garrard's Station, stated in a narrative, "...two men had been killed there before I came. One man was driving a team in at the gate and hit his head a severe blow against the bar overhead and this killed him."[4] This statement clearly indicates that the station was enclosed by a stockade.

Clements apparently was elderly when he arrived. He and Beagle were members of a hunting party out of Covalt's Station that came under an Indian attack which killed Abraham Covalt, Jr.[5] Clements met his fate at Round Bottom when attacked from ambush near the station. He was wounded in the thigh, suffering a severed artery, and died from loss of blood.[6] Martin stated that Clements was buried in the cornfield.[7]

Benjamin Stites, Jr., a resident of Columbia, acted as a scout for Covalt and Round Bottom Stations. He recalled some years later that four men were ambushed while cutting timber for the fort at Round Bottom.[8] Twenty Indians attacked the work party killing one military guard and capturing three civilians. Of the three captives, only Joseph Beagle returned.[9]

There was constant interaction between the inhabitants of the Round Bottom Station and those at Columbia, Garrard's, Covalt's and Mercer's Stations stimulated by their common desire for mutual protection and accessibility to grist mills and regular religious services.

Mary Covalt, in her reminiscences, recalled an incident in the spring of 1794 illustrating the comraderie which existed in the settlements at the time: "Two of the men had been at Columbia and were on their return to the fort (Covalt's) when the Indians attacked them. One of them, Jennings, was wounded, but he arrived at the fort. The other one, whose name was Crist, went to the Round Bottom fort to apprise them of the approach of the Indians."[10]

Round Bottom Fort was located near the south end of Miami Avenue, at the south end of present Terrace Park, and on the west side of the Little Miami River. This location is near the northeast boundary of Section 22, Township 5, Fractional Range 2, Columbia Township.[11] Mrs. Clements deeded her forty acres at Round Bottom Station to her children in 1796 but remained at the settlement with her son John until 1804. She then moved to Wayne Township in Warren County.[12]

Notes

[1] Ferris, *Early Settlement*, p. 330.
[2] Letter of General Josiah Harmar to General Henry Knox, Jan. 25, 1791, Vol. 14, Letter X, Harmar Papers, William Clements Library, University of Michigan.
[3] *Deed Book B-1*, p. 59-60, Hamilton County Recorder's Office; Narrative of Joseph Martin, quoted in Whittlesey, "Notices of Hamilton County," p. 19; Narrative of Mrs. Helen Hamilton Keck, quoted in the *Cincinnati Times Star*, March 23, 1933; Drake, "Memoir of the Miami Country," p. 65.
[4] Narrative of Joseph Martin, quoted in Whittlesey, "Notices of Hamilton County," p. 19.
[5] Jones, *Extracts from the History of Cincinnati*, p. 59-60.
[6] Narrative of Mrs. Helen Hamilton Keck, quoted in the *Cincinnati Times Star*, March 23, 1933.
[7] Narrative of Joseph Martin, quoted in Whittlesey, "Notices of Hamilton County," p. 19.
[8] Narrative of Benjamin Stites, Jr., quoted in *Cist's Weekly Advertiser*, Dec. 14, 1847.
[9] Narrative of Mary Covalt Jones, p. 7; Jones, *Extracts*, p. 64.
[10] Narrative of Mary Covalt Jones, p. 9.
[11] City of Cincinnati and Hamilton County Metropolitan Topographic Survey Maps, Hamilton County Engineer's Office, Road Records Division; U. S. Geological Survey Map, Madeira, Ohio Quad., 7.5' series.
[12] Narrative of Mrs. Helen Hamilton Keck.

Runyon's Station
1792

Henry Runyon, a Virginian who had been living in Fayette County, Kentucky since about 1784, entered warrant number 383 for 640 acres in Section 25, Township 3, Range 2 on June 19, 1789[1]. Then, on May 3, 1790, he entered warrants numbered 21 and 22 of 160 acres each in the west half of Section 19, Township 3, Range 2, in present Sycamore Township.[2]

On August 31, 1791, Andrew Round applied for one half of the northwest corner of Runyon's half of Section 19 by forfeit for non-settlement under the rules of Symmes' Miami land office.[3]

According to Runyon's son, Isaac, his father had actually settled and built a cabin in Section 19 by 1792.[4] As described by local historians, the old "Station House" stood on the east side of the Dayton Turnpike (Mad River or Reading Road) near a spring. This would place it on the north side of Hauck Road.[5]

The Runyon family may have been the only inhabitants of the original settlement but forfeitures on Runyon's property were being entered as early as February 18, 1791.[6] By 1792, roads to Runyon's were being petitioned and surveys ordered for these proposed roads. Among those listed were a road from Cincinnati up the Mill Creek to Runyon's in 1792 and a widening of the road from White's Station to Runyon's to 66 feet (four poles) in 1796.[7]

If indeed Henry Runyon built his station on the east side of the Dayton Turnpike as stated, by 1814 he had removed his residence to the west side of the turnpike in Section 25. He left the original site to Sarah Runyon, as indicated by a plat filed by a Hamilton county surveyor on June 9, 1814.[8]

Notes
[1] Olden, *Historical Sketches*, p. 98; *Symmes Purchase Records*, p. 17.
[2] Olden, *Historical Sketches*, p. 98; *Symmes Purchase Records*, p. 24, 95.
[3] Olden, *Historical Sketches*, p. 98; *Symmes Purchase Records*, p. 13-14, 95.
[4] Olden, *Historical Sketches*, p. 99.
[5] Ibid., p. 59; Greve, *Centennial History of Cincinnati*, Vol. 1, p. 293; Jones, *Extracts from the History of Cincinnati*, p. 98; *Road Record Book, Vol. 1-1B, 1790-1850*, p. 40, Hamilton County Engineer's Office, Road Records Division; map of Hamilton County by Wm. Emerson, 1847; Atlas of Hamilton County, Ohio 1884; U. S. Geological Survey, Glendale, Ohio Quad., 7.5' series.
[6] *Symmes Purchase Records*, p. 40, 60, 99.
[7] *Road Record Book, Vol. 1-1B, 1790-1850*, p. 44-45, 51, 54, 57-58, 94, 97, 110, 114, 128, Hamilton

County Engineer's Office, Road Records Division.
[8]*Hamilton County Survey Book 10*, p. 40, Hamilton County Engineer's Office, Road Records Division.

Plat of Henry Runyon's property in 1814 showing Mad River Road (Reading Road) and Lebanon Road (Route 42) in present Sharonville, Hamilton County. *(Hamilton County Recorder's Office)*

The Sugar Camp Settlement 1789

In the year 1846 the noted historian Henry Howe sketched a blockhouse on the Ohio River flood plain which had survived Indians, floods and total deterioration.[1] Howe described the blockhouse in detail and noted its location in relation to North Bend and the Ohio-Indiana state line at the mouth of the Great Miami River.

He stated that the blockhouse was "...built of logs, in the ordinary manner of block houses, the distinguishing feature of which is, that from the height of a man's shoulder, the building, the rest of the way up, projects a foot or two from the lower part, leaving, at the point of junction between the two parts, a cavity, through which to thrust rifles, on the approach of enemies."[2] Howe enumerated some thirty dilapidated structures near the blockhouse and designated the site the "Sugar Camp Settlement," but he did not name the former inhabitants.[3]

The blockhouse was situated in Fractional Section 35 in Fractional Range 1, Township 2, Miami Township on the property of John Scott Harrison.[4] Unmentioned by Howe was the fact that the blockhouse was in close proximity to Fort Finney, a garrison built in 1785 on a site about three quarters of a mile east of the mouth of the Great Miami River at Dark Hollow.[5] Fort Finney was not merely a stockaded bastion but rather a complex of structures built by the army at the request of Congress primarily as a negotiation and treaty site with the Shawnee Indians.[6]

On September 8, 1866 John Scott Harrison noted that a remnant of the old fort could still be seen in the southeast corner of the farm on which he resided. He referred to only one of the blockhouses of the Fort Finney complex.[7]

The distance from North Bend and the Ohio-Indiana state line to the Fort Finney blockhouse, as indicated on maps, places it one half mile west of the Sugar Camp blockhouse as descrbed by Howe. However, Howe merely estimated the distance[8] as he had discarded his notes while keeping the sketch. In 1889 Colonel W. H. H. Taylor, son-in-law of William Henry Harrison, supplied him with a sketch of the Harrison home and notes for use in the 1891 edition of Howe's *Historical Collections of Ohio*.

Old blockhouse near North Bend, sketched by Henry Howe in 1846 for his *Historical Collections of Ohio. (Courtesy Cincinnati Historical Society)*

Colonel Taylor had accompanied Howe on his 1846 visit to the Sugar Camp and not only remembered the sketch but asserted that the distance to the camp had been four miles below the Bend, not three as stated by Howe.[9] The location of the Sugar Camp blockhouse leaves little doubt that it was actually one of the blockhouses built at Fort Finney in 1785 and later reused as a defensive work by area settlers.

The people of Sugar Camp were not the first pioneers with that object in mind. In December 1788 a party of settlers left Limestone (Maysville), Kentucky with a thirteen-man army escort. Their plan was to make a settlement at the old fort. Unfortunately their boats were caught in an ice jam at Columbia and severely damaged. Most of their provisions were lost and the intended settlement was aborted.[10]

John Cleves Symmes had also planned to occupy Fort Finney as a temporary shelter for his settlement while he laid out his town on the point of the Great Miami River. But the Fort was inundated by a flood when Symmes arrived and his scheme failed.[11]

Throughout the nineteenth century many cabins were built along this flood plain and although Howe counted thirty Sugar Camp structures in 1846 it is possible that they were not all contemporaneous with the blockhouse. The longevity of the "Sugar Camp" name lends credence to the theory that the camp may have consisted of half-faced cabins used during the tapping of maple trees, with the blockhouse as protection against Indian incursions of the period. An observation made by an army officer in 1812 concerning some Ohio pioneer traits may help verify this theory:

> When sugar trees are a distance from the house a camp is formed in a central place among the trees and called a sugar camp. The whole family sometimes resorts to the camp and all assist in making sugar.[12]

In retrospect one can surmise the Sugar Camp blockhouse was used as a protective haven until 1795 during those few weeks when maple sap was collected and processed.

Some of the inhabitants of the settlement of Finney, which evolved near this blockhouse, were among the first pioneers to be buried in the graveyard near the old fort at Dark Hollow. A cabin belonging to the Guard family is also said to have stood near the site of Fort Finney.[13] This property is currently owned by the Cincinnati Gas & Electric Company. The blockhouse stood in an area now used for coal storage.[14]

Notes
[1] Henry Howe, *Historical Collections of Ohio*, Cincinnati, 1847, p. 236-237.
[2] Ibid.
[3] Ibid.
[4] Hon. J. Scott Harrison, *Pioneer Life at North Bend, an address to the Whitewater & Miami Valley Pioneer Association at Cleves, Ohio, Sept. 8, 1866*, Cincinnati, 1867, p. 13-14.
[5] Ibid.; Journal of General Richard Butler, quoted in *The Olden Time*, Vol. 2, p. 454; *The Military Journal of Major Ebenezer Denny, an Officer in the Revolutionary and Indian Wars*, Appendix 1, p. 59; Letter of John Cleves Symmes to Jonathan Dayton, May 18-20, 1789, Symmes Correspondence, Cincinnati Historical Society.
[6] *American State Papers, Class II, Indian Affairs*, Washington, 1832- 61, Vol. 1, p. 11-12.
[7] Harrison, *Pioneer Life at North Bend*, p. 13-14.
[8] U. S. Geological Survey maps, 7.5' series, 1914-1970, Lawrenceburg & Hooven, Indiana, Ohio, Kentucky Quads., Addyston, Ohio, Kentucky Quad.; Cincinnati and Hamilton County, Ohio Metropolitan & Topographic Survey Maps, scale 1:2400, Hamilton County Engineer's Office, Road Records Division; Howe, *Historical Collections of Ohio*, 1847, p. 236-237; Howe, *Historical Collections of Ohio*, Columbus, 1891, Vol. 2, p. 138-141.
[9] Ibid.
[10] Letter of John Cleves Symmes to Jonathan Dayton, May 18-20, 1789, Symmes Correspondence, Cincinnati Historical Society.
[11] Ibid.
[12] Lt. Jervis Cutler, *ATopographical Description of the State of Ohio*, Boston, 1812, p. 15.
[13] "Sketch of the Early Life of Baily Guard Esq.," talk delivered by Reverend Benjamin W. Chidlaw at Hunt's Grove, July 3, 1869, quoted in *The Lawrenceburg Press*, July 15, 1869.
[14] U. S. Geological Survey Map, Lawrenceburg, Ohio, Kentucky, Indiana Quad., 7.5' series.

Tucker's Station
1792

Tucker's Station was one of many early Hamilton County settlements whose founders formed their plans while living at Columbia. Henry and John Tucker, both from Passaic, New Jersey, but not related, organized a group of seven families at Columbia and in the spring of 1792 purchased from John Cleves Symmes Section 4, Range 1, Township 3 in present Springfield Township.[1]

Station improvements, including a blockhouse, were begun late that fall. Site chosen was east of present Anthony Wayne Road, north of Marion Avenue, south of the Glendale-Milford Road and west of Chester Road.[2] The blockhouse stood opposite the later residence of Manning R. Tucker, Henry's son. By the latter part of the nineteenth century the site became the property of one H. Bugher and is currently part of Woodlawn.[3]

Before station improvements could be completed, a dispute over property lines developed between Henry Tucker and Luke Foster, who returned to Columbia with his followers. The Tuckers were left with an uncompleted blockhouse and too few people with which to defend the settlement.[4]

They continued to work on the buildings for several days longer until startled by the sudden appearance of William Wells, an Indian scout who had stealthily placed himself between the working party and their weapons. Wells warned them of imminent danger, convincing the entire party to abandon the station and return to Columbia.[5]

The next spring General Anthony Wayne began forming his army near Cincinnati at Camp Hobson's Choice. During that summer the Henry Tucker party returned to their abandoned settlement and completed building the station. Although he considered his new settlement a permanent one, Tucker maintained a stable at Columbia and during the winter of 1793-1794 felt it prudent to send his most valuable horses there for safekeeping.

But the Indians stole two of his prize horses from the stable in the spring of 1794; they were recovered four days later by the Columbia militia who received a reward of eighty dollars from Tucker.[6] There is no record of Tucker's Station ever being attacked.

William J. Cook of Glendale, Ohio owns a cherry corner hutch reportedly brought from New Jersey by Henry and Mary Tucker and passed on to him by will. In the Hamilton County court records, *Will Book 6*, page 282, there is a copy of Mary Tucker's will, written April 11, 1845 and probated January 3, 1849. According to this will, the first family member to receive this corner hutch may have been granddaughter Harriet Maria N. Tucker, who received "a round stand and corner cupboard and all the ware and dishes it contained."[7]

Notes
[1]*Symmes Purchase Records*, p. 73; Teetor, *Mill Creek Valley*, p. 42-43; Olden, *Historical Sketches*, p. 113-114.
[2]Teetor, *Mill Creek Valley*, p. 42-43; Olden, *Historical Sketches*, p. 59-60, 137-138; Greve, *Centennial History of Cincinnati*, Vol. 1, p. 113-114; *Hamilton County Survey Book 16*, p. 75-76, Hamilton County Engineer's Office, Road Records Division; Ferris, *Early Settlement*, p. 329, 341-342; *Plat Book 4*, p. 84, Hamilton County Recorder's Office.
[3]Teetor, *Mill Creek Valley*, p. 43; Olden, *Historical Sketches*, p. 59-60; *Road Record Book, Vol. 1-1B, 1790-1850*, p. 141; *Road Record Book, 1844-1847*, p. 748, Hamilton County Engineer's Office, Road Records Division; maps of Hamilton County, Ohio, by S. Morrison and J. Williams, 1835; Wm. D. Emerson, 1847; Atlas of Hamilton County, Ohio, 1884, p. 4; U. S. Geological Survey, Glendale, Ohio Quad., 7.5' series.
[4]Teetor, *Mill Creek Valley*, p. 43-44.
[5]Olden, *Historical Sketches*, p. 113-114.
[6]Ferris, *Early Settlement*, p. 341-342.
[7]*Hamilton County, Ohio Court and Other Records*, Vol. 3, p. 56.

Turkey Bottom Blockhouse 1791

The only reference we have to this blockhouse is from Ezra Ferris, who stated in 1851 that during the winter of 1791-92 a few families, including the Gordons and Webbs, moved from Columbia to the north end of Turkey Bottom to be closer to their corn fields. For their protection, he said, they built a blockhouse with pickets around the door.[1]

An early account, apparently narrated by two of the participants, relates how members of the Gordon family were surprised by Indians in a maple grove on a hillside near their fort. This incident occured during the winter (probably January or February) of 1792 in a woods being tapped for sugar,[2] about 440 yards from their home.

Nancy Gordon and her brother, James, had invited a neighbor boy, John Webb, to join them in sampling the maple sap from the taps. Halfway to the grove, the boy reconsidered and returned home. Nancy was captured and never heard from again. Her brother escaped to the fort after a wild foot race with the Indians.[3] The blockhouse probably sat in Township 4, the southeast quarter of Section 14, in Columbia Township between Linwood and Red Bank, east of Wooster Pike and on the east side of Duck Creek. The property later was owned by the Langdon family.[4]

Notes
[1] Ferris, *Early Settlement*, p. 312-314.
[2] Ibid.
[3] Ibid.
[4] Maps of Hamilton County by Wm. D. Emerson, 1847, and E. Mendenhall, ca. 1877; U. S. Geological Survey, 1912, Cincinnati East Quad., 7.5' series.

Voorhees' Station 1794

In the spring of 1794 Abraham Voorhees emigrated to the Mill Creek Valley of Hamilton County. With him came his five sons—Miney, Abraham, Jr., Garret, John and Jacob—and sons-in-law Thomas Higgins and John Rynearson (or Reynerson), and all their families.[1]

The senior Voorhees was born and raised in Somerset County, New Jersey. A veteran of the Revolutionary War, he served as a drummer with the rank of private in Captain Ten Eyk's company of New Jersey militia, finally becoming a sergeant.[2] Although born a Van Voorhees, by the time he reached the Miami Country the "Van" had disappeared.[3]

The Voorhees' extended family settled in Section 33, Township 4, Range 1, in present Sycamore Township. They built a large double log cabin designed for defense as well as habitation. It stood on the west bank of the east fork of Mill Creek, a few hundred yards east of the Buck residence (Lockland), later the property of Thomas Shepherd.[4] This location today is west of Koening Park in an industrial complex, east of Shepherd Road and south of Smalley or the old Columbia Road.[5]

There were no reported hostilities at Voorhees' Station but it was well-known to the early settlers, surveyors and military personnel. On September 21, 1795 two parties of surveyors camped overnight at the station. They were on their way to the Little Miami River and the seventh and eighth ranges of the Mad River; their assignment was to survey a road and run the boundaries of land purchased by their employers.[6]

The Voorhees family was an industrious one and they continued to expand their holdings in the Mill Creek Valley, founding the settlement known as Voorhee's Town. We know it as Reading, Ohio.[7]

Notes
[1] Olden, *Historical Sketches*, p. 60, 119-121.
[2] *Official Roster of Soldiers of the American Revolution Buried in the State of Ohio*, Vol. 1, p. 379.
[3] Ibid.
[4] Olden, *Historical Sketches*, p. 60.
[5] Ibid.; *Plat Book 3*, p. 192-193, Hamilton County Recorder's Office; maps of Hamilton County, Ohio, by S. Morrison and J. Williams, 1835; Wm. D. Emerson, 1847; A. W. Gilbert, 1848; R. C. Phillips, 1865; C. S. Mendenhall, ca. 1877; *Titus' Atlas of Hamilton County, Ohio*, p. 33; Atlas of Hamilton County, Ohio, 1884, p. 5; U. S. Geological Survey, Cincinnati East Quad., 7.5' series.

[6]"Memoirs of Benjamin Van Cleve," *Quarterly Publication of the Historical and Philosophical Society of Ohio*, Vol. 17 (1922), p. 56; *Official Roster of Soldiers of the American Revolution Buried in the State of Ohio*, Vol. 1, p. 379.

White's Station 1792

Jacob White was born in Somerset County, New Jersey on May 2, 1759. In the latter part of May 1777 he enlisted in the militia in Washington County, Pennsylvania where he joined a Ranger company as a private. He eventually was promoted to Captain.[1]

Captain White stated that he had migrated to, and was defending, the Miami Country in 1790.[2] Existing official records show that on July 23, 1792, Lieutenant Daniel Griffin presented warrant number 87 for entry on behalf of Captain White. This warrant was located in Section 1, Township 3, Range 1, in present Springfield Township.[3]

White established his small settlement east of present Wayne Avenue—Harmar's and Wayne's Traces or the Great Road—and the Carthage Fairgrounds.[4] The White family, including sons Providence, Amos and Edward, arrived at their new settlement by way of Red Stone Fort in Brownsville, Pennsylvania. With them were Andrew Goble, the David Flinn family, Andrew Pryor, John S. Wallace and Lewis Winans.[5]

Captain White built his blockhouse on the south bank of Mill Creek above a fording place. Goble and the Flinn family built their cabins close by on the same side of the stream while the others chose to build their dwellings on the opposite bank, about 240 feet away.[6] At about the same time, Pryor's brother Moses and John Reily settled on adjoining tracts south of the station, which today include the Longview Hospital property.[7]

Moses Pryor and David Flinn had a business partnership. They contracted with the government to haul supplies for the army from Fort Washington to Fort Hamilton.[8] In the fall of 1792 their supply party was attacked by Indians on Pleasant Run, four miles south of Fort Hamilton. Moses Pryor was killed.[9] His widow and three children moved in with his brother Andrew at White's Station. Reily sold his 160 acres, returned to Columbia and resumed his teaching career.[10]

As one of the northernmost settlements along Mill Creek, White's Station was exposed to Indian attack. Although Jacob White built a blockhouse-style home for his family, apparently none of the other cabins were fortified. White's cabin was enclosed by a log fence "made rather for the purpose of shutting out hogs and cattle than for defence."[11] Only a rail fence provided any bulwark around the rest of the cabins.

A narrative by Thomas M. Dill, describing White's Station as it was in its infancy, reported Captain White's house as a two story double log structure with a hall connecting the second floor apartments. It was built blockhouse fashion with the second story projecting over the lower level and containing port holes to fire through. The front faced southeast and the doors were reinforced. A low fence fifty yards away extended from Wayne's Trace west of the blockhouse, east and then north to Mill Creek. A palisade reinforced a holding enclosure for livestock.[12]

On October 18, 1793 the John Wallace family was visiting in Cincinnati, leaving only six men, Captain White's twelve-year-old son, Mrs. Pryor and her three children at the station.[13] In the late afternoon, several dogs were heard barking in an adjacent woods. Thinking the dogs might have treed a raccoon, Andrew Goble left to investigate. Indians were hiding in the wooded area east of the station and along the bank of Mill Creek north of the cabins. Goble was killed as he approached the barking dogs.[14] *The Centinel of the North-Western Territory*, of Saturday, November 9, 1793 takes up the story:

> *In the twilight of Saturday evening the 19th Oct. a part of about forty or fifty Indians made an attack upon White's Station, ten miles north of this place, at the moment they were discovered, two men, a woman and three children, were outside the station, one of the men and two of the children were killed, the others could not gain their cabins but fled to some others on the opposite bank of Mill-Creek, about eighty yards distant. The Indians ran instantly into the station, which was only secured by a rail fence, between two ranges of cabins several paces apart, two of these cabins were evacuated, and only two men left to defend the whole station... they both fired, at each shot an Indian fell, the others picked up the dead bodies, and in great trepidation retreated, one of the men fired a second time as they were going off, and wounded another. The two dead have been since found and no great distance, and a rifle gun of considerable value beside*

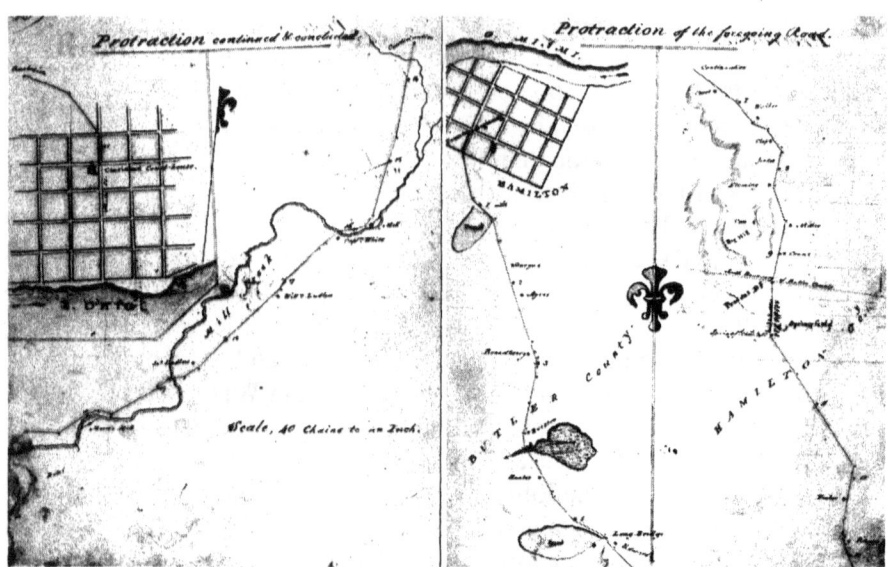

This survey depicts the protraction of a state road (Old Springfield Pike) from Hamilton to Cincinnati in 1808. This was an improvement made over the route of the Great Road (Wayne's Trace). Bruce's Station stood near the first pond below Hamilton, Tucker's house is shown near the 12-mile marker and Jacob White's Station and mill are clearly defined at the 16-mile marker. *(Hamilton County Engineer's Office, Road Records Division)*

> one of them, which was probably him who was wounded in the retreat. It is conjectured that they hastened back to their settlements, as none have since been discovered on our frontier.[15] (The actual date of the attack was Friday, October 18, 1793.[16])

Immediately following the attack, Andrew Pryor was sent to Fort Washington to petition for aid. Governor St. Clair sent twenty-four volunteer militia to engage the Indians but they failed to overtake the retreating war party.[17]

The remaining inhabitants at White's Station requested soldiers from Fort Washington to protect their settlement while they built a stockade, a project they estimated would take five or six days to complete.[18] On the morning after the attack, Governor St. Clair suggested to Captain John Pierce, commandant of Fort Washington, that a sergeant and twelve men be sent to protect the strategic supply station. He also impressed on Captain Pierce that twelve to fourteen hundred bushels of corn, which the army might need, were then stored at the station.[19]

Captain Pierce was unwilling to detach any troops without a direct order from General Wayne, but Governor St. Clair's adroit persuasion induced him to send a corporal and six men two days later.[20]

Governor St. Clair did not underestimate the importance of White's Station. As vulnerable as it may have been, the station was a holding area for army provisions and, just as important, a convenient bivouac spot for troops moving to the northeast.[21] The Great Road, which had been used extensively from Fort Washington to White's Station prior to General Wayne's Indian campaign in 1793, was a section of an alternative route to Fort Hamilton used when unfavorable weather conditions made movement of troops and supplies by way of the Great Miami River impossible.[22]

Ten days prior to the attack on White's, part of General Wayne's army, including a large contingent of Kentucky militia commanded by Major General Charles Scott and General Todd, left Fort Washington via the Great Road and bivouacked at their first camp site close to Mill Creek.[23] An officer traveling with General Todd wrote:

> *Set out in Company with Mr. (Elie) Williams (an army supply contractor), Genl. Tod & C. ordered the Bagage to follow to White's Station, got there at 6. Thursday 10 Do. the Bagage lay at Fryars (Pryor's) at White's Station Viewd. Genl Wains first Encampment on the West Side of Mill Creek.*[24]

General Wayne's 1793 campaign did not prove too effective and hostilities prevailed in Hamilton County throughout 1794. On March 15, 1794 *The Centinel of the North-Western Territory* described yet another incident involving White's Station people:

> *On Monday last, Mr. Flin (David Flinn) and Mrs. Prier (Pryor) were coming along General Harmar's Old trace, on their way from White's Station to this place (Cincinnati), was met by two Indians and chased a considerable distance, but escaped without damage. There has also been a number of horses stolen out of this town, in the corse of the present week.*[25]

On April 25, 1794 four men were attacked by Indians below White's Station; two of them were killed and their horses stolen. This was soon followed by a more daring Indian attack on a military escort, commanded by Major William Winston, between White's Station and Fort Hamilton on Tuesday, May 13, 1794. Eight soldiers were killed in the skirmish.[27]

Despite the fact that they were constantly subject to Indian raids, the settlers of the upper Mill Creek Valley were extremely active in promoting the building of an adequate road network.[28] The Great Road had been continually extended as a military road, but suitable only for the foot soldiers, the cavalry and pack horses. The citizens and army supply contractors were petitioning for roads more accessible to the settlements, mills and forts; roads which could accommodate wagons rather than the inefficient pack horse teams to expedite transport of military supplies and civilian necessities.[29] However, they had to contend with competition between settlements in obtaining permits for road surveys; many of the petitions were for personal gain rather than the public welfare.[30]

Supply posts were strung out along the new roads behind General Wayne's army during the summer campaign of 1794.[31] This army consisted of about 2600 regulars and 1600 Kentucky volunteers. They consumed at least twenty head of cattle a day and it was not uncommon to see herds as large as 400 head being driven to the supply posts.[32] One large herd intended for Fort Hamilton was driven from Cincinnati on December 6, 1794 to the supply post at White's Station, arriving there that same day.[33]

White's Station and the nearby fording place on Mill Creek were well-known to the early settlers and military personnel.[34] The White family became prominent citizens in the valley. Jacob White operated a grist mill near his station and a son, Edward, later operated a tanyard at the junction of the Hamilton and Colerain Raods.[35] Edward also was the founder of Carthage in August 1815.[36]

On February 15, 1802 Jacob White was among the first 25 subscribers for a public library in Cincinnati.[37] Despite the early success of his business ventures, Captain White eventually lost all of his property in Ohio and spent his final years in Kentucky.[38]

Notes

[1] *Official Roster of Soldiers of the American Revolution Who Lived in the State of Ohio*, Comp. Mrs. Orrville D. Dailey, Albany, Ohio, 1938, Vol. 2, p. 363.
[2] Letter of Jacob White to General James Findlay, Feb. 4, 1833, Torrence Papers, Box 28, letter 35, Cincinnati Historical Society.
[3] *Symmes Purchase Records*, p. 59; Olden, *Historical Sketches*, p.41; narrative of Luke Foster, quoted in Drake, "Memoir of the Miami Country," p. 76; *Road Record Book Vol. 1, 1793-1850*, p. 9-10, 21; *Road Record Book 1837-1839*, p. 425-432, Hamilton County Engineer's Office, Road Records Division; map of Hamilton County by R. C. Phillips, 1865.
[4] Ibid., Footnote no. 3; McBride, *Pioneer Biography*, Vol. 2, p. 154.
[5] Greve, *Centennial History of Cincinnati*, Vol. 1, p. 290; Olden, *Historical Sketches*, p.41; *History of Cincinnati and Hamilton County, Ohio*, p. 41, 419, 429.
[6] Greve, *Centennial History of Cincinnati*, Vol. 1, p. 290; *Centinel of the North-Western Territory*, Nov. 9, 1793, April 26, 1794, May 3, 1794; Hon. Samuel F. Hunt, "The Miami Valley," address at Hamilton, Ohio, July 4, 1881, p. 25.

[7]Greve, *Centennial History of Cincinnati*, Vol. 1, p. 291.
[8]Hunt, "The Miami Valley," p. 26.
[9]Greve, *Centennial History of Cincinnati*, Vol. 1, p. 29
[10]Ibid., p. 290; McBride, *Pioneer Biography*, Vol. 1, p. 39-40.
[11]Greve, *Centennial History of Cincinnati*, Vol. 1, p. 290; Cist, *Cincinnati in 1859*, p. 34.
[12]Greve, *Centennial History of Cincinnati*, Vol. 1, p. 290; *Centinel of the North-Western Territory*, Nov. 9, 1793; Narrative of Thomas M. Dill, quoted in Ford, *History of Hamilton County, Ohio*, p. 364.
[13]Greve, *Centennial History of Cincinnati*, Vol. 1, p. 290.
[14]Ibid.
[15]*Centinel of the North-Western Territory*, Nov. 9, 1793; Letter of Captain John Pierce to General Anthony Wayne, Oct. 21, 1793; Letter of Governor Arthur St. Clair to General Anthony Wayne, Oct. 21, 1793, Wayne Papers, Vol. 30, p. 28-30, Historical Society of Pennsylvania.
[16]Letter of Captain John Pierce to General Anthony Wayne, Oct. 21, 1793, Wayne Papers, Vol. 30, p. 28-30, Historical Society of Pennsylvania.
[17]Olden, *Historical Sketches*, p. 108-109.
[18]Letter of Captain John Pierce to General Anthony Wayne, Oct. 21, 1793; Letter of Governor Arthur St. Clair to General Anthony Wayne, Oct. 21, 1793, Wayne Papers, Vol. 30, p. 28-30, Historical Society of Pennsylvania.
[19]Ibid.
[20]Ibid.
[21]Letter of Governor Arthur St. Clair to General Anthony Wayne, Oct. 21, 1793, Wayne Papers, Vol. 30, p. 28-30, Historical Society of Pennsylvania.
[22]Hunt, "The Miami Valley," p. 26; Olden, *Historical Sketches*, p. 136-138; Fletcher, *Dearborn and Ohio Counties*, p. 96.
[23]"Two Journals of the Kentucky Volunteers, 1793 and 1794," Ed. Richard C. Knopf, *The Filson Club History Quarterly*, Vol. 27 (1953) p. 251.
[24]Ibid.
[25]*Centinel of the North-Western Territory*, March 15, 1794.
[26]Ibid., May 3, 1794.
[27]Ibid., May 17, 1794.
[28]Olden, *Historical Sketches*, p. 138-148.
[29]Ibid.; Letter of Robert Elliot and Elie Williams to the Secretary of War, Nov. 17, 1792, Anthony Wayne Papers, Manuscript Collection, Cincinnati Historical Society.
[30]Olden, *Historical Sketches*, p. 138-148.
[31]"Two Journals of the Kentucky Volunteers, 1793 and 1794," p. 248.
[32]"Memoirs of Benjamin Van Cleve," quoted in *Quarterly Publication of the Historical and Philosophical Society of Ohio*, Vol. 17 (1922) p. 53.
[33]Ibid., p. 55.
[34]*Road Record Book Vol. 1, 1793-1850*, p. 59, 116; *Hamilton, County, Ohio Survey Book 1*, p. 21, 97, 110; *Road Record Book 1837-1839*, p. 425-432, Hamilton County Engineer's Office, Road Records Division;
[35]Ibid.; *The Western Spy and Hamilton Gazette*, May 26, 1815.
[36]*The Western Spy and Hamilton Gazette*, Aug. 18, 1815.
[37]Charles Cist, *Western General Advertiser*, Sept. 18, 1844.
[38]*Cist's Daily Advertiser*, Oct. 1, 1847.

Wood's and Manning's or Miller's Station 1796

It was reportedly during the fall of 1795, after General Anthony Wayne had imposed a peace treaty on the Indians of the Northwest Territory, that Joshua, Nathan, and Richard Manning, with their brothers-in-law, David, John, and Jeriah Wood and their respective families, established a settlement in the Virginia Military District in today's Clermont County.[1] However, the settlement *may* date from several years later, since the Woods and Mannings are on Mason County, Kentucky tax lists as late as 1797.

Their settlement was a "squatter" community, since the settlers were living on land actually owned by Thomas Buckner in survey number 1087.[2] Their closest neighbor at that time may have been Colonel Thomas Paxton at his settlement to the northwest, near today's Loveland.[3] The William Buchanan family may also have been located nearby, isolated and vulnerable to Indian attack.[4] The Wood's and Manning's Station site was near a copious spring which today is located west of Collier Road in Washington Township, Clermont County, about a mile east of the Calvary Methodist Church on Route 756.[5]

The families at the station, having Pennsylvania roots and having emigrated from Washington, Kentucky, were well acquainted with the method of building "station" forts in Kentucky. The Woods and Mannings reportedly built a double cabin residence enclosed by a stockade, with an open area cleared around the station to eliminate cover for any attacking Indians.[6]

Folklore says that famous Indian fighters such as Daniel Boone, Simon Kenton, and Cornelius Washburn frequently visited Wood's and Manning's Station. It is also said that William Buchanan on many occasions brought his family and cattle within the stockade when Indian war parties were seen in the area.[7]

In the early 1800s, Nathaniel Massie, Deputy Surveyor for the Virginia Military District, apparently asserted the ownership of the actual proprietor of the Buckner survey. However, the Woods and Mannings reportedly received title bonds to neighboring property to compensate them for the improvements they had made.[8] By 1813, Martin Miller had acquired 710 acres in the Buckner

Survey, including the area upon which the station stood. He removed the stockade and used the timber for other purposes, but maintained the double cabin.⁹ By that time various members of the Buchanan family had bought large areas of land in the adjoining Survey Number 1064 belonging to Beverly Roy.¹⁰

There were no actual attacks on Wood's and Manning's Station by the Indians, but small parties of warriors often caused alarm while traveling to the various crossings of the Ohio River on horse-stealing raids into Kentucky.¹¹

Notes
¹Rockey and Bancroft, *History of Clermont County*, p. 280, 363; Mason County KY, tax lists, 1795-1797, Kentucky State Archives, Frankfort.
²Ibid., p. 42, 363; *Atlas of Clermont County, Ohio*, p. 8-9.
³Rockey and Bancroft, *History of Clermont County*, p. 280.
⁴Ibid., p. 36, 280, 363.
⁵Ibid.
⁶Rockey and Bancroft, *History of Clermont County*, p. 280, 363.
⁷Ibid., p. 36, 280, 363.
⁸Ibid., p. 363.
⁹Ibid.; *Deed Book M11*, p. 239, 490; *Deed Book L10*, p. 311; *Deed Book N12*, p. 92, Clermont County Recorder's Office.
¹⁰*Deed Book A1*, p. 105-108, Clermont County Recorder's Office; Rockey and Bancroft, *History of Clermont County*, p. 364.
¹¹Rockey and Bancroft, *History of Clermont County*, p. 36.

Bibliography

Manuscript Sources

The Cincinnati Historical Society contains a rich variety of sources on the early Miami Country settlements. Among the most significant are:

The correspondence, legal papers and land sale records of John Cleves Symmes, which provide an invaluable record of Symmes' troubled and eventually tragic leadership in the early settlement of this area.

The papers of John Stites Gano and his family, prominent settlers at Columbia.

The Lytle Papers, containing a tremendous amount of raw information relating to early development and land sales in the Virginia Military District, where William Lytle was deputy surveyor.

The Torrence Papers, with a wealth of material on the organization of early militia units in Southwestern Ohio, and on the various expeditions against hostile Indians.

The Robert Clarke Papers contain many transcriptions and original documents concerning early midwestern history.

Charles Whittlesey's "Historical, Topographical and Geological Notices of Hamilton County, Ohio," includes newspaper clippings of some of the best memoirs of early settlers.

The memoirs of Mary Covalt Jones and General James Taylor and the diary of Major Winthrop Sargent are extremely important manuscripts relating to the Miami Country settlements.

The William Clements Library of the University of Michigan at Ann Arbor contains the Harmar Papers, the collected correspondence and official records of General Josiah Harmar. This collection is outstanding in helping to grasp the problems of frontier defense all along the Ohio Valley.

The Historical Society of Pennsylvania has made available an excellent microfilm edition of the papers of Anthony Wayne, which give an interesting look at the importance of the Miami Country stations as supply depots and rest stops for Wayne's army.

The Wisconsin Historical Society contains the broadest in scope and best-known collection of early pioneer papers and reminiscences in the Lyman Draper Collection. Especially helpful are the papers of Daniel and Benjamin Drake (The Drake Papers, Microfilm Series O), which deal with the early settlement of Cincinnati and the Miami Country.

County Records

The Butler County Recorder's Office, Hamilton, Ohio, contains *Transcript Records* of early land sales, and *Deed Books* on land transfers.

The Clermont County Recorder's Office, Batavia, Ohio, has on file *Deed Books* for all county land sales, and some *Transcript Records* of sales previous to the formation of the county.

The Dearborn County Engineer's Office, Lawrenceburg, Indiana, has field notes of Israel Ludlow and other surveyors of early surveys in the county.

The *Hamilton County Courthouse*, Cincinnati, holds many of the early survey, road and land sale records of the Southwestern Ohio region. A study of these records is essential to gaining an idea of the true location of the area's first settlements. Especially important are the *Road Record Books*, the *Survey Books*, the *Plat Books* and *The Restored Records, Decrees & Plats Affecting Real Estate, 1798-1863*, all in the County Engineers office, Road Records Divison; and the early *Deed Books* and *Plat Books* in the Recorder's office.

The Warren County Recorder's Office, Lebanon, Ohio, holds the *Warren County Commissioner's Journals*, which contain invaluable records of early surveys and petitions. This office also has *Transcript Records* of land sales, deed and lease transactions prior to formation of the county. The county courthouse in Lebanon holds the early *Wills and Administrations*. The *Auditor's* and *Engineer's Offices* contain the official land and road surveys.

Newspapers

Some of the newspapers especially useful to researchers interested in the early history of Southwestern Ohio include:

The Centinel of the North-Western Territory, the first newspaper published in Ohio, printed in Cincinnati between 1793 and 1796. The *Centinel* contains many advertisements relating to land sales and the establshment of new stations. Its news articles reported in great detail Indian raids and counterattacks in the Miami Country, and provide the only written sources for many of these incidents.

Cist's Weekly Advertiser, 1844-1853, and *Cist's Daily Advertiser*, 1847-1848, both published in Cincinnati, are valuable sources of reminiscences by some of the Miami Country's earliest settlers. They also contain many short articles illustrating the early history of the region.

Liberty Hall and Cincinnati Gazette, printed in Cincinnati from 1819 to 1827, is an important source in tracing developing industry and agriculture in Southwestern Ohio.

The Western Spy, printed under various names in Cincinnati from 1799 to 1822, provides valuable evidence of the growth of population and industry in the Miami Country, even though publication was begun after the initial wave of settlement and Indian hostilities were over.

The Western Star, the oldest continuously published newspaper in the country west of the Allgehenies, is still being published in Lebanon.

Books

American State Papers, Washington, D. C., 1832-1861 (38 Vols.).

Anburey, Thomas, *Travels Through the Interior Parts of America: In a Series of Letters From An Officer,* London, 1789 (2 Vols.).

Ashe, Thomas, Esq., *Travels in America, 1806,* London, reprinted Newburyport, Massachusetts, 1808.

Atlas of Clermont County, Ohio, Philadelphia, 1870.

Atlas of Clermont County, Ohio, Philadelphia, 1891.

Baily, Francis, *Journal of a Tour in the Unsettled Parts of North America in 1796 and 1797,* London, 1856.

Bartlow, Bert S., Todhunter, W. H., Cone, Stephen D., Pater, Joseph I., Schneider, Frederick, Etc., Eds., *Centennial History of Butler County, Ohio,* Cincinnati, 1905.

Benzing, Esther, *Fairfield, Ohio,* Mt. Healthy, Ohio, 1978.

Beveridge, Albert, *Abe Lincoln in Indiana,* Boston, 1928, Reprinted Ft. Wayne, Indiana, 1953.

Bond, Beverly W., Jr., Ed., *The Correspondence of John Cleves Symmes,* Cincinnati, 1926.

Bond, Beverly W., Jr., Ed., *The Intimate Letters of John Cleves Symmes and His Family,* Cincinnati, 1956.

Bone, Frank A., *Complete Atlas of Warren County, Ohio,* Lebanon, Ohio, 1891.

Brien, Lindsay M., Ed., *A Genealogical Index of Pioneers in the Miami Valley, Ohio: Miami Co., Montgomery Co., Preble Co., and Warren Co., Ohio,* Dayton, Ohio, 1970.

Brien, Lindsay M., Ed., *Miami Valley Will Abstracts: Miami, Montgomery, Warren and Preble Co., 1803-1850,* Dayton, Ohio, 1940.

Burnet, Jacob, *Notes on the Early Settlement of the North-Western Territory,* Cincinnati, 1847.

Burress, Marjorie Byrnside, Ed., *Early Rosters of Cincinnati and Hamilton County, Ohio,* Cincinnati, 1984.

Burress, Marjorie Byrnside, *It Happened 'Round North Bend, a History of Miami Township and its Borders,* Cincinnati, 1970.

Carter, Clarence Edwin, Ed., *Territorial Papers of the United States*, Washington, D. C., 1934 (17 Vols.).

Cary, Samuel F., *History of College Hill and Vicinity*, College Hill, Ohio, 1886.

Centennial Atlas of Warren County, Ohio, Lebanon, Ohio, 1903.

Cist, Charles, *Early Annals and Future Prospects of Cincinnati in 1841*, Cincinnati, 1841.

Cist, Charles, *Skteches and Statistics of Cincinnati in 1859*, Cincinnati, 1859.

Collins, Lewis S., *Historical Sketches of Kentucky*, revised by Richard H. Collins, Covington, Kentucky, 1874 (2 Vols.).

Collot, Victor, *A Voyage in North America*, Paris, 1826, Reprinted New York, 1974 (2 Vols.).

Cone, Stephen D., *A Concise History of Hamilton, Ohio*, Middletown, Ohio, 1901.

Conover, Charlotte Reeve, Ed., *Dayton and Montgomery County, Resources and People*, New York, 1932 (4 Vols.).

The County of Butler, Ohio, an Imperial Atlas and Art Folio, Richmond, Indiana, 1895.

Craig, Robert D., *Revolutionary War Soldiers in Hamilton County, Ohio*, Salt Lake City, 1965.

Crout, George C., Ed., *Middletown, U. S. A., All American City*, Middletown, Ohio, 1960.

Cummins, Virginia, Comp., *Hamilton County, Ohio, Court and Other Records*, Cincinnati, 1966-1969 (3 Vols.).

Cutler, Jervis, *A Topographical Description of the State of Ohio*, Boston, 1812.

Denny, Ebenezer, *Military Journal of Major Ebenezer Denny, an Officer in the Revolutionary and Indian Wars*, Philadelphia, 1859.

Des Cognets, Anna Russell, *Governor Garrard of Kentucky, His Descendants and Relatives*, Lexington, Kentucky, 1898.

Doddridge, Joseph, *Notes on the Settlement and Indian Wars, of the Western Parts of Virginia and Pennsylvania, from the Year 1763 Until the Year 1783, Inclusive*, Wellsburgh, Virginia, 1824.

Downes, Randolph C., *Council Fires on the Upper Ohio, A Narrative of Indian Affairs in the Upper Ohio Valley until 1795*, Pittsburgh, 1968.

Drake, Benjamin, *Tales and Sketches of the Queen City*, Cincinnati, 1838.

Durham, Samuel, *The Pioneer Settlers of the Lower Little Miami Valley*, privately printed, 1897.

Durrett, Reuben T., *Bryant's Station and the Memorial Proceedings Held on its Site*, Filson Club Publication No. 12, Louisville, 1897.

Edgar, John F., *Pioneer Life in Dayton and Vicinity, 1796-1840*, Dayton, Ohio, 1896.

Elliott, James, *Poetical and Miscellaneous Works of James Elliott, A Non-Commissioned Officer in the Legion of the U. S.*, Greenfield, Massachusetts, 1798.

Everts, L. H., *Combination Atlas Map of Butler County, Ohio*, Philadelphia, 1875.

Ferris, Ezra, *The Early Settlement of the Miami Country*, Indiana Historical Society Publications, Vol. 1, No. 9, Indianapolis, 1897.

Fletcher, Charles W., *History of Dearborn and Ohio Counties, Indiana*, Chicago, 1885.

Ford, Henry A. and Kate B., *History of Hamilton County, Ohio, with Illustrations and Biographical Sketches*, Cleveland, 1881.

Garber, Dwight Wesley, *Water Wheels and Millstones; A History of Ohio Grist Mills and Milling*, Historic Ohio Buildings, Series 2, Columbus, 1970.

Green, James A., *William Henry Harrison, His Life and Times*, Richmond, Virginia, 1941.

Greve, Charles, *Centennial History of Cincinnati*, Cincinnati, 1904 (2 Vols.).

Guthman, William, *March to Massacre, A History of the First Seven Years of the United States Army, 1784-1791*, New York, 1970.

Gwathmey, John H., *Historical Register of Virginians in the Revolution, 1775-1783*, Richmond, Virginia, 1938.

Hamilton County, Ohio, Business Directory, Cincinnati, 1911-1912.

Harding, Marjorie Heberling, Comp., *George Rogers Clark and His Men: Military Records, 1778-1784*, Frankfort, Kentucky, 1981.

Harrison, John Scott, *Pioneer Life at North Bend, An Address to the Whitewater & Miami Valley Pioneer Association at Cleves, Ohio, Sept. 18, 1866*, Cincinnati, 1867.

Harrison, William Henry, *A Discourse on the Aborigines of the Valley of the Ohio*, Cincinnati, 1838.

Hayes, Royal S., *The Hayes Family Origin, History and Genealogy*, Cincinnati, 1927.

Heckwelder, John, *A Narrative of the Mission of the United Brethren Among the Delaware and Mohegan Indians*, Ed. William Elsey Connelly, Cleveland, 1907.

Heiser, Alta Harvey, *Hamilton in the Making*, Oxford, Ohio, 1941.

Heiser, Alta Harvey, *West To Ohio*, Yellow Springs, Ohio, 1954.

Heiss, Willard, and Mayhill, R. Thomas, Eds., *Census of 1807, Butler County, Ohio*, Knightstown, Indiana, 1968.

Henderson, Frank D., Rhea, John D., Dailey, Jane Dowd, Eds., *The Official Roster of Soldiers of the American Revolution Buried in the State of Ohio*, Columbus, 1929 (3 Vols.).

A History and Biographical Cyclopedia of Butler County, Ohio, Cincinnati, 882.
History of Cincinnati and Hamilton County, Ohio, Cincinnati, 1894.
The History of Warren County, Ohio, Chicago, 1882.
Hook, George W., Weakly, H. H., Parrott, H. E., Shuey, E., Shuey, W. A., Winters, Mrs. John A., Steele, Robert, *History of Dayton, Ohio*, Dayton, 1889.
Horn, W. F., *The Horn Papers*, Scottsdale, Pennsylvania, 1945 (3 Vols.).
Houser, Howard R., *Wilderness Doctor: The Life and Times of Dr. John Hole*, Centerville, Ohio, 1980.
Howe, Henry, *Historical Collections of Ohio*, Cincinnati, 1847; Cincinnati, 1850; Cincinnati, 1888 (2 Vols.); Columbus, 1890 (2 Vols.).
Hunt, Samuel F., *The Miami Valley*, address at Hamilton, Ohio, July 4, 1881.
Hutslar, Donald, *The Log Architecture of Ohio*, Columbus, 1972.
James, Rev. William H., *79th Anniversary of the Presbyterian Church, Springdale, Ohio*, Cincinnati, 1876.
Johnson, Rev. William M., *175 Years at the Lebanon Presbyterian Church, 1806-1981*, Centerville, Ohio 1981.
Johnston, John, *Recollections of Sixty Years*, Ed. Charlotte Reeve Conover, Piqua, Ohio, 1957.
Jones, A. E., *Extracts from the History of Cincinnati*, Cincinnati, 1888.
Jones, A. E., *Reminiscences of the Early Days of the Little Miami Valley*, Cincinnati, 1878.
Jones, Robert Ralston, *Fort Washington at Cincinnati, Ohio*, Cincinnati, 1902.
Kellogg, Louise Phelps and Thwaites, Reuben Gold, Eds., *The Revolution on the Upper Ohio, 1775-1777*, Madison, Wisconsin, 1908.
Kellogg, Louise Phelps, Ed., *Frontier Advance on the Upper Ohio, 1778-1779*, Madison, Wisconsin, 1916.
Kellogg, Louise Phelps, Ed., *Frontier Retreat on the Upper Ohio, 1779-1781*, Madison, Wisconsin, 1917.
Kjellenberg, Marion S., *Blue Ash, 1968 History and Directory, 1793-1968. The Fastest Growing City in Southwestern Ohio*, Montgomery, Ohio, 1968.
Loveland...From its Beginnings, Loveland, Ohio, 1976.
Mastin, Bettye Lee, *Lexington, 1779: Pioneer Kentucky as Described by Early Settlers*, Cincinnati, 1979.
McAllister, J. T., *Virginia Militia in the Revolutionary War*, Hot Springs, Virginia, 1913.
McBride, James, *Notes on Hamilton, From an Original Manuscript Written in 1831*, Hamilton, Ohio, 1898.
McBride, James, *Pioneer Biography, Sketches of the Lives of Some of the*

Early Settlers in Butler County, Ohio, Cincinnati, 1869 (2 Vols.).

McHenry, Chris, Ed., *Symmes Purchase Records*, Lawrenceburg, Indiana, 1979.

Mansfield, Edward, *The Annual Address Delivered Before the Cincinnati Astronomical Society*, Cincinnati, 1845.

Mansfield, Edward, *Personal Memories: Social, Political and Literary with Sketches of Many Noted People, 1803-1843*, Cincinnati, 1879.

Mills, William C., *Archaeological Atlas of Ohio*, Columbus, 1914.

Moessinger, George and Bertsch, Fred, *Map of Hamilton County, Ohio*, New York, 1884 (Atlas).

Olden, J. G., *Historical Sketches and Early Reminiscences of Hamilton County, Ohio*, Cincinnati, 1882.

Pennsylvania Archives, Harrisburg, Pennsylvania, 1874-1935 (119 Vols.).

Putnam, Rufus, *The Memoirs of Rufus Putnam*, Ed. Rowena Buell, Boston and New York, 1903.

Phillips, Hazel Spencer, *Richard the Shaker*, Oxford, Ohio, 1972.

Prucha, Francis Paul, *The Sword of the Republic: The United States Army on the Frontier, 1783-1846*, Bloomington, Indiana and London, 1977.

Rauck, George W., *Boonesborough: Its Founding, Pioneer Struggles, Indian Experiences, Transylvania Days and Revolutionary Annals*, Filson Club Publications, No. 16, Louisville, 1901.

Report of the Commission to Locate the Site of the Frontier Forts of Pennsylvania, Harrisburg, 1896 (2 Vols.).

Robinson, E. and Pidgeon, R. H., *Atlas of the City of Cincinnati, Ohio*, New York, 1884.

Rockey, J. L. and Bancroft, R. J., *History of Clermont County, Ohio*, Philadelphia, 1882.

Shaw, Archibald, *History of Dearborn County*, Indianapolis, 1915.

Sherman, C. E., *Original Ohio Land Subdivisions*, Mansfield, Ohio, 1925, (Volume 3 of *The Ohio Cooperative Topographic Survey*, Mansfield, Ohio, 1916-1933, 4 Vols.).

Simmons, David A., *The Forts of Anthony Wayne*, Ft. Wayne, Indiana, 1977.

Smith, Thomas, *The Mapping of Ohio*, Kent, Ohio, 1977.

Smith, William E., *History of Southwestern Ohio: The Miami Valleys*, New York, 1964 (2 Vols.).

Smith, William Henry, Ed., *The St. Clair Papers*, Cincinnati, 1882 (2 Vols.).

Soil Survey of Hamilton County, O. 1975-1979, Cincinnati, 1979.

Spencer, Oliver M., *Indian Captivity of O. M. Spencer*, New York, 1834.

Squier, E. G. and Davis, E. H., *Prehistoric Antiquities of the Mississippi Valley*, reproduction by AMS Press, New York, 1973 (2 Vols.).

Teetor, Henry B., *Life and Times of Israel Ludlow*, Cincinnati, 1885.
Teetor, Henry B., *The Past and Present of the Mill Creek Valley*, Cincinnati, 1882.
Thornbrough, Gale, Ed., *Outpost on the Wabash*, Indiana Historical Publications, Vol. 19, Indianapolis, 1957.
Thwaites, Reuben Gold and Kellogg, Louise Phelps, Eds., *Frontier Defense on the Upper Ohio, 1777-1778*, Madison, Wisconsin, 1912.
Titus' Atlas of Hamilton County, Ohio, Philadelphia, 1869.
Wallace, Joseph, *Past and Present of the City of Springfield and Sangamon County, Illinois*, Chicago, 1904 (2 Vols.).
Williams, Byron, *History of Clermont and Brown Counties, Ohio*, Milford, Ohio, 1913 (2 Vols.).
Williams, Edward G., *Fort Pitt and the Revolution on the Western Frontier*, Pittsburgh, 1978.
Year Book, Revolutionary Ancestors of the Sons of the Revolution in the State of Ohio, 1895.

Periodicals

Beaver, R. Pierce, "The Miami Purchase of John Cleves Symmes," *Ohio Archaeological and Historical Society Quarterly*, Vol. 40 (1931).
Butler, Richard, "Journal of General Richard Butler," *The Olden Time*, Ed. Neville B. Craig, Pittsburgh, 1846-1847 (2 Vols.).
Drake, Daniel, "Memoir of the Miami Country, 1779-1794," Ed. Beverly W. Bond, Jr., *Quarterly Publication of the Historical and Philosophical Society of Ohio*, Vol. 18 (1923).
Dudley, Charlotte W., "Jared Mansfield: United States Surveyor General," *Ohio History*, Vol. 85 (1976).
Evans, Nelson W., "Colonel John O'Bannon," *Ohio Archaeological and Historical Society Publications*, Vol. 14 (1905).
"Extracts of B. Van Cleve's Memoranda," *The American Pioneer*, Cincinnati, 1843-1844 (2 Vols.).
Faries, Elizabeth, "The Miami Country, 1750-1815, as described in Journals and Letters," *Ohio Archaeological and Historical Society Quarterly*, Vol. 57 (1948).
Green, James A., "North Bend, Ohio," *The Ohio Social Science Journal*, Vol. 4 (1932).
Hall, Virginius C., "Richard Allison - Surgeon to the Legion," *The Ohio State Medical Journal*, Vol. 48 (1952).
King, Arthur G., "The Earliest Map of Cincinnati, 1792," *Bulletin of the Historical and Philosophical Society of Ohio*, Vol. 15 (1957).

www.ingramcontent.com/pod-product-compliance
Lightning Source LLC
Chambersburg PA
CBHW020829020526
44118CB00032B/402